GRACE
HOPPER

**Additional titles in the Library of Naval Biography
series, edited by James C. Bradford**

Confederate Admiral: The Life and Wars of Franklin Buchanan
by Craig L. Symonds
Andrew Foote: Civil War Admiral on Western Waters
by Spencer C. Tucker
Thomas ap Catesby Jones: Commodore of Manifest Destiny
by Gene A. Smith
Joshua Barney: Hero of the Revolution and 1812
by Louis Arthur Norton
Matthew Calbraith Perry: Antebellum Sailor and Diplomat
by John H. Schroeder
Mad Jack Percival: Legend of the Old Navy
by James H. Ellis
*Commodore Ellsworth P. Bertholf:
First Commandant of the Coast Guard*
by C. Douglas Kroll
Thomas Macdonough: Master of Command in the Early U.S. Navy
by David Curtis Skaggs

LIBRARY OF NAVAL BIOGRAPHY

GRACE HOPPER

Admiral *of the* Cyber Sea

Kathleen Broome Williams

Naval Institute Press
Annapolis, Maryland

This book has been brought to publication by the generous assistance of Marguerite and Gerry Lenfest.

First Naval Institute Press paperback edition published 2012.

ISBN 978-1-59114-978-1

Naval Institute Press
291 Wood Road
Annapolis, MD 21402

Library of Congress Cataloging-in-Publication Data

Williams, Kathleen Broome, 1944–
    Grace Hopper : admiral of the cyber sea / Kathleen Broome Williams.
            p. cm.
    Includes bibliographical references and index.
    ISBN 978-1-55750-952-9 (alk. paper)
    1. Hopper, Grace Murray. 2. Women admirals—United States—Biography.
3. Admirals—United States—Biography. 4. Women computer engineers—United
States—Biography. 5. Computer engineers—United States—Biography. I. Title.
    V63.H66W55 2004
    359'.0092—dc22

                        2004007942

Printed in the United States of America on acid-free paper ∞

24 23 22 21 20   8 7 6 5 4

For Chlöe, a loving friend

Contents

Foreword xi

Preface and Acknowledgments xiii

1   Remember Your Great-Grandfather the Admiral 1

2   You're in the Navy Now 25

3   Women Enter the World of Technology 68

4   A *WAVE* Ordnance Officer? 99

5   I'm in the Reserve, Retired, and on Active Duty 114

6   The Navy's Best Recruiter? 150

7   Amazing Grace 172

Notes 197

Bibliography 221

Further Reading 231

Index 235

Foreword

On 6 September 1995, the U.S. Navy commissioned its newest Arleigh Burke–class destroyer, the USS *Hopper* (DDG-70). Bristling with the most advanced electronic weapons systems, it was fittingly named for Rear Admiral Grace Hopper, a pioneer computer scientist and the officer who contributed most to the standardization of the navy's computing systems.

Arleigh Burke was Hopper's senior by five years. He graduated from the Naval Academy with a degree in engineering in 1923; Grace Hopper, a student of math and physics, graduated from Vassar five years later. The year 1943 was pivotal for both Burke and Hopper. In May of 1943 Burke was promoted to captain and transferred from the Bureau of Ordnance, where he had been testing guns in the Naval Gun Factory in the Washington Navy Yard, to command of a destroyer squadron in the Solomon Islands. In December 1943 Grace Hopper entered the navy, was assigned to the Computation Project of the Bureau of Ships at Harvard University, and began writing programs for the Mark I, the navy's most advanced computer. Eighteen years later Burke retired from the navy as Chief of Naval Operations and entered the business world where Hopper, a systems engineer, had risen to become Director of Automatic Programming Languages for the Univac Division of the Sperry Corporation. Five years after Burke retired from the navy, Hopper was placed on the retired reserve list, but within a year was recalled to active duty to spend the next nineteen years working on the navy's computer systems. When Hopper retired again in 1986, this time as a rear admiral, she was the navy's oldest serving officer. Both Burke and Hopper served in the navy for forty-two years.

Unlike Burke, Hopper has not until now been the subject of a scholarly biography. This is due in part to the reading public's preference for studies of individuals with political or combat careers, and in part to a shortage of personal papers left by Hopper. Kathleen Broome Williams is the perfect individual to correct this lacuna in both naval history and the history of technology. She brings to this study an understanding of women in the navy and naval technology gained through her previous books, *Secret Weapon: U.S. High-Frequency Direction Finding in the Battle of the Atlantic* (1996) and *Improbable Warriors: Women Scientists and the U.S. Navy in World War II* (2001). Thus, I was more than pleased when she responded positively to my invitation to contribute this volume to *The Library of Naval Biography* series.

The Library of Naval Biography provides accurate, informative, and interpretive biographies of influential naval figures—men and women who have shaped or reflected the naval affairs of their time. Each volume explains the forces that acted upon its subject as well as the significance of that person in history. Some volumes explore the lives of individuals who have not previously been the subject of a modern, full-scale biography, while others reexamine the lives of better-known individuals adding new information, a differing perspective, or a fresh interpretation. The series is international in scope and includes individuals from several centuries. All volumes are based on solid research and written to be of interest to general readers as well as useful to specialists.

With these goals in mind, the length of each volume has been limited, the notes placed at the end of the text and restricted primarily to direct quotations, and a brief essay on "Further Reading" provided to assess previous biographies of the subject and to direct the reader to the most important studies of the era and events in which the person lived and participated. It is the intention that this combination of clear writing, fresh interpretations, and solid historical context will result in volumes that restore the all-important human dimension to naval history and are enjoyable to read.

James C. Bradford

Preface and Acknowledgments

In 1983 Grace Murray Hopper, then seventy-six years old, was made a commodore by special presidential appointment. Two years later the title of that rank was changed to rear admiral. In 1987 the navy named its new computer center in San Diego for Hopper and in 1996, four years after her death, it launched the newest Arleigh Burke–class destroyer *Hopper*. The recipient of numerous medals, awards, and honorary degrees, Hopper was esteemed both for her intellect and for her energy. Her message to everyone was above all to innovate and never to be tied to the old or customary way of doing things. Even when she finally retired in 1986—the oldest serving officer in the navy—Grace Hopper continued working as a consultant for Digital Equipment Corporation. She died in 1992 and was buried with full military honors in Arlington National Cemetery.

Hopper had a long and distinguished civilian career, first as a professor of mathematics and later as a computer scientist in a major corporation. Her greatest source of pride, however, was always her service in the U.S. Navy. After earning a PhD in mathematics from Yale in 1933, Hopper went on to teach mathematics at Vassar College in New York. After World War II, she moved into commercial computing, entering the new field on the ground floor and helping to define the meaning of systems engineering. In 1949, she joined the Eckert-Mauchly Computer Corporation, remaining with the company through its various permutations until 1967. During her years in private industry, Hopper became well known and respected for her role in the invention of the compiler and in the creation of COBOL, a programming language in wide use today. Her pioneering work in the development of programming languages is considered her major contribution to computing, earning for Hopper the nicknames "Grandma COBOL" and "the Grand Lady of Software."

The pivotal point in Hopper's life, however, and the catalyst for all her later successes, was her military service in World War II. The navy introduced her to the emerging world of computing, where she spent the rest of her long and productive life. Years later, Hopper admitted that she had never thought of going into computer work because there were no computers to go into—not until she met the Mark I at the navy's Computation Laboratory at Harvard. Hopper began her computing career writing programs for the Mark I, the first automatically sequenced digital computer in the United States. After the war, she spent twenty years in the naval reserve using what she was learning in her civilian career to help establish the navy's emerging computer systems. Then, in 1967, Hopper was recalled to active duty, serving a further nineteen years standardizing navy computer programming languages.

In 1944, the Mark I could complete three operations a second. Nine years later, Hopper was writing programs for the UNIVAC, the first commercial large-scale electronic computer, which completed 1,000 operations a second. In 1963, when Hopper still had twenty-three working years ahead of her, the fastest computer around, the CDC 6600, could execute over three million instructions a second. Hopper not only kept up with these changes, she was also forward looking and quick to anticipate where the field would go next. For much of the second half of the twentieth century, she played an important part in the computer revolution. Always pushing the limits of conventional thinking and finding innovative approaches to problem solving, Hopper left her mark not only on navy computing, but also on the information processing profession as a whole. Today, U.S. Navy computing is so ubiquitous that at a cost of about a million dollars a year a civilian firm provides secure Internet message boards where officers at sea can post information, recount experiences, ask questions, and receive answers. Anticipating such developments, Grace Hopper would not have been surprised.

In part because of her gender and her age, Hopper attracted considerable media attention. Because she spent nineteen of her last working years in uniform, she became the symbol of navy computing, and many people know a little about her. She herself was the author of dozens of papers and articles on computing, and she was the subject of dozens more, as well as of print, radio, and television interviews. Two biographies have been written about Grace Hopper. Both are good but limited because they are intended for young readers. Two dissertations have looked more closely at Hopper's career: one deals with her as a teacher and the other is an examination of her pioneering computing work. Her experiences in the navy, however, have been treated only superficially.

This biography focuses on Hopper's navy career, examining the skills she possessed that were so valuable to a male-dominated military bureaucracy that she overcame the barriers of gender and age so often inhibiting to others. Hopper had nothing to offer the navy but her understanding of computers. Yet the navy had emerged from World War II so dependent on advanced information systems that Hopper's area of expertise was exactly what was needed. In a fast-developing field and with growing competition from industry, there was a shortage of people in the navy with her ability, knowledge, and experience. Once back on active duty, her strength of character and energy ensured her continuing relevance in a rapidly changing young person's game.

Perhaps it is inevitable that someone who attracted such media attention should be the subject of numerous myths. Among the most persistent of these are that Hopper invented the computer term "bug"; that her husband had been killed in World War II; that she created the computer language COBOL; and that she was the first woman to achieve the rank of rear admiral. While she herself did not start these stories—found in sources as reputable as the *New York Times,* the *Navy Times, Time* magazine, and the Baltimore *Sun*—neither does she seem to have discouraged them.

Another of the errors that has persisted, and to which Hopper herself really did contribute, was that the Harvard Computation Laboratory was taken over by the Bureau of Ordnance (BuOrd) during World War II. In fact, as all primary documents make clear, it was the Bureau of Ships that ran the Computation Lab, handing it over to Bureau of Ordnance control only on 1 January 1946. Perhaps Hopper's carelessness on this point in later interviews stems from the fact that she continued to work at the lab for three years after the war, during which time it was, indeed, under BuOrd.

Regrettably, very little of Grace Hopper's personal correspondence has survived. Her voice can be heard clearly, however, in the several lengthy oral history interviews she granted over a fifteen-year period. Her energetic personality and her strong views also emerge in the hundreds of less formal interviews she gave to newspapers and journals and in her interviews on *Sixty Minutes* and the *David Letterman Show.* The extensive professional writing she left is infused with her unmistakable vigor, and the hundreds of thank-you letters she received for her speeches and presentations ring with repetition of her memorable phrases and ideas. Both sources demonstrate the range and depth of her influence. Hopper donated many of her professional papers to the Smithsonian Institution, which has the best collection. Additional papers are scattered among the Howard Aiken Papers at Harvard University and other civilian and navy collections, particularly at the various branches of the National Archives and Records Administration, and at the Hagley Museum and Library in Delaware. Hopper also left a large collection of memorabilia to the navy. It is housed in the Grace M. Hopper Building, Naval Computer and Telecommunications Station, Naval Air Station North Island, San Diego, California. Two huge crates contain all her plaques, awards, trophies, honorary doctoral hoods, and framed certificates, as well as a large collection of photographs and newspaper clippings. The navy maintains a small gallery in the building featuring a rotating exhibition from among its Hopper collection. The Charles Babbage Institute at the University of Minnesota in Minneapolis is the best source for documents on the history of computing and has an excellent oral history collection. Finally, the recollections of Hopper's colleagues, family, and friends have added valuable insights and little-known facts.

I am most indebted to members of Grace Hopper's family, who have been generous in sharing their memories in interviews and correspondence and in giving me access to family papers. I regret that Grace's sister Mary Murray Westcote did not live to see this book, but I thank her three sons, Walter, William, and John Westcote. Grace's brother's son, Roger F. Murray III, graciously showed me around the family camp at Wolfeboro, New Hampshire, and spent hours talking to me on a rainy afternoon sitting on the porch looking out at the lake that Grace loved so much. Once more I am indebted to the late Bob Campbell and the late Dick Bloch, who were there to help when I began research on Grace Hopper and who were very keen to have her story told. Ruth Brendel Noller has also given generously of her time and her memories of the early days at the Harvard Computation Lab. Rita Yavinsky, Grace's close friend at Digital, shared her many recollections with me and gave me access to her large collection of papers and news clippings from Grace's later years. Dick Fredette, who worked closely with Grace in the navy for almost nineteen years, very kindly allowed me to plague him with innumerable questions, always responding patiently, as did Norma Gealt, Grace's navy secretary.

There are a number of other people to whom I owe a debt of gratitude; without their cooperation this book could not have been written. When I had hit several brick walls, Tim Nenninger of the National Archives found accessions that included Hopper documents from the 1960s and 1970s at the Washington National Records Center, Suitland, Maryland. The navy's Jim Jenson and Lt. (jg) Steve Boatwright made it possible for me to access these collections. While at Suitland, Taiqua Wormley and Sean Brown cheerfully helped me with the masses of boxes. As so often in the past, Kathy Lloyd and Gina Akers at the

Naval Historical Center were of great assistance. Capt. Susan S. Jannuzzi, Lt. Cdr. Sandra Jamshidi, Lt. Cdr. Marianna Magno, and James E. Becker made me very welcome at Naval Computer and Tele-communications Station (NAVCOMTELSTA) San Diego, where they went to considerable trouble to enable me to spend a day browsing happily among all the Hopper memorabilia. The U.S. Navy has been both cooperative and helpful in advancing this project. I also wish to thank the many archivists whose assistance made my work so much easier: Sandy Smith and Barry Zerby at the National Archives; Michael Nash at the Hagley Museum and Library; Ronald Hindman and Eric Voelz at the National Personnel Records Center, St. Louis; David Wright at Unisys Corporation; Alison Oswald and Kay Peterson at the Smithsonian; Harley Holden and Dean Martin at the Harvard University Archives; Sylvia McDowell and Ellen Shea at the Schlesinger Library, Radcliffe Institute for Advanced Study; Dean Rogers at the Vassar College Library; Emilyn Brown and Nancy Cricco at New York University Archives; Christine Fipphen at the Wolfeboro Historical Society; Dawn Stanford at IBM Archives; Maggie Dixon at the Collegiate School, as well as David Smith and Marcia Eldridge at Brewster Academy, and Jim Hollister and Jill Rouse at Bloomsburg University. My thanks also go to the late I. Bernard Cohen, Winifred Asprey, Nancy Whitelaw, Charles Bates, the Hon. John F. Lehman, and Fred Stott, each of whom contributed help and encouragement, to Kurt Beyer for kindly allowing me to read his unpublished dissertation on Grace Hopper, and to Frank Delano for the title of this book. Beverley Ben Salem made it possible for me to spend many weeks each year at the various archives around Washington, D.C. I could not have done it without her kind hospitality. As always, my children make all endeavors worthwhile.

Doubtless there are errors and omissions; for these, alas, I have no one to blame but myself.

GRACE HOPPER

1

Remember Your Great-Grandfather the Admiral
Early Years: 1906–1944

One summer afternoon when she was young, Grace Murray climbed into her little sail canoe and shoved off from the dock. She had already acquired a considerable nautical proficiency, and her mother watched indulgently from the porch as she progressed down Lake Wentworth. Suddenly, a sharper than usual gust of wind caught the little craft, capsizing it. As Grace was to recall later, in this much-repeated tale, her mother merely picked up the megaphone she kept handy for such occasions and called to her daughter, "remember your great-grandfather, the admiral." With this stout admonition not to abandon ship, Grace clung to the upturned canoe and kicked it safely back to shore.[1]

This adventure was to become one of Grace Murray Hopper's signature tales of her youth, told and retold in talks, interviews, and articles. The story of the clocks was another in her standard repertoire. It usually ran something like this: Seven-year-old Grace had always been fascinated by the alarm clock that woke her up each morning. One day she determined to find out what made it ring. Unscrewing the back caused the wheels, springs, and cogs to cascade to the floor before she could see how they all fit together. Undeterred, Grace took apart each of the remaining six alarm clocks in the seven-bedroom house, but without any better luck than the first time. Her mother's reaction was to restrict Grace's experimentation to one clock only—a degree of restraint calculated not to dampen her daughter's enthusiasm for investigation. In later years, Grace obviously cherished this incident as indicative of her early passion to find out how things worked. She often told interviewers that she had always had a "basic drive towards technology...."[2] Both stories, moreover, reflected her view of herself as plucky, resourceful, inquisitive, and unstoppable. Later in life she was often described as "feisty" and " strong-willed," and she said of herself that she was a maverick. What she did not recount, perhaps because it did not fit this image, was that she was also much attached to a dollhouse with flowered wallpaper, a blue mansard roof, and dormer windows. She kept the dollhouse all her life.[3]

On a snowy day in December 1906, Grace Brewster Murray was born in her grandparents' brownstone in New York City, the first child of Walter Fletcher Murray (1873–1947) and Mary Campbell Van Horne (1883–1960). The baby, named for her mother's best friend, was ushered into a well-to-do, upper middle class family and had a privileged upbringing in a harmonious home. A few weeks after her birth, she and her parents moved into a fashionable new apartment building on 95th Street, off Riverside Drive, just north of the Soldiers and Sailors Monument. Grace's arrival was followed three years later by the birth of a sister, Mary Campbell (1909–2000), and two years after that by a brother, Roger Franklin Murray II (1911–98).[4]

Both sides of the family were by then well established in New York and New Jersey, of Dutch and Scottish ancestry. Walter's father, John W. Murray, had moved with his parents from Kirkubright, Scotland, to America when he was eleven, settling on the north side of 20th Street between Eight and Ninth avenues in New York City. John's father had been a builder who worked on the reservoir that used to be behind the Fifth Avenue New York Public Library. John Murray attended New York Free Academy (later City College) and moved up to what was then the countryside at 125th Street. He had a strong sense of community, joining both the Volunteer Fire Department and the New York 7th Militia Regiment, soon to be the National Guard. When his regiment was mustered into the regular army in April 1861, at the outbreak of the Civil War, John Murray, who had been elected a first lieutenant, accompanied it to Washington where it was detailed to protect the capitol. John's military career was cut short, however, when he contracted typhoid that June and was mustered out. Returning home, he moved to Plainfield, New Jersey, prospered in the insurance business, and sent his two sons to Yale University. Eventually, he became president of the German American Insurance Company. During World War I, the company was confiscated from its German owners and became the Great American Insurance Company.[5]

Grace's mother's side of the family traced its lineage back to the revolution through Russells as well as Campbells and Van Hornes. Grace would later tell interviewers that one of her ancestors was a privateer with a "well-armed brig"[6] and that another, " Samuel Lemuel Fowler, picked up his musket on 19 April 1775 and marched from Newbury to Concord Bridge to stand up to the British."[7] More recently, a maternal great-grandfather, Alexander Wilson Russell, had fought the Barbary pirates in Africa and saw action under Gen. Winfield Scott in the Mexican War of 1846–48. During the Civil War, he fought at Mobile Bay and

Vicksburg in the Union Navy and eventually retired as a rear admiral. Alexander's grandfather and namesake had been a lieutenant in the Seventh Pennsylvania Regiment during the Revolutionary War, and Alexander's brother, John H. Russell, also distinguished himself in the Union Navy in the Civil War and retired as a rear admiral in 1886. John's son and namesake, an Annapolis graduate who began his career in the navy, became commandant of the Marine Corps in the 1930s. His daughter, Brooke Russell, a distant cousin of the Murrays, married Vincent Astor, heir to the fortune of John Jacob Astor.[8]

Although she was barely two when she met him before his death, Grace retained a lifelong impression of Great-grandpa Russell—a big man with white muttonchop whiskers and a silver-topped cane. She often referred to a meeting at his home in Philadelphia as the source of her early reverence for the naval service. The incident was surely fixed in her mind more by being told about it than by memory, but Grace was never one to miss an opportunity to use a good story. Another of her stock-in-trade tales was that Great-grandpa Russell took a dim view of women and cats in the navy. When she was commissioned, she put some flowers on his grave to comfort and reassure him.[9]

John Garret Van Horne, Grace's maternal grandfather, was born in 1853 and lived until 1932. The original American branch of the family had come to Jersey City (then part of New Amsterdam) at the time of Petr Stuyvesant. John Van Horne graduated from New York University and became the chief civil engineer for the City of New York. He helped to lay out the streets in Pelham and the Bronx. Grace loved to accompany him on these expeditions and recalled with pleasure being allowed to help him by holding up the red-and-white-striped surveyor's pole and watching him figure angles and intersections. Mary Van Horne, Hopper's mother, grew up in a brownstone on 69th Street. One of her friends was Marie Borden of the Borden milk family.

Surrounded by books in their home at 316 West 95th Street, Grace was raised in a family where intellectual curiosity was encouraged and acumen rewarded. Like his father, John, Walter Murray was an insurance broker. He was a graduate of Andover Academy and a Phi Beta Kappa graduate of Yale. He started out in his father's German American Insurance Company but later formed his own company, R. F. Murray & Bro., with his older brother Roger. Grace's mother, Mary, is remembered for her love of mathematics and intellectual games and puzzles of all sorts. She used to do the *New York Times* crossword every Sunday, carefully copying it onto graph paper first, so that someone else could use the original. She, too, like her daughter after her, had sometimes accompanied her engineer father on his surveying trips in New York City. Although special arrangements had been made to allow her to study geometry in school, her formal mathematical education went no further. Nevertheless, she was very intelligent and well informed and had strong opinions on everything, particularly world politics, and delighted in expressing her views freely. Her son once remarked that, during his mother's youth, it was unthought of for a girl to go on to college but that she was determined her daughters should do just that. This notion was reinforced in 1915 when her husband, who suffered from hardening of the arteries, submitted to the only procedure then available, amputation of his leg. His children were eight, five, and three.[10]

Soon, Walter Murray's other leg was also removed at the knee. At a time when few women drove, his wife went right out and bought a car, a Model-T Ford, and when he was well again, drove her husband to work every day. Throughout his long recovery, Mary took up much of the burden of running the household that would normally have fallen to Walter. It was she who paid the bills, balanced the accounts, and figured the taxes. " She was Dutch, you know," her daughter Mary said of her mother years later, as though that was sufficient to explain her fortitude.[11]

Against the odds, Walter Murray survived for many years after his double amputation, dying in 1947 at the age of seventy-four. His insurance business thrived and he got around on wooden legs and two canes, even continuing to play golf. Totally unselfconscious about his legs, he loved to tease his children about how seldom he had to change his socks—only when they got dusty. A slender, bald man with just a fringe of hair, he was very self-sufficient and seldom asked anyone to do anything for him. He never complained about anything and was always cheerful. Still, he was also aware of his shortened life expectancy because of his poor circulatory system and was insistent that his daughters be educated to support themselves should they need to. In the early twentieth century, middle-class young women were generally prepared only for marriage and motherhood. The Murrays' determination to see their daughters schooled for employment was rare.[12]

All three children adored their father and seem to have felt a pressure to live up to his high standards. After all, if he could thumbtack his socks to his mahogany legs, then there was no obstacle they should not be able to overcome. Looking back after more than eighty years, Grace's sister Mary remembered what fun she and her brother Roger had had together. Grace, however, she pronounced to be "kind of a bore."

Perhaps she became that way, her sister speculated, because from an early age their mother put on Grace the burden of taking care of her younger siblings. " We always had maids and everything," recalled Mary, " but Grace was supposed to tell us what to do."[13]

As was customary in that day and for people of their circumstance, the Murrays also employed a nanny to help care for the children when they were young. Grace remembers being taken with her sister to play in Riverside Park in the afternoons. Every couple of months or so, Grace and her family would take a ferry across the Hudson—there were no bridges nearby, and no tunnels yet—and then ride the Jersey Central down to Plainfield to spend the weekend with their Murray grandparents. The extended family was close and everyone went, all the children and grandchildren. The Walter Murrays were also frequent visitors at Grace's maternal grandparents' on 69th Street. On the weekends, Mary Murray would pile all the children into the car and take them to historic or cultural sites in the city. Later, they had a subscription to the Saturday morning lecture series at the Natural History Museum and the Philharmonic Children's concerts. Mary pursued her determination to have her children know their city well with the same sort of persistence later seen in her oldest child. Years later, Grace remarked that she had probably been to every single museum in New York. The Murray children were never spoon-fed, though; they were encouraged to have new ideas and to innovate. Their ideas were taken seriously, carefully evaluated, and good ones were rewarded with a pat on the back. The children were also expected to hold their own in the debates the whole family enjoyed so much. Grace learned at the dinner table how to make an argument and back it up convincingly.[14]

Like many girls of her time and class, Grace attended private girls' schools. She went to the Graham School at 42 Riverside Drive, a few blocks from home. The school, which marked its centenary when Grace was nine, was one of the oldest for girls in New York City and was older than the well-known Seven Sisters women's colleges, to which many Graham School graduates aspired. Nearby Barnard College, for example, was barely twenty-five years old that year, and Vassar College, just up the Hudson River, which Grace would later attend, was only fifty-five years old. The Graham School boasted an illustrious faculty: Elihu Root, later secretary of state, secretary of war, and U.S. senator from New York, was one of many well-known former teachers. The school was also just around the corner from the venerable Collegiate School for boys, the oldest independent school in the United States, where Grace's brother went. The Collegiate School was affiliated with the West End Collegiate Church next door—an outgrowth of the Dutch Reformed Church—that the Murrays attended.[15]

In general, women's career opportunities were highly circumscribed until major changes began to occur in the 1960s. Yet even at a time when there were still many restrictions, it had been possible to view progress with optimism. In an address celebrating the Graham School's centenary, noted educator of women Dean Virginia Gildersleeve of Barnard College contrasted her present educational preoccupations with the prevailing attitudes of one hundred years earlier. To make her point, she quoted a member of the Board of Aldermen of Plymouth, Massachusetts, who in the early nineteenth century had emphatically declared himself " opposed to educating girls. A woman might come into the room when I was writing a letter and look over my shoulder and say, 'that word is spelled wrong.' I should not like that." Dean Gildersleeve pointed out to the listening girls the advances that had occurred in women's education since then. Nowadays, she explained, she had constantly to " grapple with the complexities of a college curriculum and try to figure out how much calculus and psychology and anthropology Sarah Smith may reasonably be expected to absorb in a given time." Moreover, she continued, energetic reformers were at that very moment urging on her "the necessity of providing courses in vocations for women, advisers to inform our students concerning the multifarious courses open to women today, and psychological tests to determine which they should enter." Twenty-seven years later, Gildersleeve, still a Barnard dean, played an important part in opening the way for women to join the navy.[16]

Much has been made of the early twentieth century focus of private schools on training girls for marriage and motherhood. Dean Gildersleeve was another side of the academic environment in which Grace grew up, and she was a very different sort of role model. Grace herself gave an early hint of her independence with a rhyme published in the Graham School yearbook in 1916:

Faithfulness in all things
My motto is you see;
The world will be a better place
When all agree with me.[17]

The self-confidence—as well as the humor—of these lines remained life-long attributes. Years later, interviewers noted Grace's low-key voice and her initial reserve, as though she were summing them up before deciding what to say. Everyone seemed to agree that she was generally a quiet person, one who got her own way not by force but by persuasion. But everyone also agreed that she generally did get her own way. Patience and persistence were notable characteristics, but when she spoke she could be very direct. Her nephew, Roger, easily recalled many instances of this. He never found her intimidating at all but, for example, when she was on the phone and had had enough of the conversation she would just say so and hang up.

Although its members were reserved and not prone to show emotion, Grace's family gave her a firm and loving childhood, which stood her in good stead. Both sides of the family were steeped in commerce and believed in its value. Grace's mother used to say that her father was a self-made man and had done it all on his own, without help from the government. The Murrays were firmly Republican and inclined to dislike Democratic social welfare schemes, although they also instilled in their children a strong sense of public service. In this environment, Grace grew up secure and self-reliant. She was never one to flounder. No one recalled her acting tentative or, indeed, anything other than focused. In all the many interviews she granted later in life, in all the articles about her, as well as in the recollections of those who knew her well, there was no suggestion that Grace was beset by doubts about her course in life, about where she had been or where she was going.

Summers in New Hampshire were an important part of this solid foundation, and even though Grace did not often return later in life, they remained for her a fond recollection of a happy youth. In 1896, her grandfather—John—who liked to fish, bought some property on Lake Wentworth in Wolfeboro, adjacent to Lake Winnipesaukee, because of the excellent bass. Wolfeboro billed itself as the oldest summer resort in America because it was the location of a summer home owned by Gen. James Wolfe. Eventually, John Murray gave a lot next door to his daughter, Minnie; another child bought property on an island in the lake; and his son Walter, Grace's father, bought a neighboring property, Oak Bluff. Soon the eight Murray children and relatives by marriage owned most of the property along that edge of the lake, creating what became known locally as the "New York" shore of Lake Wentworth. Mary Van Horne and Walter Murray had met in Wolfeboro, and Grace and her siblings spent every summer there with more than thirty cousins. They called their summer homes "camps" because they were originally rustic and somewhat primitive. For a long time it remained an idyllic spot because it was too far for most people to travel.[18]

Summers in Wolfeboro stretched from around Memorial Day until just after Labor Day. Grace went every year from the time she was six months old until World War II. In the early days, the trip took a day and a half. They rode the night boat out of New York to Fall River, Massachusetts, and then took a train to South Station in Boston. They caught a trolley across Boston and took another train from North Station to Sanbornville, New Hampshire. From Sanbornville, they took a little railroad around the north side of Lake Wentworth to Wolfeboro. Later, when they started driving to New Hampshire, the trip took even longer, the travel being mostly over unpaved dirt roads.[19]

Besides sailing and swimming, summers in Wolfeboro were also dedicated to the acquisition of what Grace's mother viewed as essential life skills. All three children kept vegetable plots and learned to cook and to sew. Even young Roger had to learn how to sew on buttons. Grace mastered needlework, knitting, and crocheting, accomplishments to which she remained attached for the rest of her life. The children were also encouraged to be sturdy and independent, and they had a great deal of freedom, although the Chief Warden (mother) posted house rules that they all had to obey. Canoes could be taken onto the lake, for example, only with the permission of the Chief Warden or the Warden (father). Even at a young age, Grace was a keen hiker, climbing Tumble Down Dick and Copple Crown and other nearby hills, regaling the friends who accompanied her with local Indian lore that she learned from books in the Wolfeboro library.[20]

When Grace's strong-willed mother got too bossy, everyone dispersed, often to sail. Even Walter would go tooling around in his specially built inboard-motor canoe. He also retreated to his workshop in an old boathouse, where he made all sorts of things out of wood, including cabinets and model houses for the children. Grace got from him a handiness with tools. As a child, she spent a great deal of time making things out of a Structiron construction kit of nuts, bolts, and pieces of metal. She also learned to play the piano and played until she was in her thirties. Her favorite pastime, though, was reading, and in the summers she could always be found sitting on the front steps with her nose in a book. Books were always at the top of her Christmas wish list.[21]

When Grace was fifteen, her cousin Sadie graduated from Vassar. From then on, apparently, Mary Murray planned to have her daughters attend the same college in Poughkeepsie, New York, one of several well-known private women's colleges catering to the bright daughters of the affluent. At seventeen, Grace failed the Latin entrance exam for Vassar, so she went to the Partridge School in Plainfield, New Jersey, for a year. Walter Murray had grown up in Plainfield, and Miss Partridge, the school principal, was a Vassar trustee. She prepared her students very well, and Vassar seldom rejected any of them. The Murray sisters were no exception. Although Grace enjoyed being a weekly boarder at the Partridge School, it must have been difficult for someone as competitive as she to have failed to get into college on her first try. She was not one to back down, however, and such episodes in her life were marked by persistence and eventual success.[22]

In September 1924, Grace finally took the train up the Hudson to begin her college career. Vassar, like other leading feminist institutions, had originally modeled its curriculum on that of Harvard and Yale, and four of the first eight professors taught science. One of the most frequent reasons for wanting a Vassar education, given by women who graduated before World War I, was the desire for a career. Among postwar graduates, however, it was much more common to hear that Vassar's popularity with their friends was a deciding factor. This reflected a pronounced shift away from the gains made by the suffrage movement in the first two decades of the century. It also signified a slackening interest in the employment opportunities opened up by the First World War. In Grace's freshman year, Vassar followed this postwar trend in women's education away from pioneering efforts at equality with men's colleges, introducing instead subjects aimed at preparing women for marriage and children. That very year the college created a School of Euthenics, offering courses such as "Husband and Wife," "Motherhood," and "The Family as an Economic Unit." These were designed "to raise motherhood to a profession worthy of [women's] finest talents and greatest intellectual gifts." Hopper's sister Mary, who followed her to Vassar in 1926, had a double major in economics and child studies although, after her children were in school, she went back to work as a statistician for an insurance company. The Depression further hastened the drift away from the goal of equality in education and economic opportunity between women and men. Widespread unemployment raised the notion that working women were selfishly taking jobs away from men on whom families depended for their support.[23]

Disregarding the trend, Grace concentrated on mathematics and physics at Vassar. Inspired by her grandfather, she had thought about studying engineering in college but knew "there was no place for women in engineering at that time."[24] Still, this bent toward the practical and for applied mathematics was a core characteristic of her life. Suggestive of this interest was her later fascination with Stonehenge. She made several visits to the prehistoric ring of giant stones in England and delighted in being photographed standing next to them. "You go back and look at Stonehenge," she told an interviewer in 1975, "and you marvel that some 4,000 years ago men could move those stones.

Then step back and see the pattern . . . the concept. And then you consider they not only had the concept but the will to make it happen." It was not only the early astronomical and mathematical notions represented at Stonehenge that gripped her, but also the extraordinary feat of engineering. As she put it, "there still had to be a guy that moved the first stone."[25]

At Vassar, Grace's inspiration in mathematics came from Professors Henry Sealy White and Gertrude Smith. White, affectionately known (although not to his face) as "Pop White," had been trained in Göttingen, Germany, the center of European mathematics, like eminent mathematicians and physicists such as J. Robert Oppenheimer, Richard Courant, Max Born, Enrico Fermi, John von Neumann, Edward Teller, and Werner Heisenberg.[26]

Before World War II, mathematics in the United States was still generally behind Europe. Until the end of the 1920s, mathematics had not yet come of age, and promising American mathematicians often went to Europe to obtain doctorates. After that, more graduate students in mathematics began to choose American universities. The mathematics being developed in the United States, however, was different in emphasis from that in Europe: it tended to be highly abstract. Applied mathematics was not strongly represented, and, in general, applied mathematicians were looked down on by their colleagues in pure mathematics. There was a widespread belief that "you turned to applied mathematics if you found the going too hard in pure mathematics." Among the few proving otherwise was Richard Courant, who had come to the United States from Europe in 1934 and who had pulled together a small group to study applied mathematics at New York University. William Prager—another fugitive from Hitler's Europe—established a program of advanced instruction and research in applied mechanics at Brown University in Rhode Island in 1941. But attitudes toward applied mathematics did not change much until World War II, when the war work of Courant, Prager, and many others, including Grace herself, proved its indispensability.[27]

As an undergraduate, Grace was not politically involved and did not run for any class offices at Vassar. Nor was she particularly interested in competing in team sports, other than water polo, which was not then an organized activity. At Wolfeboro, everybody swam, of course, as well as sailed, and she lived a vigorous outdoor life in the summer, but she did not transfer any of these interests to college. Although she had a number of close friends, she was generally not inclined to join groups. Her ambition, it seems, was just to do well for herself scholastically. She also started smoking while at college, a habit she refused to relinquish for the rest of her life.[28]

Grace was asked once, years later, about Vassar students' career goals, and she answered that most of her classmates had no goals other than to get married. If they expected to work at all, it was assumed they would become schoolteachers. She, too, therefore, "just naturally expected to teach." Grace knew of a few women with graduate degrees who were actuaries, and one or two who worked in laboratories, but they were very few. Fifty years later, Hopper attended her class reunion at Vassar and found that not much had changed among her peers. Most of them were married and, if they worked outside the home, they were mostly occupied with volunteer work. "After I'd been there about twenty minutes," Hopper recalled a few years later, "I found myself being very polite to all the nice old ladies." What she was too circumspect to say was that she found those housewives dull.[29]

Grace's flair for teaching first came out while she was still an undergraduate. One of Vassar's trustees had a daughter who was failing physics at the college, to the consternation of the administration. Hopper was asked to tutor the girl and was such a success that she soon had students lining up for help. Years later, that girl wrote to the alumnae magazine of her gratitude to Grace. "With her help," she wrote in 1996, "I suddenly began to understand the approach to science." From failing the midterm, she inched her way up to an A at the end of the year thanks to "a great teacher." From the beginning, Grace had understood that abstract concepts inaccessible to many can be made comprehensible by practical demonstration. When she taught displacement, for example, she would take her tutees into the bathroom and have someone climb into a tub full of water.[30]

Hopper graduated from Vassar with honors in 1928, majoring in both math and physics. She had also taken a great many courses in economics, public finance, money and banking, business cycles, and that sort of thing. This business background would stand her in very good stead later when she worked in industry. On graduation, Hopper won a fellowship to study mathematics at Yale, where she earned a master of arts two years later. Her father had gone to Yale, and her brother was in the undergraduate class of 1932. He, too, like his older sister, graduated Phi Beta Kappa, but with a major in economics.

While still at Vassar, Grace met Vincent Foster Hopper in Wolfeboro. His family had a home there, and he had a car before the Murray girls were old enough to drive. He would take everyone to the movies, packing them in, with some even standing on the running board and hanging on to the outside of the car. More than seventy years later, Grace's sister Mary recalled that it was she who knew Vincent first. He was a student at Princeton when they were at Vassar, and Mary remembered with obvious pleasure that when letters arrived from him "you could hold them up and everybody would see the Princeton seal there." But Grace was the one he took to the prom and whom he married.[31]

Vincent, whose father was the Rev. Dr. Abram Hopper of Trinity Reformed Church in New York City, was a brilliant young man, an English major elected to Phi Beta Kappa in his junior year. Although he was just a few months older than Grace, he graduated from Princeton with highest honors in 1927, a year ahead of her. In 1928, he received a master's degree at Princeton and that same year joined the faculty at New York University's School of Commerce, teaching courses in general literature.[32]

Grace and Vincent were married on 12 June 1930 in a traditional wedding. Her sister Mary was her maid of honor and her brother served as an usher. Grace wore a white wedding gown that had been in the family a long time. Vincent was teaching at New York University and studying for a PhD at Columbia while Grace started a PhD program in mathematics at Yale. She studied under James Pierpont and with algebraist Oystein Ore, whom she described to her sister as a very demanding Scandinavian. She also studied with Howard T. Engstrom, with whom she would have continuing contact over the years.[33]

One of her experiences at Yale was typical of Hopper. She needed to pass a German language exam but did not want to take lessons. She had not forgotten, however, the humiliation of failing Latin. So she bought a mathematics textbook in both English and German versions and taught herself enough German to get her degree. Years later, she admitted that although she could not learn foreign languages by studying grammar and could not really speak any language other than English, she had discovered that with dictionary in hand she could rather easily make sense of any foreign text she needed to understand. Later on, she used her language skills to impress generations of students. She would stand facing the blackboard and, with chalk in her left hand, would begin writing in German. When her hand arrived directly in front of her nose she would switch the chalk to her right hand—she was ambidextrous—and continue writing in French.[34]

In 1931, Grace returned to Vassar to teach, joining an almost all-female faculty. She started at eight hundred dollars a year as an assistant in mathematics and wrote her doctoral thesis in absentia from

Yale. The first courses she was assigned to teach were those with the largest sections, and those nobody else wanted, such as mechanical and architectural drawing, basic trigonometry, and calculus. Inheriting courses that were unpopular with her senior colleagues was not all a bad thing for Grace. Although she knew nothing about finite differences, she tackled a course in it, staying just one jump ahead of her students and at the same time acquiring knowledge that later sent her into computing. Because she had had one course in probability at Yale, she also picked up the probability course at Vassar. This gave her background for operations research and game theory—also to prove useful in her computing career.[35]

Hopper always maintained that she had been brought up to write things out and that she had been well trained in writing. Because she thought it was a very important skill, she used to "bug" her students about it. She started her probability course, for example, by giving a lecture on Sterling's formula. Then she would have her students write up the lecture. She marked what they handed in, covering their submissions with red ink in the process of correcting their writing. The students were generally indignant, letting her know that they were taking a math course, not English. Unfazed, Hopper replied that they would never get anywhere in math or in any other subject unless they could communicate and write clearly.[36]

At the beginning of her working life, Hopper established the patterns that were to stay with her for the next forty-five years. She brought to her job an intense focus, a tireless dedication, and an irrepressible urge to innovate. While teaching mechanical drawing to a left-handed student, she spent after-hours in the lab finding out how to reverse T-squares and triangles. She brought new texts and new materials into each course and devised new applications to catch the students' interest. The mechanical drawing course had been "deadly" before, Hopper admitted, so she livened it up by having the students do map projections, ultimately creating a whole mythical country with cities and populations. Inspired by the new Disney cartoons that were appearing, she had her students develop drawings for animation and she also taught them how to draw graphs of the sort that were beginning to be used in the newspapers. The standard calculus textbooks always had some ballistics problems, but as rocketry was just developing and catching the public attention, Grace substituted rockets for bullets. Little did she dream that soon she herself would be running such calculations on a computer for a real war. Courses that had previously had an enrollment of ten became so popular that students from all different majors signed up to take them, eventually swelling the ranks to as many as seventy-five.

These unorthodox courses had the wholehearted support of Henry White, who still chaired the department when Grace returned to teach. Her former calculus teacher, Gertrude Smith, who was still there too, also supported her. Many of the younger faculty, though, objected to Grace's methods saying she was not teaching traditional mathematics. Perhaps they were envious of the popularity of her courses. As any academic knows, however, as long as she brought students into the department, her position was unassailable. Grace, moreover, was scrupulous about taking on additional departmental and college responsibilities. She served as guidance counselor for freshmen, sat on a number of faculty committees, and was a member of the college marking committee.

Faculty at Vassar could audit courses freely, and Grace took full advantage of this, regularly sitting in on two classes a semester. She learned the basics of astronomy, statistical astronomy, geology, philosophy, bacteriology, biology, zoology, plant horticulture, architecture, and much more. She later said that this broad background in many different disciplines was invaluable to her career in computing. Each discipline had its own language and symbols, and she became increasingly interested in how computers could be used to further the interests of each. She came to see computers as tools that could be harnessed to solve problems in all subjects—for example, weather and earthquake prediction. Later, this interest propelled her into compilers and languages and other software.[37]

In the early years of their marriage, both Grace and "Hopper," as she called her husband, were extremely busy teaching, studying, and writing dissertations, but they also played badminton regularly at the faculty badminton club, and once in a while they played golf. In 1932, they added to the Murray family compound in Wolfeboro when Grace and Vincent bought and fixed up a dilapidated nineteenth-century farmhouse, Kent Farm, on nearby Brackett Road. The house was on sixty acres of land, and it cost them the $450 dollars they had remaining from a wedding gift. They worked on the house during the summers, doing much of the carpentry themselves, as well as plastering and painting. Whatever time she had left, Grace spent on hooking rugs for the farmhouse and knitting for family and friends. Although the farmhouse had no indoor plumbing, electricity, or heat, Grace and Vincent stayed there every summer until 1941. After the war, Grace traveled so much that she seldom had occasion to use the farmhouse in Wolfeboro. In 1972, she gave it to her brother's son, Roger III, who had settled in Wolfeboro permanently.[38]

During her years at Yale, Grace had won two prestigious Sterling Scholarships. In 1934, she was awarded a PhD in mathematics and election to Sigma Xi. Her dissertation topic was "New Types of Irreducibility Criteria." Between 1930 and 1934, only 396 mathematics PhDs were awarded in the United States. Of these, 334, or 84.3 percent, went to men and 62, or 15.7 percent, went to women. Between 1990 and 1994, sixty years later, the number of mathematics doctorates awarded had gone up to 5,253, but those earned by women had increased to only 20.2 percent. Yale awarded seven doctorates in mathematics between 1934 and 1937. Grace was the only woman who received one. During the 1930s, the percentage of women earning doctorates actually declined, and this was especially true in male-dominated fields such as the sciences and mathematics. The only other woman going through the doctoral program in math at the same time as Hopper was a nun. Social pressures on women to marry and have children rather than a career were an effective deterrent for many. Family influence was important, and women who went ahead with their careers were usually those who had the approval and even encouragement of their parents, as in Hopper's case, or at least their tacit acceptance.[39]

Even with a distinguished degree in hand, as she had predicted, Grace had little choice but to continue in one of the few professions open to her, the traditional female one of teaching. It should also be noted, however, that most men with PhDs in mathematics took the same route. In 1930, only 15 percent of all math PhDs were in nonacademic employment. Even in teaching, though, women were losing ground; in the 1930s, the percentage of female college teachers fell 6 percent to 26.5 percent, the decline affecting private and all-female schools as well as public coeducational ones. But Hopper was never one to fuss about lack of opportunity. Years later, when asked whether she had missed out on any career objectives because she was a woman, her response was typically terse. "Back in those days you didn't have career objectives," she said. "You had a job and you did a job."[40]

Only a minority of women with a PhD in mathematics in those days ever married and even fewer had children. Of those who married fellow academics, the man's career was almost always given priority.[41] Grace was unusual in maintaining the momentum of her career, but perhaps the effort was too much for the marriage. She and Vincent built a house on the Vassar campus where they were together most weekends during the academic year, commuting back and forth from the city to Poughkeepsie up Route 9 along the Hudson River in Grace's 1928 Model-A Ford, which she named Dr. Johnson. Such an arrangement must have put a strain on the marriage. So, too, did the immense amount of work they packed into those years. In addition to teaching full time, for the first eight years that they were married Vincent was working on his dissertation on medieval number symbolism. Grace recalled becoming fascinated with the subject herself and helped him with the research. Vincent finally received his PhD in 1938; his dissertation was published soon after.

There was also the added strain of the Depression, which was dispelled only by the rigor of living in a country at war. When wartime rationing was imposed in 1942, it made housekeeping a chore, requiring time and energy to keep track of food points and other allowances. Like other housewives, Hopper had to figure out how much meat they could have, and she was also concerned to save extra sugar points for her father "because he loved it." That is when she learned to take her drinks without sugar, "so that Dad could have it." Driving between New York City and Poughkeepsie became increasingly difficult because of gasoline rationing. They had to plan every trip very carefully.[42]

Meanwhile, moving on from the Collegiate School, Grace's brother Roger had been sent to another prestigious boys' school, Phillips Academy in Andover, Massachusetts. From Andover, Roger beat the traditional path to Yale from which he graduated in 1932 with a degree in economics and election to Phi Beta Kappa. According to his sister Mary, Roger would have liked to continue on to graduate school, but the Depression was on and he figured that his father had already spent enough money sending three children through college. One of Walter Murray's college friends was a partner at J. P. Morgan, so Roger applied for a job there first, but there were no openings. As it happened, Roger's Uncle Bert was the president of Banker's Trust Company, but it would not have done for Roger to go directly to him. Instead, he applied the usual way and was admitted to the Banker's Trust trainee program. Over the years, he worked his way up to senior management, eventually becoming head of economics at the bank.

For some time, most of the Murrays lived in the same building at 316 West 95th Street. Walter and Mary lived on the seventh floor, Grace and her husband moved into the third floor until she built the house in Poughkeepsie, and her sister and her husband moved into the sixth floor before moving to New Jersey. Brother Roger and his family lived just across the street at the corner of 95th Street and West End Avenue, and stayed there until he retired. Roger's son Roger III also attended

Andover, and Roger's nephew, Walter Westcote, went to Yale, eventually also going to work at Banker's Trust. While working for Banker's Trust, Roger spent ten years attending night school at New York University, obtaining both an MBA and a PhD in the winter of 1941.[43]

That same year, Grace won a faculty fellowship at Vassar, which allowed her to teach half time and study half time while receiving her full salary. She spent part of each week at the Courant Institute for Mathematics at New York University taking graduate courses with Richard Courant, whom she greatly admired. In part, she felt right at home with him because he was in the same Göttingen tradition as her mentors at Vassar and at Yale. He was also, according to Hopper, "a terrific teacher.... The sheer delight and inspiration of a teacher like that was fascinating." She worked with Courant on the calculus of variations and also in the area of differential geometry. According to Grace, Courant did have what she called "one trick." He made his students write up his lecture notes and that was what he put together and published "to make those books." But that did nothing to dampen what she called "a perfectly gorgeous year." Nor did the fact that at intervals Courant scolded her in his "cute accent," because, as she put it, "I kept doing unorthodox things and wanting to tackle unorthodox problems."[44]

Part of Hopper's work with Courant had involved one of the first government-sponsored defense training courses. It was on finite differences and solutions to partial differential equations. Grace later found out that this course showed up on her navy job classification punch card and was undoubtedly one of the reasons for her wartime assignment to the Harvard Computation Laboratory.

Hopper remembered Pearl Harbor vividly. She and Vincent were in their study. They had what she called a "great" double desk, and each had a window and books all around. There was a little radio nearby, and that is how they heard the announcement of the attack. Whatever problems already existed in her marriage, however, had not been resolved by the opportunity of the sabbatical to spend more time together. She and Vincent separated at the end of 1941 and were divorced in 1945. That same year, Vincent married Mabel Sterling Lewis, who had been a friend of Grace's, a year ahead of her at Vassar, and a bridesmaid at her wedding. That must have been bitter indeed. Over the next forty-five years, Vincent carved out an illustrious career at New York University. In addition to his teaching he was a specialist in Renaissance literature, a literary critic, author, editor, compiler, and translator. He died of cancer in 1976 at the age of sixty-nine.[45]

Grace continued to use her married name, never spoke of the divorce, and disliked mention of it in articles about her. Many articles, in fact, stated that she was a widow, and some, including the venerable *New York Times,* even went so far as to say that her husband died during World War II. In those days, divorce was not acceptable, it was a stigma, and if Grace was not intentionally misleading about her husband, she apparently did nothing to correct the erroneous stories.[46]

According to her sister, Grace had other relationships later on, one in particular with a navy reservist who was a telephone company engineer. It was a serious and long-lasting romance, but by then Grace was already beginning to travel extensively for the navy, giving talks. She also outranked him, which was awkward. Eventually, he married someone else. Meanwhile, the senior Murrays maintained a close family even after the children were grown and moved away. Grace's sister's sons remember gathering at Grandma Murray's in New York City every Christmas. Uncle Roger and his family were there, and Aunt Grace would arrive from Boston or Philadelphia or wherever she was then living. After her mother died, Grace usually celebrated Thanksgiving and Christmas with her brother or her sister. Mary did not think her sister missed having children but whatever the truth of her feelings, of which she left no record, she was devoted to her nephews and their families. She used to knit all the time, keeping the boys well supplied with sweaters and socks, eventually extending the gift list to her grand-nephew and -nieces. Many of her colleagues noted that later in life Hopper sat busily embroidering or knitting through board and committee meetings. Beware the person who took this industry for inattention, however. She never missed a point, from time to time interjecting an apt comment without interruption to the clicking of her needles.[47]

Had it not been for World War II, Grace might never have left her settled life at the genteel campus in New York where she was teaching. The war brought an end to her Vassar career and to everything predictable about her future.

When the Japanese attacked Pearl Harbor, there were no women in the U.S. Navy, or in any other military service. In early 1942, a generally reluctant navy was driven to consider admitting women, especially when the newly created War Manpower Commission declared itself unable to supply a sufficient number of men to satisfy the needs of the projected naval expansion. Uncertain how to proceed, the navy appointed Dean Virginia Gildersleeve, long an advocate of women's causes, to chair an advisory council for the Women's Reserve United

States Navy. Gildersleeve was directed to draw up the initial plans for a women's naval force, although, as she expressed it later, ". . . if the Navy could possibly have used dogs or ducks or monkeys, certain of the older admirals would probably have greatly preferred them to women." [48]

On 30 July 1942, Congress authorized the establishment of the Navy Women's Reserve. Gildersleeve's national reputation had attracted a remarkable group of very able women to head the proposed new force, including forty-two-year-old Mildred McAfee, the president of Wellesley College in Massachusetts, who soon became the first director of the WAVES—Women Accepted for Volunteer Emergency Service. Stringent limitations were imposed on navy women. They would be temporary emergency personnel only, signed on for the duration of the war plus six months, and restricted to serving ashore within the forty-eight states. No numerical limits were set, but Rear Adm. Randall Jacobs, Chief of Navy Personnel, had told the Senate that he thought numbers "will probably go up around 10,000 before we get through with it." In the end, the total number of women who served in the navy reached almost one hundred thousand. There was also a cap on promotions: McAfee was to hold the top post with the rank of lieutenant commander. Only 35 WAVE lieutenants were authorized, and no more than thirty-five percent of the remaining officers could be lieutenants (junior grade).[49]

Still, Grace was eager to join. Although she eventually spent almost forty-three years in the navy, initially she had to fight to get in. In 1942, Hopper was already thirty-five and considered old for enlistment. To make matters worse, she failed the physical exam because she weighed in at only 105 pounds, 16 pounds under the navy weight guidelines for her height of 5 feet 6 inches. She was not thin because she ate too little; neither she nor her sister ever weighed more than 106 pounds their whole adult lives, and her brother weighed only 130 pounds. She tried to tell the navy her weight was the result of her Scottish ancestry; she was lean and tough, she said, and did not need to weigh 120 pounds. Her sister explained that Grace liked food and she also liked to cook, although when she was commuting back and forth from Poughkeepsie to New York City, her mother-in-law, who lived with them in the city, did the cooking for Vincent.[50]

An even more significant impediment to joining the navy than weight or age was her profession. Mathematics was crucial to the war effort; as a professor of mathematics, Grace was in a classified occupation and had to apply and then wait six months for a release. She persevered, however, later explaining that she had wanted to serve more directly than by teaching. Because of Great-grandpa Russell, Hopper said, she "naturally. . .went navy." Already separated from Vincent, the navy must have seemed a natural escape from a messy situation.[51]

Grace's determination to serve was expected in her family, of course. In World War II, as she put it, "...we were all in...everybody was in something." One of her cousins was a navy nurse, and another joined the WAC (Women's Army Corps). Another cousin was an architect with very poor eyesight and very thick glasses. He applied and was rejected by the Marine Corps, the navy, and even the army. He finally got into the Seabees in Houston, as a carpenter, and went on to design some of the finest latrines in the Pacific. A second cousin, Alexander R. Bolling, was in the army. He retired after the war as a lieutenant general. Grace's brother Roger, who had just received his doctorate that winter of 1941, tried for a commission but was rejected for poor eyesight as well as—like his sister—for being underweight. He finally found that because of the draft he could get in as an enlisted volunteer, which he did. He was quickly accepted for Officer Candidate School training in Florida, earned a commission, and served in the army air forces until 1946. He reached the rank of captain, receiving a letter of merit and the medal for merit for his work as secretary of the Air Coordinating Committee. After the war, he returned to his job as vice president of the Banker's Trust Company. Roger's wife worked at the Office of Scientific Research and Development (OSRD).[52]

Grace's sister, who could not join the military because of her three young sons, ran the nursery at the General Electric plant in Bloomfield, New Jersey, for all the women who were working there making proximity fuses for the defense industry. Vincent, who was also overage at thirty-five, tried to get a commission but kept getting turned down, mostly because of poor eyesight. Like his brother-in-law, he finally got in as an enlisted volunteer. The Granite State News, of Wolfeboro, which like many local papers had a column recording the wartime service of its native sons and daughters, announced that on 8 December 1943 Vincent Hopper graduated from the Army Administration School with superior honors. He served until 1945 as an enlisted classification specialist with the army air corps/army air forces. Grace Hopper's mother, Mary, served on a ration board, and even her father, who had retired before the war, went back to work for his insurance company when all the young men left. He also served on the local draft board.[53]

Many other people of all ages prepared for war in different ways. Hopper's mentor, Richard Courant, did much valuable war work on gas bubble phenomena in underwater explosions, commissioned by the

Applied Mathematics Panel. This work, done in consultation with the navy's David Taylor Model Basin, was described as "of the most direct and immediate importance in connection with the underwater protection of ships." After the war, his institute continued to do work under navy contracts.[54]

As early as October 1940, Congress appropriated nine million dollars for the cost of condensed college-level engineering courses designed to meet the shortage of engineers trained in fields essential to the national defense. The Federal Security Agency of the U.S. Office of Education administered the program known as ESMDT (Engineering, Science, and Management Defense Training), and in 1941 over 2,300 ESMDT-sponsored courses were offered in 144 engineering schools in the United States and Puerto Rico. The following year, Congress voted an additional $17,500,000 to expand the program to include training for chemists, physicists, and production supervisors. Once the war began, the program accelerated, changing its name to ESMWT, for war training. Although courses had educational prerequisites, there were no restrictions on participants regarding their "age, sex, race, or color."[55]

Under the driving force of Dean Gildersleeve, Barnard College established its own Faculty National Service Committee to examine the contents of all courses that might be of value as "war minors" to students majoring in the various departments. As far as possible, such courses were to be related to "requirements of Civil Service, Army, Navy, or other war works demands," to help prepare students to join the war effort. Barnard's geology department identified meteorology, geological survey work, work in photogrammetrics, and courses in topographical drafting as suitable war minors. For each of these, a good foundation in mathematics and physics was required. On 19 February 1942, professor of engineering Frank Lee suggested to Dean Gildersleeve that they institute an ESMDT course in statistical drafting. This was in response to "a request . . . by the Navy Department for chartists for immediate employment by the navy."[56]

Similar ESMDT/ESMWT and war minor courses were offered at many women's colleges including Bryn Mawr, Manhattanville, New Jersey College for Women, Sweet Briar, Goucher, Pembroke, Skidmore, Radcliffe, and Wellesley. The Committee on College Women Students and the War, under the American Council of Education, was also active in promoting "significant plans or programs for the higher education of young women to prepare them to meet the specific needs already developed in the war period." One of the most successful of these programs was the joint New York University/Vought–Sikorsky venture instituted to train women as aeronautical engineers. The Vought–Sikorsky Aircraft Division of the United Aircraft Corporation produced, among other navy items, shipboard fighter planes such as the F4U-1 Corsair.[57]

Disappointed in her first attempt to join the navy, Hopper spent the summer of 1942 in New York City teaching mathematics at Barnard to women enrolled in the special war preparedness courses. All that summer she watched midshipmen from the training ship on the Hudson River march past her window, and every day she longed even more to join the navy. She felt even worse the following year when everybody was contributing to the war effort and there she was, a comfortable college professor. She finally persuaded Vassar to approve a leave of absence by telling them she was joining the navy no matter what. The navy then gave her a waiver for the weight requirement—which she carried around with her for the next several years. Her marital status was not an impediment because she had no children. In December 1943, having just turned thirty-seven, Hopper was sworn in to the U.S. Navy Reserve. Although she did not know it at the time, she was about to embark on a new career that would absorb the rest of her life.[58]

Looking back ten years later, Grace, then working in Philadelphia and still in the naval reserve, said that her life since graduation seemed divided into two parts, the dividing line being the date she applied for a naval reserve commission. "Part one now seems very long ago," she said. "At the time it seemed like a very busy life, teaching at Vassar. From here it looks like a pleasant, smooth, almost pastoral life. And, it seems very far away, and legend like."[59]

Grace was sent for WAVE officer training to the Northampton Midshipmen's School at Smith College in Massachusetts where, unlike male officers who were trained as "90-day wonders," women officer candidates received only sixty days' indoctrination. "Thirty days to learn how to take orders, and thirty days to learn how to give orders, and you were a naval officer," Grace recalled with amusement. For the first thirty days they were all apprentice seamen and learned to take orders. If they washed out, as some did, they could still be in the navy as enlisted personnel. Grace could not afford to wash out though, because she was too old to enlist. If she failed the second part of the course, she was out of the navy completely. During the second month, WAVE officer candidates, now midshipmen, learned how to give orders. They were trained to do this in a level voice, clearly and without shouting. They also learned to march, to compose navy letters and reports, and to recognized ships and aircraft, among many other things.[60]

To her surprise, Grace enjoyed the drill most of all. It seemed just like dancing to her, which she had always loved. She turned out to be very good at drill and was made the battalion commander. Officer candidates also studied the organization of the navy, its history, and its traditions and customs. "We had to have good enough sense to talk about the deck and the overhead and not the floor and the ceiling and we had to talk about bulkheads and try and make those crusty old admirals happy," Hopper recalled. The midshipmen were trained in navy protocol and in the proper demeanor. Hopper learned the lessons well and later this caused problems. As she explained, "I had the darndest time trying to let admirals go through doors ahead of me and they tried to treat me like a lady and get me though the door first and we usually ended up going through together which was bad."[61]

The WAVES were divided into two battalions, the campus battalion and the so-called hotel battalion for the women who lived in the Northampton Inn. Grace was in the hotel battalion. Always fastidious about her clothes and sensitive to fashion, Hopper was appalled at the "horrible lisle stockings" they had to wear. Nylon stockings had just become available, but all nylon was needed for parachutes and other defense efforts, so the WAVES were issued thick cotton stockings. They also had heavy black navy shoes, much to the disgust of many.[62]

Hopper was older than most of the other officer candidates, and in fact there were numbers of her former students among them. She had not had to study for exams in years and found all the memorization difficult. "I could figure out anything that derived itself logically, but that wasn't logical—you just memorized it and tried to put it together," she recalled. In many ways, though, Hopper saw that she had a much easier time than "the youngsters," as she called them. She had had a very hectic life over the past few years, juggling teaching at Vassar and Barnard, taking courses at New York University, commuting between New York City and Poughkeepsie, writing, running a home, and taking care of a husband and parents. She had always had to assign priorities and strictly manage her time and resources. In the navy, all the minor decisions were made for her. She did not have to fuss over what to wear and she did not have to think about what to fix for dinner. Best of all for Hopper, because of the wartime meat shortage, the WAVES were served fish every night for dinner, and lobster on Sundays, which she loved. Whereas the youngsters rebelled against the uniforms, the lack of freedom, and the food, once Hopper got over the cotton stockings, she reveled in the life. She relaxed into it "like a featherbed and gained weight and had a perfectly heavenly time."[63]

Although she later said she should probably have studied harder, Hopper graduated at the head of her class of eight hundred WAVE officer candidates at the end of June 1944. Because of her PhD she was commissioned a lieutenant (junior grade [jg]), whereas most of the women became ensigns. Her commission read: "I do hereby appoint *him* a Lieutenant (jg) of the U. S. Naval Reserve." Hopper believed had she in fact been a man she would have been sent to sea, but women were restricted to shore duty and, at that time, still within the continental United States. Hopper thought she knew where the navy would assign her. One of her instructors at Yale, Howard Engstrom, was in the naval reserve running what was misleadingly termed the Communications Supplementary Activity in Washington, D.C. It was, in fact, the navy's cryptographic center, where they were working on machines to break enemy radio codes. At the time, of course, Grace had no idea they were building code-breaking computers; that was a closely guarded secret. But she thought her math background would make her suitable for working with Engstrom, whatever he was up to. During the war, in addition to taking advantage of ESMWT courses, the navy had devised its own correspondence courses for civilians who wanted to help the war effort. When a course on cryptanalysis was sent out to college math departments, including to Vassar, Grace and three or four colleagues took it. Then Grace spoke to Engstrom and thought it was all arranged for her to join him in Washington as soon as she finished midshipmen's school.[64]

What she did not know was that while she was in Northampton, the navy had taken over the use of a computer at Harvard, and the director of the project had informed the Bureau of Naval Personnel (BuPers) that he needed a crew of mathematicians with experience in finite differences. Grace's course with Courant in the solution of partial differential equations was a strong qualification. Her orders were changed, and at the beginning of July she was sent to the Bureau of Ships Computation Project at Harvard.[65] Long after the war, when asked how she was selected for that duty, Hopper's answer was characteristically succinct: "The Bureau of Naval Personnel's punch cards turned me up with a PhD in mathematics. So they shot me to Harvard."[66]

2

You're in the Navy Now
The Harvard Years: 1944–1949

"My orders read 'Navy Liaison Office,'" Grace Hopper recalled later, describing her arrival at Harvard on 2 July 1944. After hunting around the campus she finally found the navy office in the basement of a university building on Divinity Avenue. At least they had heard of the Bureau of Ships (BuShips) Computation Project, but they were not sure where it was. A letter confirming their responsibility for liaison with the new project had been sent only the week before. Finally, at about 2 o'clock in the afternoon Hopper was directed to another basement—protected by navy armed guards—in the Cruft Laboratory.[1] She still did not know why she was in Cambridge, Massachusetts, rather than Washington, nor what she was expected to do once she arrived. A guard escorted her downstairs to the Computation Project where she reported for duty to Cdr. Howard H. Aiken. An exasperated Aiken immediately demanded to know where the hell she had been. At six feet four inches tall, with piercing gray eyes and wild eyebrows, Hopper's new boss was a formidable sight. As Hopper tried to explain that she had been allowed weekend leave and then had spent most of the present day trying to find the lab, he brushed her excuses aside. No, he said, he meant where had she been for the past two months? He had told the Bureau of Personnel that she did not need midshipmen's school because she already had a doctorate. Besides, in this job she would have no use for enemy aircraft recognition skills. To his disgust, Hopper had been sent to Northampton anyway.[2]

Aiken had some reason to be upset. He was already swamped with work. Even before BuShips had figured out the administrative details of the Computation Project, news of its existence somehow got around and requests for help with difficult or lengthy mathematical computations poured in. On 14 June Capt. T. A. Solberg, head of Research and Standards at BuShips, had already been forced to write to the director of the MIT Radiation Lab to explain that "with the limited number of personnel, and the existing work load," he did not expect the Harvard facility to be available for MIT computations for several months. "It has been necessary to set up a system of priorities," he concluded.[3]

Now that Hopper had arrived at last, Aiken asked if she had a place to live. When the reply was "no," instead of being concerned he only barked: "Well, get to work and you can find a place to live tomorrow." Then he took her into the machine room. "That's a computing engine,"[4] he announced, pointing to a large, loud mass of machinery. After briefly explaining what the machine was for, Aiken told her he would be delighted to have the interpolation coefficients for the arc tangent series by the following Thursday. He handed her a slim codebook and gave her one week to learn, as she put it, "how to program the beast and to get a program running."[5]

Thirty years later, when she was asked how she became interested in computing, Hopper replied that she had had no choice in the matter. "I was ordered to the first computer in the United States by the United States Navy," she said, "and I reported to the Mark I computer."[6]

U.S. Navy computing got its start in two major but unconnected efforts in World War II. Each effort flowed from a particular navy imperative. One was for extensive computation of ordnance firing tables. The other was for radio intelligence derived from reading enemy radio codes and ciphers. The urgent need for firing tables instigated BuShips' takeover of the Computation Laboratory at Harvard University in 1944. While the Allies were fighting in Normandy, navy mathematicians were running numbers for ballistics tables on the Harvard Mark I, a digital computer, in Cambridge, Massachusetts.

The dependence of modern navies on long-range radio communication secured from eavesdropping by codes and ciphers spawned the navy's other major wartime computing operation, the Communications Supplementary Activity—Washington (CSAW, pronounced see-saw), presided over by Howard Engstrom. This was the navy's main cryptologic agency during the war, where Hopper had thought she was headed. Until public disclosure in the 1970s, few knew of the navy's secret World War II code-breaking computers at CSAW. Much of the construction of those single-purpose computers—derived from the British Turing Bombes—was conducted in association with National Cash Register in Dayton, Ohio, at the Naval Computing Machine Laboratory.[7]

Between the two world wars the growth of large-scale businesses had already sparked efforts to come to grips with modern calculation and record-keeping needs. Work progressed in several industrial as well as academic laboratories on improved calculators, and one or two early computer designs were produced. By 1930, Dr. Vannevar Bush and his colleagues at MIT had developed a differential analyzer—a general-purpose, automatic analog computer made up of a mass of wires, tubes, and gears, and driven by electric motors. Copies of the analyzer were eventually widely used in the war effort, especially to solve some of the navy's complex ballistics problems. Similar, but simpler, analog machines were also used during the war for radar and gunnery.

Dr. George R. Stibitz was engaged in a parallel effort at Bell Telephone Laboratories (BTL). In 1940 Stibitz put into operation a digital device called a "partially automatic computer" using as its basic elements the standard relays and switches that had been developed for dial telephone exchanges. It was capable of performing addition, subtraction, multiplication, and division of complex numbers. By the mid-1940s BTL had also completed machines roughly comparable to the Mark I in overall performance. At the same time, at Iowa State College, mathematician John V. Atanasoff was working on a device he described as a matrix multiplier. Some have argued that this was the first electronic digital computer, at least in America, but it never became operational.[8]

Overseas, advanced computer developments were also in progress, accelerated by the war. In Germany in 1938, six years before the Mark I, engineer Dr. Konrad Zuse completed his Zuse 1, an electromechanical relay computer. By 1943 he had completed the Zuse Z3, which was probably the first fully functional general-purpose digital computer and which was used—although too late to affect the outcome of the war—in the German aircraft industry and in the engineering of V2 rockets. In Britain impending war brought a rush of computer developments focusing on code-breaking applications. The electromechanical Turing Bombes were succeeded by the Colossus series, also produced by mathematician Alan M. Turing for cryptanalysis. The first Colossus, an electronic protocomputer, became operational in January 1944, just at the time the Mark I was installed at Harvard, and was undoubtedly one of the most important computer developments of the war.[9]

The Mark I was Howard Aiken's brainchild, the culmination of a project he began in 1937 as a graduate student at Harvard. He had been studying the ionosphere, particularly with regard to radio reflections, but had become frustrated by the tedious and time-consuming mathematical calculations required for his doctoral dissertation. Hoping to speed up this work Aiken sketched out a design for a mechanism to perform the calculations he needed automatically. His idea was to join together a large number of calculators to operate simultaneously so that data could be passed from one to the next in sequence. It was a kind of assembly line concept, according to Hopper, and very innovative.[10]

Engineers at International Business Machines—IBM—built Aiken's device under his guidance but using many of their own patented parts and guided by their long experience with calculating machines. Aiken gave up his rights to the design in exchange for IBM's assistance in creating the device. What emerged from the collaboration, the Automatic Sequence Controlled Calculator (ASCC), or Harvard Mark I, was the first functional, large-scale, automatically sequenced, general-purpose, digital computer to be produced in America. The press called it a "Robot Brain" and sometimes even an "algebraic superbrain," but Aiken, by then a professor of physics and applied mathematics, called it "just a lazy man's dream," intended for use in scientific numerical computation.[11]

By the time the Mark I was finally completed at the IBM facilities in Endicott, New York, at the beginning of 1944, America was at war and what had begun as the timesaving concerns of a graduate student had assumed a much larger significance. In light of the national emergency, IBM president Thomas J. Watson Sr. gave the computer to Harvard as a gift and in May 1944 the Mark I was taken over as a project of the navy's Bureau of Ships. Desperate for gunnery and ballistics calculations and recognizing the importance of the Mark I, the navy leased it from Harvard for the duration of the war.[12]

Meanwhile Aiken, "the fighting professor," who had joined the U.S. Naval Reserve already, had been called to active duty in mid-1941.[13] He took up a commission as a lieutenant commander and went to teach magnetic mine technology in Yorktown, Virginia. While at the Mine Warfare School Aiken made many trips to Washington, D.C., most probably to advertise that his machine was under development by IBM and to arrange for its use by the navy when it was ready. In the interim he needed someone in Cambridge to act as his deputy on the project and as liaison with IBM. That winter he recruited and hired Robert V. D. Campbell, a graduate student in the Harvard Physics Department, to work closely with the IBM engineers to bring his machine to completion. Campbell's main tasks were to check circuit diagrams and to develop programs to test each component of the computer as it was built. There was no precedent for much of what he was doing nor any training; everything done on the Mark I was being done for the first time.[14]

In January 1944, with Aiken still stuck in Yorktown, the Mark I had been disassembled at Endicott, transferred to Harvard, and set up in the old battery room in the basement of the Cruft Laboratory by a team of IBM technicians. On one of his trips to Washington, Aiken had visited the Naval Research Laboratory in Anacostia, where much of the navy's research on radar, radio, and sonar was conducted. While there, Aiken recruited Richard Bloch, a naval reserve ensign and recent mathematics honors graduate of Harvard. It did not take much to persuade Bloch to return to his alma mater to work for the navy on a unique new calculating machine. Finally, in June 1944, Aiken was promoted to commander and sent to run the BuShips Computation Project at Harvard where he became, as he put it, "the only man in the world who was ever commanding officer of a computer."[15]

The computing machine taken over by BuShips in 1944 was unique in many ways. In appearance it bore no resemblance to the computers of sixty years later. First of all it was enormous, some fifty feet long, eight feet tall, and eight deep, filling an entire room. It had more than 750,000 parts, used 530 miles of wire, and had 3,000,000 wire connections, and its main assembly weighed about five tons. A four-horsepower electric motor and a drive shaft that extended the length of the machine drove all the mechanical parts by a system of interlocking gears, counters, switches, and control circuits. Over a thousand ball bearings kept its components moving. Built to exploit the ideas of Charles Babbage, a nineteenth-century professor of mathematics at Cambridge University in England, the Mark I was a rare creature. It was an electromechanical digital computer—destined to dominate the field for only a year or two, briefly bridging the gap between calculators and electronic computers.[16]

Aiken described the Mark I as a "general arithmetic machine capable of addition, subtraction, multiplication, division, and the transfer of numbers." He explained that the machine could add and subtract in three-tenths of a second and took only 14.7 seconds for division. Calculating logarithms took the machine fifty-nine seconds and working out trigonometric functions could be done in eighty-eight seconds. Most impressive, however, was the machine's automatic functioning, which enabled it to proceed through a series of arithmetic operations by means of relays and step counters without human intervention.[17] It had one very unusual characteristic, however, not found in later computers. The machine would stop dead at the end of an operation unless the number seven, or some other automatic signal, had been entered to tell it to go on to the next operation. According to Hopper, this had its uses, especially for debugging, but she never heard of another computer that stopped at the end of every single operation without that signal.[18]

When problems were brought to the lab they had to be put into language the machine could read—machine code—using the codebook that covered all types of mathematical problem. Once a problem was coded, the operator, usually an enlisted man, punched the appropriate code holes in a four-inch-wide tape on a manual tape punch. The tape punch perforated the streamers of paper that, when fed into the calculating mechanism, dictated its operation in a manner not unlike that of a player piano's music roll. After the problem was run the tape was preserved so that it could be used again on future problems.[19]

Automatic sequence control was accomplished according to the coded instructions on the punched paper tape. The holes in the tape were recognized by mechanical feelers, which controlled the closing of electric relays. These relays set up the electric circuits necessary to route numbers and to initiate the various procedures. The code on the paper tape gave the machine three jobs to do: it told the machine which storage device to go to to get a given number or series of numbers, where to put those numbers, and then what to do with the numbers. Items of information might read, for example, "Take the number out of counter A; deliver to counter B; start grouping operation." The result, the output, was handled either by punch cards or by two electric typewriters. Thus began the concept of programming, central to Aiken's understanding of computing, and perhaps the most important lesson Hopper learned from him.[20]

The multiple-purpose capabilities of the Mark I—the fact that it could be set to accomplish a wide range of different types of numerical calculations—was one of its great strengths and set it apart from other contemporary computing devices. Among the types of problems it could tackle were problems of integral calculus, solution of ordinary differential equations, solution of simultaneous linear algebraic equations, harmonic analysis for problems of vibrations and oscillations, and statistical analysis. Aiken also predicted that his machine would enable statisticians to work with many more variables than had previously been possible and that it held the key to the solution of differential equations. It could also be used in the evaluation of integrals and would be useful for all phases of applied mathematics. Concerned about making a contribution to the war effort, Aiken correctly foresaw that the Mark I could be used in the fields of atomic physics, radio research, investigations of the ionosphere for information on the reflection of radio waves, and optics and electronics.

For Aiken—who always wanted practical results—flexibility, accuracy, and reliability were even more important than speed, although he estimated that the Mark I was nearly a hundred times faster than a manually operated calculator. The Mark I attained its accuracy by representing numbers to twenty-three significant digits, and it had built-in error-checking procedures. It ran twenty-four hours a day, functioning 90 to 95 percent of the time with few interruptions for fifteen years.[21]

Aiken was well aware of ongoing experimental work using vacuum tubes to replace the relatively slow mechanical relays, but he believed it was better to sacrifice some speed for a device that could be put to use immediately. A postwar history of wartime computing developments bears him out: "electronic equipment held great promise in the high speed computing field but it appeared that the established techniques ... [of] relays would permit earlier completion of large scale computing equipment."[22] Hopper agreed, noting that vacuum tubes were not reliable enough until at least two years after Aiken started work. "He couldn't afford to fiddle around with circuits yet," she said. She further observed that Aiken's concepts were so far ahead of the material resources then available that they were later transferred to electronics when suitable equipment was finally produced.[23]

In the beginning, Aiken's crew was very small. By the time Hopper arrived in July, Bob Campbell had joined the navy and become an ensign. In addition to Ensign Bloch there were only four enlisted men and Ruth Knowlton, Aiken's civilian secretary. It is a testament to Hopper's toughness that she was not rattled by her first encounter with Aiken. In fact she quickly came to respect him and to regard him very highly, although she did refer to those early days as her "sufferings." She freely admitted that she would not have accomplished the task Aiken so abruptly assigned to her on the first day without the help of the whole crew. Before she arrived, Campbell and Bloch had been trying to bribe each other to take the desk next to hers. They had heard that a gray-haired old schoolteacher was coming and neither of them wanted to sit near her. Hopper thought she remembered that Campbell had actually paid Bloch five dollars to take the desk next to hers. Both men quickly discovered their error, however. Hopper was no stuffy schoolmarm, so they set to work to teach her coding, as programming was then called.[24]

Ens. Ruth A. Brendel arrived at the laboratory in August. She too had had trouble finding it. Its location was still a mystery to many on campus, and her orders had told her to report to the Radio Research Laboratory, which was even more confusing. As it turned out, the Navy Liaison Office—the one Hopper finally found on Divinity Avenue—had been set up initially to supervise the Radio Research Laboratory at Harvard. With the takeover of the Mark I by BuShips in spring 1944, the Computation Lab was assigned to the same liaison office, although almost nobody seemed to know that.[25]

Brendel had been an instructor in mathematics at the University of Buffalo and had joined the navy in spite of the fact that at twenty-one she already had two degrees and a good job. Keen to contribute to the war effort, she had wanted to enlist earlier but could not do so until she was twenty-one without her mother's permission. Her mother had been very reluctant to see her go because she was a widow and Brendel's brother and uncle were both in the navy already. Brendel's father, too, had been in the navy in World War I and there was a navy tradition going far back in the family, so Brendel was determined to sign on in spite of her mother's misgivings. She had fully expected an assignment teaching mathematics and was very disappointed when she received orders to the Computation Laboratory. Like Hopper, Brendel had grown up in a family that encouraged her to excel in whatever field she chose. As Brendel put it years later: "My parents were very open with me and I didn't know that girls weren't good in math."[26]

Hopper was always sure that Aiken's only concern was to get the job done, and if there were only women available with the requisite skills to do that, it was fine with him. She knew he could be equally critical of all his staff, male or female. Young and inexperienced Ruth Brendel, however, remained convinced that Aiken did not care for women, and she often found his harshness almost impossible to take. Years later, the emotion still in her voice, she described "the commander," as they all called him, as a huge, very gaunt, overpowering individual. "You didn't ask him questions," she said emphatically. According to Brendel, Aiken was not a teacher and did not see himself as one. In fact he had nothing but scorn for academics and told Brendel repeatedly: "If you know something, you can teach it." He regarded himself as a researcher and expected everyone else who worked with him, or under him, to emulate him. Many people differed with Brendel on Aiken's teaching skills, Hopper in particular. In 1964 Aiken won a prestigious award for computing and he was honored, among other things, for "the knowledge and inspiration imparted to many as a teacher." His biographer, I. Bernard Cohen, went even further, asserting that "the galaxy of students who received degrees under his direction may, in the long run have been his greatest contribution to the developing computer age." Brendel could not get on with Aiken and could not see in him any of the qualities of a good teacher that she so much admired.[27]

Many times Brendel determined to seek a transfer; she was especially keen to go to Alaska or Hawaii when they were opened to WAVES, but Aiken would not hear of it. He once told her that if she submitted an application for a transfer he would not process it. "We're all a part of this unit, and you're not going anywhere else," he growled.[28]

Hopper was the best antidote to Aiken. Brendel described the older woman as "a wonderful teacher, a mentor, a companion," who always shielded her from the commander and made her life at the lab bearable. "Grace and I were congenial," Brendel recalled years later, "we had a good friendship, she was like an older sister to me. I was in awe of her in the sense that she had as classmates [at Yale] the men who had written the books I was studying from." Hopper taught Brendel coding and helped her get her problems onto the machine. Brendel said Hopper mentored just about everyone there "but I worked shoulder-to-shoulder with her, elbow-to-elbow." Whenever a new problem came in to prepare for the machine, Hopper would sit and explain it to Brendel in a way she found easy to understand. Even though most of the problems involved differential equations of a more complex nature than Brendel had faced before, Hopper was "just as patient as she could be." Over the years many people found Hopper an invaluable supporter and teacher.[29]

Hopper also got on very well with Aiken. According to Brendel this was because "she catered to him and when he was temperamental, she would calm the rest of us down. She was the peacekeeper, and she was such a marvelous person." Brendel particularly recalled Hopper's sense of humor: "Everybody liked Grace and she liked everybody," she said. Hopper also had "an eye for the young men," as Brendel put it. Everyone knew Hopper was separated or recently divorced and had no commitments. At one point Brendel and the others thought Hopper and a certain navy captain "were going to be an item," but in the end "they weren't."[30]

Rank was generally not an issue at the lab; the commander ran a tight ship as far as computing went, but he was interested in performance, not hierarchy. Those present in the early days, like Campbell, remembered that "even though it was a navy organization . . . Aiken didn't stand on ceremony very much, and it was quite informal." As one petty officer recalled, "Personal relations were atypical for a navy unit." Certainly Hopper found the atmosphere great fun, and even Brendel admitted that the commander was "security conscious, but not insignia-conscious."[31]

The navy assigned enlisted men as well as officers to work at the lab. Some who had had three or four years' experience repairing IBM equipment were made petty officers with the rating of "Specialist-I" (for IBM) and were assigned to the Mark I as machine operators.

Among these were the original four, Delo Calvin, Hugh Livingston, John Mahoney, and Durward White. They did not have to have mathematical training; they installed the coded program tape, installed or changed the functional tapes, changed the specified values, set switches, and physically controlled the machine's operation. Another petty officer came not from IBM training but via the navy's Class A Electrician's Mate School. Today the Specialists-I would be known as data processors and data systems technicians. A bright young yeoman, Frank Verdonck, brought some order into the administrative operation of the lab. There was also a very tough chief, back from the Pacific, who according to Hopper never managed to learn much about the computer but was an excellent electrician, especially good at tracking down problems. He also tried to keep the crew in order, but in that he was handicapped by the rather freewheeling officers.[32]

The formal dedication of the Mark I at Harvard on 7 August 1944 was to have been a gala event with Harvard president James B. Conant accepting the machine from Thomas Watson on behalf of the university. Unfortunately, misunderstandings and a clash of egos not only marred the occasion, but poisoned Watson's relationship both with Harvard and, more particularly, with Aiken. A press release put out by the University News Office failed to do justice to the essential part played by IBM and its engineers in the implementation of Aiken's original design. For his part, Aiken introduced the Mark I to the press the day before the ceremony and gave a dramatic demonstration of its capabilities that left them with the impression of his primary role in its creation. The Boston *Daily Globe* showed a photograph of the "World's Greatest Calculator," noting that it was invented by Cdr. Howard H. Aiken, U.S. Naval Reserve. The *New York Herald Tribune* ran a large photograph of Aiken standing beside the Mark I under a banner headline reading "The Greatest of Mathematical Calculating Machines and Its Designer." Watson objected angrily to Aiken being singled out as sole inventor. It is true that some of the articles did not even name the IBM engineers without whose skill the device might never have been built. Other articles, though, like that in the *Herald Tribune,* spoke of the "joint direction" of the research on the machine. "The Commander," the paper wrote, referring to Aiken, "said that his three co-workers all contributed greatly to the construction of the machine."[33]

The Mark I had cost IBM $250,000 to build and it had taken eight years. It seemed to Watson that, compounding his other omissions, Aiken completely overlooked this generous sponsorship. Symbolic of their different agendas was the issue of the Mark I's appearance. Aiken wanted the machine left open, all the works exposed, for ease of access. Watson, on the other hand, wanted to encase it in a handsome, modern steel and glass case designed by Norman Bel Geddes. Watson won that round, and it certainly cut down the noise the machine made, but once it was under Aiken's control and fully operational, the cover was quickly discarded. President Conant was gracious at the ceremony, Watson kept himself under control and gave Harvard an additional gift of one hundred thousand dollars to help maintain the Mark I, but Aiken was unrepentant. Watson's relationship with Harvard never recovered from his perceived slights and he bore Aiken a personal grudge for the rest of his life.[34]

While some of the staff of the Computation Lab felt IBM had not been treated fairly, Hopper, who participated in the demonstration of the Mark I to the press and who later witnessed Watson's anger, always retained a negative attitude toward IBM. Almost thirty years later she recalled that some time after the dedication, when Watson visited the Computation Lab, his people took pictures of Watson and the former IBM enlisted men but not of the officers who ran the machine. She claimed "IBM never gave the credit they should have to Aiken. They gave credit to their own engineers but they did not give it to Aiken." When pressed for specifics, Hopper admitted that the multiplier, later incorporated into the Mark I, had already been invented by IBM. But, she continued, "the overall concept and in particular the secret mechanism and the interpolator, were pure Aiken." Writing to Aiken in September 1944, Harlow Shapley, director of the Harvard Observatory and an old friend, echoed Hopper's view. Returning to New York after the dedication of the Mark I, Watson had written a report of the events for *Think,* the IBM in-house magazine. Shapley had discussed the article with a friend who agreed that it was "not only totally inadequate, but unfair and misleading."[35]

Hopper was never dispassionate about Aiken, as she had not been about Courant. Nor was she to be, later, about John Mauchly, for whom she worked after the war and whom she also greatly admired. Her feelings for people ran deep and she remained intensely loyal, frequently overlooking weaknesses that seemed obvious to others.

The navy was uninvolved in, and perhaps unaware of, the tensions with IBM. The importance to them of the Mark I's numerical computing ability was indicated by the presence of many senior naval officers at its inauguration. These included Rear Adm. Edward L. Cochrane, chief of the Bureau of Ships; Rear Adm. A. H. Van Keuren, director of the Naval Research Laboratory (NRL); and Rear Adm. Julius A. Furer, coordinator of research and development.[36]

The Bureau of Ships contract for the Computation Project, which was to last until "six months after the cessation of present hostilities," was part of a pattern of increased military and government involvement with industry and academe. As war threatened, intellectual resources all over the country—especially scientific and mathematical resources—had been enlisted to tackle the challenge of a vast technological expansion. In June 1940, the National Defense Research Committee (NDRC), headed by Vannevar Bush, was established to mobilize and direct engineering and scientific talent. It was joined a year later by the OSRD. Eventually, more than thirty thousand people worked on such NDRC/OSRD projects as radar, fire-control mechanisms, proximity fuses, and the atomic bomb. At first, both the navy and the army opposed the control of wartime scientific research by a civilian organization, even though they each had representation on NDRC. By the time the Mark I was operational, however, NDRC's influence on navy science was well established, made more palatable by generous research and development grants.[37]

Traditional navy suspicion of academic labs receded once it became clear to many that this war, unlike previous ones, might be won by technical and scientific advances made during the course of the war itself. As a result, most navy bureaus worked rather smoothly with the civilian scientific structure. This cooperation was facilitated by the very large proportion of scientists—civilians and former civilians temporarily in uniform—who were involved in war-related research in academic and corporate as well as in military laboratories. Of Hopper's acquaintances, for example, Howard Engstrom headed a large group of top mathematicians, engineers, and physicists from all over the country, while Richard Courant worked as a civilian on navy applied mathematics projects.[38]

Many academic and corporate applied science facilities were under some form of supervision by both NDRC and the navy (or the army) although the chain of command was often less than clear. This was certainly true in the case of the Harvard Computation Lab. Howard Aiken technically reported to Cdr. David T. Ferrier, navy liaison on campus, for local issues. His orders, though, came from BuShips, where his contact was Cdr. Eugene Smith. In addition, he also received instructions from the NDRC's Applied Mathematics Panel (AMP) on projects to be assigned to his lab. The Mark I technically belonged to Harvard, but during the war its use was devoted exclusively to military purposes; the navy paid for its operation, all the salaries, and even an eight-hundred-dollar monthly rent to Harvard.[39]

This situation was at times confusing but hardly unique during the war. Such mixtures of civilian and military authority occurred in research facilities all over the country, including at other Harvard laboratories. Nor was the Computation Lab the only case in which the navy took over a whole organization. In 1942, the Naval Computing Machinery Laboratory was formed at National Cash Register's (NCR) plant in Dayton, Ohio. Eventually, the navy took over all NCR's cryptanalytic work. But at the Computation Lab—an entirely naval reserve outfit— civilian and military leadership were fused in the person of Howard Aiken; the navy put him in command of his own laboratory. Also, perhaps because of the small number of people involved and the innovative nature of the work, which few outsiders understood, Aiken was essentially autonomous locally, running his nominally navy facility in his own idiosyncratic way.[40]

By contrast with Germany, Britain, and Japan, American science benefited from a late entry into the war. Vannevar Bush had time to create an organization capable of connecting a wide variety of military and civilian resources in the solution of problems whose component parts were farmed out to many separate and otherwise unconnected entities. The navy's Computation Lab became one of those entities, running calculations whose results formed part of the answers to many different kinds of technical military questions.[41]

Of course, Aiken's lab was not the only one addressing the country's computing needs. During World War II, the United States manufactured approximately 45 percent of all armaments produced by all parties engaged in the conflict. Scientists and technicians worked at a feverish rate on the design, testing, modification, and analysis of these weapons, and their efforts required extensive numerical calculations. Trained specialists—usually women called "computers"—produced many of the numbers, using desk calculators. The time required to solve a problem this way was often expressed in "girl hours." Wartime pressure, however, generated government contracts to create better and faster methods of computation. Experimental work to improve computing was being done in commercial labs, most prominently at Westinghouse, General Electric, Radio Corporation of America (RCA), NCR, BTL, and IBM. In addition to Harvard, innovative computing work was also being done in academic labs at MIT and at the Moore School at the University of Pennsylvania. Different approaches were explored including relay-type computers, electronic computers, analog differential analyzers, punch-card computing, and other mechanical techniques.[42]

Although Grace Hopper left Vassar to work in uniform at Harvard in a lab taken over by the navy, there were also civilian scientists there from many other places. Harvard took on over one hundred research contracts during the war, worth 33.5 million dollars. OSRD contracts employed 1,759 people, mostly civilian, with 69 additional personnel engaged in non-OSRD work. Projects ranged in size from the 808-person Radio Research Laboratory, which occupied a whole wing of the biology building, to 454 people at the Underwater Sound Laboratory, to a lone researcher working in his own office. The Computation Laboratory was one of Harvard's smallest contracts in terms of personnel.[43]

The situation at MIT was similar. The director of the giant Radiation Lab was from the University of Rochester, while the associate director had come in from the University of Illinois. This mass relocation of scientists and mathematicians meant that many were pressed to work on problems well outside their fields and about which they had previously known little or nothing. It was not just the navy that made such demands on people.[44]

Mathematicians who found themselves in uniform were lucky if they were sent to serve in an army or navy research installation; not everyone was so appropriately assigned. Like Grace Hopper, Herman Goldstine was one of the fortunate ones. Capt. Goldstine, a University of Chicago mathematician, was ordered to the Aberdeen Proving Ground in Maryland, where he became the army's liaison with the Eckert-Mauchly team working on the ENIAC (Electronic Numerical Integrator and Computer) at the University of Pennsylvania. The ENIAC connection brought him in touch with the celebrated mathematician John von Neumann, who consulted on the project. Goldstine's wartime assignment had a profound effect on his subsequent career, just as Hopper's did. After the war he went to work in computing with von Neumann at Princeton.[45]

For other mathematicians there was work in operations research groups, some attached to various air commands or to navy units such as the Antisubmarine Warfare Operational Research Group (ASWORG), directed by the MIT physicist Philip M. Morse. Still others were associated with British and Canadian research efforts. There were also posts in industry. Bell Telephone Laboratories was perhaps the largest wartime employer of mathematicians, but others worked at RCA, Westinghouse, Bell Aircraft, and other companies with war contracts. There were also mathematicians working on the Manhattan Project.[46]

As soon as the war began the navy had moved to secure the services of eminent scientists because in some quarters, at least, there was already an understanding of the importance of maintaining a technological edge. Columbia University astronomer Dr. Wallace Eckert with his IBM machines was recruited for secret work at the Naval Observatory in Washington, working directly for the navy but as a civilian. In 1942, John Atanasoff left Iowa State College to join the staff of the Naval Ordnance Laboratory (NOL) and he, too, remained a civilian, although he was three years younger than Aiken. In June 1944, the navy tried, unsuccessfully, to lure physicist John W. Mauchly away from the University of Pennsylvania's Moore School of Electrical Engineering to work at NOL. He was told that "the Laboratory's need for men with the proper qualifications is urgent," but he declined the offer, even though he was only thirty-six (a year younger than Grace Hopper) and would have remained a civilian.[47]

The U.S. Army also recognized the importance of civilians and civilian facilities to serve its scientific war needs. It, too, funded work at many academic and industrial laboratories, recruiting a formidable group of scientists. One of the most productive of these collaborations was between the Moore School and the Army Ordnance Department's Ballistic Research Laboratory at Aberdeen, resulting in the ENIAC, designed for ballistics analysis. The navy's Computation Project at Harvard was part of this larger picture of America's mobilization for war.[48]

When Dick Bloch moved to Cambridge from the NRL in March, he had been told to get the Mark I operational as soon as possible. Bloch had never taken an engineering course and had to teach himself on the job. This was what they all had to do in the early days. Bloch's particular assignment was to learn how to develop sets of operational instructions for the Mark I. These operational instructions were written in machine code, which is why the task was referred to as coding. Hopper always believed that coding more accurately described what they were actually doing, and she regretted that the term changed to programming, which she thought should have been reserved for a higher-level operation. The first codebook, covering many types of mathematical problems, was compiled by Aiken and Bloch and was essential for the operation of the computer. According to Aiken, it was already out of date by the time of the dedication of the Mark I, but he hoped to have a new one out soon. He intended to distribute it to scientists with whom the lab would be cooperating, so they could see what the machine could do.[49]

Working at the lab exposed Hopper to many people who remained involved with computers after the war just as she did. One she considered a good friend was Eugene Smith, the navy commander who was BuShips' liaison with the Harvard Lab. She also met Dr. Mina Rees, who was with the Applied Mathematics Panel. After the war, Rees ran the Mathematical Sciences Division of the newly formed Office of Naval Research and was responsible for providing navy funding to support research in computing. John von Neumann, one of the founding professors of the school of mathematics at the Institute for Advanced Study at Princeton, appeared at the Computation Lab periodically, using the Mark I to run numbers for his atomic energy computations. Although he soon became involved with the ENIAC project and later had a great influence on the architecture of electronic computers, when he came to Harvard he still knew nothing about computing. Hopper remembers him going over and peering at the typewriter printouts, waiting for his results and frustrated by a procedure that seemed so slow.

Mathematician Norbert Weiner of MIT, who was formulating his theory of cybernetics, was fascinated with the Mark I. He visited the Computation Lab often to argue with Aiken about whether the brain functioned like a machine or the machine was created to function like the brain. According to Brendel, Weiner wanted to recruit Aiken's crew for the first society of cyberneticians, but Aiken would have nothing to do with it. Hopper was not impressed with Weiner either and did not have much good to say about him. She may well have been concerned about his pessimistic views of the impact of technology on society. Harlow Shapley agreed. In February 1945 he wrote Aiken in his usual sprightly fashion "Your friend Norman [sic] Weiner is up a stump, what with personalities and the like at MIT and too great grandeur of his ideas. . . ." Plenty of other grandeur visited the lab too. Lots of gold braid paraded through, impressing everyone working there with the importance to the war effort of the work they were doing. They also noted that Harvard's President Conant visited frequently and talked at length with Aiken. Through these contacts Hopper got to know many of the people who would play key roles in postwar computing.[50]

Years later, when asked whom she enjoyed most of the many brilliant people she had worked for in her long career, Grace Hopper chose Howard Aiken. He "always said you could make any mistake in the world once," she recalled. But "if you made the same mistake twice, heaven help you." Hopper thought Aiken an "excellent leader," who kept the group moving forward at a formidable pace while maintaining high standards, both teaching and challenging his young staff. Everyone acknowledged that he was not easy to work for, though. He would go and stand behind Hopper and growl, "So you don't know programming yet?" But she was self-confident and -assured and never minded his quirky humor. Even those most devoted to Aiken, such as Dick Bloch, described him as a "tough hombre"; at times he would bring Ruth Brendel nearly to tears.[51]

Dick Bloch was constantly getting into trouble with Aiken because he made innovative changes to the machine that improved the running of his programs, but then he would forget to change things back again, messing up the computer for the others. Hopper tried to explain to him that Aiken was exactly like a computer: he was just wired in a certain way. But Bloch was young and would insist that his way was right. "I don't care what's right or wrong," Hopper would respond, "he's wired that way. If you are going to work with him you must realize how he is wired." Being older, Hopper was particularly sensitive to the time and to the task. She pointed out that Aiken never demanded any more of anybody than he would have aboard a ship, and while it was true that they were on dry land, Hopper saw that "we needed this, and required this same discipline." Ever the pragmatist, Hopper accepted Aiken the way he was and found him excellent to work with. However, not everyone did.[52]

Numerous anecdotes about Aiken support this view. At a Harvard faculty meeting years later, according to legend, someone mentioned that Aiken was not present because he had gone to the dentist. "To have his teeth sharpened I suppose," was the quick response. Prof. Bernard Cohen, who knew Aiken and Harvard well, wrote, "Only such a man could have made a reluctant Harvard become a center for the new science and art of computing."[53]

Everyone at the lab worked compulsively long hours (although theoretically operating in three shifts), personnel and machine pushed to the limit, focusing intensely on the war effort. Most of them lived in rooming houses nearby, only a quick walk away from the lab. There were no navy quarters at that time and they could not live in Boston, where there was more choice of accommodation, because the subways stopped running at night because of the war. Hopper and Brendel lived in the same house for a few months until Brendel and Ruth Knowlton, Aiken's secretary, found an apartment to rent together and lived there for the rest of the war. At twenty Knowlton, a recent graduate of Simmons College, was even younger than Brendel, and neither of the women had ever lived away from home before. The two became lifelong friends.

In Hopper's rooming house, an old building with a center entrance, she had a big room on the first floor to the left of the front door, and a bath behind that. Brendel had a tiny room upstairs, over the door, and Hopper would tease her about her large estate on the second floor. They had no way of cooking in their rented rooms, so getting food was a problem. There was a small cafeteria around the corner from the lab, and most of the time they ate there. Brendel usually had breakfast and lunch with Hopper, and very often dinner too. But in spite of the time they spent together, Hopper never spoke much about personal things, including her husband. Brendel knew Hopper was separated, but she never knew exactly when the divorce went through.[54]

Usually, the crew at the Computation Lab felt rather like navy stepchildren, although Aiken did not mind the benign neglect at all. No one at the lab got food ration stamps because they were supposed to eat at the main mess in the nearest navy facility, the Supply School, but it was too far away and they had no way to get there. Once a week one of the enlisted men made a run over to the Supply School to buy cigarettes and whatever else they needed, but otherwise they were on their own as far as navy support was concerned. Since the lab was directly under the authority of Washington, when staff members needed medical or dental work, for example, and asked what navy facility to report to, they were told, "Go anywhere." Tucked away among surrounding ivory towers, Aiken's Computation Lab was really isolated, made even more so by twenty-four-hour armed protection.[55]

Cooped up listening to the Mark I's constant clicking (some thought it sounded like a giant sewing machine and others like knitting needles), the young staff formed a close fraternity, relieving the pressure with smoking and with practical jokes. Most of the crew smoked, but Hopper was a chain smoker. Her clothing reeked of cigarette smoke, as did her room. Many of the jokes played at the lab were at the expense of an unpopular lieutenant, who, being the most senior after Aiken, became the computation project's executive officer. The man was something of a health fanatic and had food fetishes scoffed at by all the rest. They constantly made trouble for him, including hiding all his carefully guarded bottles of carrot juice. He denounced his fellow officers to Aiken as insubordinate but in response the commander dressed him down for failing to assert his authority and maintain control. Looking back, Hopper agreed that she and her colleagues had been insubordinate, but she could not resist adding that he had asked for it.[56]

They also enjoyed making fun of Lt. Edmund Berkeley. Hopper later worked with him closely and had great respect for him, but in the hothouse atmosphere of the Computation Lab nothing was sacred. Berkeley, a former civilian "computer," had been sent up from the ballistics section at the Dahlgren Naval Proving Ground in Virginia on special assignment and he did not know much about the navy. In the beginning he was scared to death of Aiken and started sending Hopper little notes asking for help. He always stamped and dated everything, and soon began writing Aiken little memos that he left on his desk. Half the time Aiken just threw them away and when Berkeley found out he was furious with Hopper and the others for not having had the guts to tell him sooner. "We used to plague the hell out of Berkeley," Hopper recalled years later with obvious glee. One day they got a roll of toilet paper and dated and stamped each sheet and then sent it to Berkeley. They also started the story circulating that before he went to bed at night he would date and stamp the sheets so that he would know where he was when he woke up next morning.[57]

Even the old hand Dick Bloch came in for his share of ribbing. Bloch had been irritating everyone for a while, and they all knew that a naval officer cannot go outdoors without his cap. One day, when Bloch was heading out for a date, they hid his cap up on the pipes in the machine room and no one would tell him where it was. That was good for a long laugh, but the most fun was socking it to the army. The back way to an army storeroom in the basement of Cruft was next to the area occupied by the Mark I, and the army had lots of nice paper of the sort that was very hard to come by in wartime. One day Hopper and Verdonck found a whole carton of graph paper. They were just in the process of liberating it when Aiken appeared and asked what they were doing. They told him they were getting some graph paper. Almost thirty years later Hopper had no trouble remembering his reply. "Well, you better leave one pack," said the commander. "The army may not be able to count but they can tell the difference between some and none."[58]

Aiken, whom Hopper considered "a superb mentor," was constantly attentive, in his office at all hours with the door open and his back to the machine; if it stopped, he was out in a flash to see what was wrong, quickly pitching in wherever necessary to help get it going again. The greatest help, though, in finding why the machine had stopped came from an unexpected quarter: Hopper's navy-issue handbag. Machine problems, called bugs, were very often caused by fraying of the brushes on the counters, which caused them to spark. When this happened, the operators would go to Hopper and borrow the little mirror from the handbag she always had with her. Then they turned the lights off and held the mirror down into the machinery to locate where the counters were sparking. At such times the tension was palpable because everyone knew, as Dick Bloch put it bluntly: "Howard was only at peace with the world when the Mark I was producing numbers."[59]

There were so many odd quirks that could stop the machine that Hopper and Bloch experimented with what were some of the earliest systematic debugging procedures. In a lighter vein, Hopper also created a whole cartoon menagerie to explain the problems. Among the different sources of bugs was the dragon who chewed holes in the paper tape. There was also a whole set of gremlins, including the one who had a long snout with which he picked up the small dots of paper that had been carefully punched out of the tape and that had fallen to the floor. The gremlin put them back in the tape, causing the machine to malfunction. This was not wholly fanciful: it had happened that if the tape got on the floor and there were any punched-out dots lying around, those things somehow got back into position in the tape and stayed there. "Frequently we did find bugs that were nothing but the fact that a hole had gotten back into a hole," recorded Hopper with some amusement.[60]

In spite of this infestation of bugs, the Mark I produced numbers very reliably. Dick Bloch noted that Bob Campbell "was really responsible for getting the machine into productive operation," but Campbell called Bloch "the primary force as far as I'm concerned." Bloch became so skilled at programming that Hopper used to call him the Mozart of computers—the only person who could write a program, flawlessly, in ink, and have it run the first time. "He drove us nearly crazy because he could do that," she admitted. Hopper later said Bloch was the mathematician, the theory man, whereas Campbell was both theorist and realist; he could both design the machines and build and make them work.[61]

The Computation Lab had completed twenty-three reports for BuShips in less than two years when the project was transferred to the Bureau of Ordnance in January 1946. Aiken's crew had achieved a remarkable record of efficient productivity. Most of the reports were purely technical, often in the form of laboratory records, and many did not even mention the practical use to which the computations would be put. The projects were so secret that even the coders usually identified them only by letters of the alphabet. Because the machine was much more powerful than almost everything else then available, many of the new scientific developments occurring during the war passed through the Computation Lab. The personnel there were very much involved in the rapid advances in aircraft, missiles, guided missiles, and new types of depth bombs, among many other things. Radar, too, was undergoing revolutionary change, as were many other technologies. Many of the calculations run on the Mark I were essential to these new developments.

To deal with the workload as well as the rapid pace of changing weaponry and devices, Aiken had created a dynamic, innovative atmosphere that Hopper found fascinating. "It was a hotbed of ideas and concepts and dreams and everything under the sun," she later said. But there was also intense pressure. Everyone who submitted problems to the lab was in a hurry for the answers "because you see," as Hopper put it, "we hadn't had rockets, we were just beginning to have rockets. We had no firing tables for them. We had new torpedoes. Nobody knew what they were going to do. All these things had to be computed." On a table next to Aiken's desk was a telephone connected directly to the Bureau of Ordnance in Washington. They used to shake every time it rang because it would invariably be someone asking when the numbers would be ready.[62]

Aiken kept tight control of the work at the lab and it was he who handed out job assignments. He himself was kept busy running the outfit and working with Washington on a contract and specifications for a new computer, the Mark II. There was no adequate equipment at Dahlgren Proving Ground for computing range tables. After the Applied Mathematics Panel conducted a comprehensive study of the best available computing devices, the navy had selected Aiken to build an updated version of the Mark I for $250,000.[63]

Normally, in a research lab the workload would be distributed among teams, but there were not enough people to have teams at the Computation Lab so they each worked on their own problems individually. At first there were just the three of them—Campbell, Bloch, and Hopper—but they were soon joined by others. By then Bob Campbell was mostly working with Aiken on the designs for the Mark II, as was Ed Berkeley, representing Dahlgren. Lt. Harry E. Goheen, who joined the computation project from a research group, handled run-of-the mill computations as they came in, as did Lt. (jg) Brooks Lockhart and Ens. Brendel. Later they were joined by Lt. Joe Harrison and Lt. Frederick Miller and others. Robert Rex Seeber, a navy civilian, also joined the technical staff. Even Aiken's wife, Agnes, helped out at the lab, punching and checking sequence tapes.[64]

One of the first problems to occupy Dick Bloch was Problem E, which had to do with ballistic analyses for a 5-inch 38-caliber antiaircraft gun. The completed solution accommodated key input variables provided by the navy including target bearing, elevation and range, the ship's angle of pitch and roll, drift angle, time of flight, and residual projectile velocity. High-capacity projectiles had been developed so much faster than the corresponding range tables that in 1942 the

navy was already some five hundred tables behind. The advent of proximity fuses also meant extensive recomputation of existing tables. Until
the Mark I became operational, the navy had to rely on what Hopper
described as "acres of girls down at Aberdeen [U.S. Army Proving
Ground] using hand-driven calculators" to create such tables.[65]

A very big classified problem, Problem K, also took up much of
Bloch's time that first year. Early in August, when von Neumann came
to the Computation Lab for calculations he needed, Hopper and the
others at the lab knew von Neumann's work on spherical shock waves
came from the Los Alamos National Laboratory in New Mexico and
correctly assumed it dealt with atomic fission. In fact, von Neumann
was wrestling with the difficult implosion problem for detonating plutonium, which involved him in lengthy mathematical calculations. Because no programming languages existed yet, von Neumann had to
rely on Dick Bloch for the huge task of writing the machine code and
sequencing for his problem. The Mark I was at that point fully scheduled for operations twenty-four hours every day, and only a sense of
the urgency of von Neumann's problem allowed it to be squeezed in,
one day at a time, between other projects. Capt. Solberg of BuShips
acted as liaison between the Computation Lab and the Applied Mathematics Panel, which oversaw this aspect of von Neumann's work. In
July, he expressed his concern to the AMP head. "I'm rather hoping," he
wrote to Warren Weaver, "that Dr. von Neumann's requirements will
not become excessive in as much as we already have established a priority of work at this station and it will not be desirable to have any
more interruptions than absolutely necessary." The numbers run on
the Mark I were needed to complete von Neumann's work, which resulted in the plutonium bomb exploded at Alamogordo, New Mexico,
on 16 July 1945—the first atomic detonation—and the "Fat Man" device dropped on Nagasaki, Japan, on 9 August.[66]

Bloch also programmed Problem L to generate a massive set of
Bessel functions requested by the NRL. A number of advanced research projects the navy was undertaking needed those functional
values for applications as diverse as radio- and sound-wave propagation, heat flow, and bandwidth of frequency-modulated transmitters.
The production of Bessel tables became a huge baseload project at
the Computation Lab, lasting through 1945 and well into 1946. The
Bessel functions ran all the time, especially at night, except when
problems of greater urgency took precedence. The electric typewriters for the output from the Mark I produced such clear results that
the tables could be printed directly in a photo-offset process; avoiding

retyping contributed powerfully to one of Aiken's chief concerns, which was reliability.[67]

The Computation Lab also computed tables of Hankel functions. These had been requested by NRL but were also used by other naval research activities, such as NOL, the U.S. Navy Radio and Sound Laboratory, and the David Taylor Model Basin, for solution of problems of radio-wave propagation and radiation, underwater sound propagation, and the like.[68] Another early Computation Lab problem run for BuShips involved solving ten simultaneous algebraic equations for a multiple regression. The purpose of the calculation was to determine the tensile strength of steel plates with varying quantities of minuscule impurities, from information submitted by a number of different plants including Sparrows Point, Carnegie-Illinois, and Johnstown. The results affected the many uses to which steel was put during the war, especially in ship construction.[69] The Mark I also worked on the theory of coupled antennas, evaluated the accuracy of experimental fire-control computers designed and built by NRL, ran numbers for the MIT Radiation Lab that could not be handled by MIT's own differential analyzer, and worked on calculations for a new type of lens for the air forces. They also ran numbers for Brown University's work on flow patterns. As one example of the Mark I's effectiveness, in three weeks it accomplished the computing that the Radiation Lab had figured it would take their own computing room eighteen weeks. This was a substantial saving that indicated the value of the Mark I to the war effort.[70]

In a Computation Project Report of Activity for the Bureau of Ships dated 16 August 1944, Aiken described Bloch's work on the 5-inch 38-caliber gun, which had consumed thirty hours of machine computation time. Work on rotation of the coordinate axes in the solution of the fire-control problem had taken sixty hours; basic analysis of fire-control computer test data took eighty hours; and the calculation of Class B errors of a fire control computer required one hundred hours. The rest of the projects mentioned illustrate the difficulty of determining the practical application of much of the work of the lab. Report #2, for example, was described merely as "Evaluation of Integral," which required fifty hours of computer time. Report #4, which took 120 hours of machine computation, involved "Multiple Regression; together with 8 analyses." "Evaluation of Infinite Series," Report #5, consumed thirty hours. The total hours of machine computation time for this reporting period was 570 hours. As Aiken concluded, "A mean ratio of machine operation to manual time is probably 50 to 1. Hence, the total manual hours of computation would be approximately 25,000 hours, giving an over all ratio of machine to manual time of about 10 to 1." In other words, the Mark I was earning its keep.[71]

By October 1944, Aiken's lab was undertaking computations for the Bureau of Ordnance on spherically and cylindrically symmetric underwater blast problems. The problems, dealing with the pressure increases that occur in convergent detonations, were carried out in conjunction with the computing section at Columbia University. At first it had been thought possible to carry out all the computations on Columbia's IBM punch-card equipment, but the volume of material produced was too extensive. A numerical computing scheme was therefore set up that seemed "suited for the Harvard machine. Conferences with Lieutenant [Commander] Aiken at Cambridge confirmed this," and permission was sought from BuShips to use the Mark I.[72]

In March 1945, Dr. Philip M. Morse, an MIT physicist who headed the Antisubmarine Warfare Operations Research Group, suggested that the Mark I might be used on the tables of Mathieu Functions he needed urgently to complete one of his studies. Morse's group had firmly established the new field of operational research that was instrumental in the defeat of the German U-boats, among other things. Yet during the war there were those who doubted the value of calculations of mathematical tables. Hunter College mathematician Mina Rees, at that time technical aide to the AMP, explained that "it is seldom possible to justify in advance the computation of extensive and fundamental tables in terms of military necessity; yet those tables when they have been computed are found to be of wide and important usefulness, both for military and for other research."[73]

By comparison, most of what Hopper worked on was fairly small. The first problem she remembered was the one Aiken thrust at her that first day on the job. It involved finding the interpolation coefficients for applications of the arc tangent series. This was a fairly elementary problem except that it had to be computed to twenty-three digits for the Mark I. The purpose of the task was to compute rocket trajectories. Instead of shooting inert objects (shells), the navy was now firing self-propelled missiles (rockets) for which there were no firing tables. Another problem Hopper worked on concerned magnetic mines that were set off by metal ships. The navy had to know the extent of the effect of the mines and over how large an area they could detect ships in order to know how close together to sow them. The same variables applied to the new acoustic mines. The navy also needed to know what kind of a dipole to tow behind a ship to sweep the mines when they had to be removed. The sweeper had to know the influence of the dipole and how much strength it would take to detonate the mines. At first the navy said it needed the numbers for every foot of distance, but Hopper figured it would take paper stacked to the size of a cord of wood to print out all those results. She successfully argued that a less detailed report would suffice. Still, she filled a whole book of computations to send to the navy.[74]

Hopper also wrote a number of smaller programs for special jobs involving partial differential equations and things of that sort. Then, part way through that first year, Aiken walked up to her desk and told her she was going to write a book. When she protested that she had never written a book before, Aiken's response was a laconic, "Well, you're in the navy now." So she went to work (against her wishes) writing a manual for the Mark I.[75]

Handicapped by her lack of engineering background, Hopper took copious notes from Dick Bloch at the lab or over late dinner at the Coach Grill in Harvard Square. She had to understand all the basic circuits of the Mark I so that she could explain its coding procedures and the plugging instructions. Hopper wrote about five pages daily. At the end of each day she had to read the pages out loud to Aiken, and if he did not like them she had to do them over. Ultimately, she did a formidable compilation job putting together a 561-page manual that gave a full and detailed description of the Mark I: all its parts, all its circuits, and samples of all kinds of programming and coding.[76]

According to Hopper the historical introduction to the manual was rather rough because wartime restrictions prevented her from traveling to find sources. Instead, she had to rely on what she could dig up at the Widener Library at Harvard. She found histories of mathematics, of course, which included information on the abacus and mentioned Pascal and Leibnitz, but there had not been anything written on the history and development of computers. At this point Hopper's computing education under Aiken took an interesting twist. He insisted that she read Charles Babbage's autobiography for the origin of most of the basic computing concepts. Aiken also wanted her to familiarize herself with the work of Lady Ada Lovelace, whom Hopper always remembered for having written the first loop. Hopper did have access to the original Babbage papers, which she found delightful reading. In fact, she thought they were still worth reading by anyone interested in computers because Babbage had some novel ideas that had not yet been implemented.[77]

Hopper herself wrote out all the instructions for the manual and made all the circuit drawings. Much of the information existed already in notebooks that were used to run the computer, but Hopper designed a new type of timing chart with circuit diagrams corresponding to it, to show the sequencing of operations. "Back in those days," Hopper explained, "you really had to know every relay and how they were working or you couldn't debug a program. Because you never knew if it was a relay or your program." The timing on relays could slip; one might hold too long so it did not pick up the next one soon enough, and then the following one would not get picked up. These things happened and had to be checked for, hence Hopper's detailed diagrams. "All-in-all [though]," Hopper concluded with emphasis, the Mark I "ran *amazingly* well."[78]

Yeoman Frank Verdonck and Ruth Knowlton typed the whole manual and Ruth Brendel helped with the proofreading. The chapter headings were composed very carefully, half tongue-in-cheek, to reflect credit on whomever was making the major contribution in that area. Chapter one, for example, referred to Aiken, while Aiken himself chose to put Hopper's name on the chapter on coding since by then she was in charge of the programmers. "We had a lot of fun finding ways to give credit," Hopper recalled. "This was a very happy crew."[79]

There was only one exception. Lt. Hubert A. Arnold, by all accounts, never fit in at the Computation Lab. He never became a real naval officer—a severe critique from Hopper—because, according to her, he remained too much of a college professor. He was a real mathematician who could never divest himself of his academic training. "He absolutely refused to admit that there could be both a positive and a negative zero. As far as he was concerned zero was positive and that was that," Hopper recalled. Since the computer test register indicated both positive and negative zero, Arnold's programs often would not run. Arnold would flail around at the computer and Aiken would storm into Hopper's office and ask her to find out what was wrong with Arnold's routine. He had usually ignored a negative zero.[80]

Arnold was also, according to Ruth Brendel, a ballet dancer. One day the commander caught him doing ballet exercises in front of the computer. It is not hard to imagine the resulting scene. Hopper tried to intervene to convince Aiken to be nice to the executive officer, but to no avail. From then on Aiken referred to him as "that damned dancer." This problem was finally solved by assigning Arnold the task of writing the bibliography for the Mark I manual. From then on he stayed at the Widener Library, well clear of the lab, eventually producing a very extensive bibliography of computing information and techniques.[81]

Despite Hopper's success, Aiken, ever practical, was convinced that an engineering education was the most useful for the new field of computing. When a scientist from the Aberdeen Proving Ground visited the Computation Lab in March 1945, Aiken impressed on him very forcefully "that . . . [he should seek] not mathematicians but engineers" for his Ballistics Research Laboratory. In fact, this view reflects the blurring of the boundaries between science and technology that characterized much of wartime science. Everything was done at such a fast pace, and there were so many new developments that few could afford the luxury of specializing. People just pitched in wherever they were needed, often working directly on machines and devices while at the same time helping to construct their theoretical framework.[82]

Years later, when she was asked about her first days at work at Harvard and how she had learned to program the Mark I, Hopper's reply was as straightforward as her approach to the problem must have been. "Well they gave me a code book and told me to do it," she said. "We were all in the navy," she would often say later, and "we didn't have time to react or think or anything. We just had to go ahead and do things." Hopper was always ready to tackle any problem, so it is easy to see how she thrived at the Computation Lab. She spent the rest of her life impatiently pushing ahead, at the cutting edge of the rapidly developing new field to which the navy had introduced her.[83]

As Hopper described it, the very early programming was actually extremely basic. Programmers had to tell the computer exactly what to do, step by step. All of the mathematical processes had to be broken down into very small steps of addition, subtraction, multiplication, or division and put into a sequence, and this is still the essence of programming today. After figuring out how to write the machine instructions, Hopper then punched them on tape, put the tape in the computer, and hoped it would run.[84]

One of the major challenges faced by Hopper and her fellow programmers was that the Mark I only had seventy-two words of storage. There was one instruction input, up to three data inputs, two typewriters, two card readers, and a card punch to handle a range of computations including some extremely large and complex partial differential equations and statistical problems, all of which had to fit into only seventy-two words of storage. Working within such tight parameters at the top speed demanded by the war required an intense focus of energy and intellect. It was a challenge that Hopper found fascinating, and one that she thought might well defeat the "so-called sophisticated programmers" of more recent times.[85]

Hopper was not particularly interested in hardware and had very little concern with it. By her own account she was happy to leave this up to others. Her interest was always in software and during the war she had been frustrated by the slowness of the progress. This occurred in large part because each person wrote with specific problems to solve and they wrote their own programs. Hopper's interest in the Mark I, therefore, quickly focused on methods to speed the process of writing coding instructions to run her own individual problems. She was always looking for shortcuts, which in the early days meant assembling collections of subroutines. A subroutine was a clearly defined, easily symbolized, often repeated program. Similar work putting together a library of mathematical subroutines was also being undertaken in England by M. V. Wilkes of Cambridge University, although during the war there was relatively little information around about different systems, even within the United States, because of security restrictions. Compartmentalization was the norm, even at the Harvard lab.

In spite of its relative isolation, a surprisingly steady stream of visitors found their way to the lab to see the amazing automatic brain at work and to consult on possible problems to feed it. Dick Bloch had written a magnificent program to use when admirals and other VIPs came by. "It would display everything: cards would read, cards would punch, the tapes would all move, lights would flash," recalled Hopper, "and it didn't do a darn thing in computation, but it put everything in motion. That was very reliable for display when necessary." Other visitors had a more serious interest, especially people at MIT. They knew that the Mark I was functioning twenty-four hours a day and they were having trouble keeping their differential analyzer operational. One day someone from MIT came to the lab to ask whether Aiken would lend some of his staff to help them out. Aiken turned to Brendel and, in a humorous play on words that stunned her, said: "If they would make you a Gigadeer Brendel, I would loan you to them." "You never knew what would come out of his mouth," Brendel concluded, years later.[86]

Somehow, in the midst of all this frantic activity, Hopper developed the seeds of what was later to become her most creative work on a universal computer language. The inspiration, as she candidly admitted, was her own difficulty in writing loops: codes that would instruct the machine to repeat the required operation a specified number of times. If she wanted to do something twelve times, for example, Hopper found she usually ended up doing it eleven or thirteen times because she could not remember whether she had started with a zero or a one. Then, too, there was the problem of copying. When she worked out a useful piece of code for a specific problem, Hopper wrote it down in her notebook so that it could be used again. An example of this was the code she wrote for a problem involving the roll of a ship. Because a ship cannot roll more than 90 degrees either way, there was no need to compute the angle for anything greater. So Hopper wrote a little piece of code within those parameters and filed it away in her notebook. Soon, both she and Bloch had built up quite a collection of their own small subroutines—for example, a routine to compute the cosine or the square root, which they could reuse and which they could borrow from each other. Still, each time they reused a subroutine it had to be copied into the new program and all the addresses had to be added up.

At this point Hopper recognized that two weaknesses came into play to which all programmers were subject—especially late in the day— that injected a good deal of error into the process. The first was that they could not copy correctly, and the second was that they had trouble with addition. Frequently, in the process of copying, a Δ (delta) symbol, which was used to indicate a space, it could turn into a 4 (number four), and the letter B had the annoying habit of turning up as the number 13. When compounded by elementary errors of addition, this could turn the best subroutine into a guaranteed failure for the program into which it was inserted. As long as subroutines had to be copied into other programs by fallible humans, such program-stopping errors would persist. It was perfectly clear to Hopper that the machine sitting nearby was an expert at both copying and adding, so her idea was to make the computer do the work. Eventually, after the war, this insight led to her work on compilers.[87]

With the Mark II already on the way to commissioning, Aiken sent Hopper and one or two others from Harvard to Pennsylvania to see the ENIAC and find out what was going on with it. Promotional material put out by the machine's inventors a few years later claimed that with the ENIAC, "Babbage's dream had come of age." While the electronic equipment provided a speed and flexibility unimaginable to Babbage, the "functional theory was," according to them, "amazingly similar." Thus Babbage was claimed as inspiration for both of the two giants of early computing, the ENIAC and the Mark I. ENIAC was indeed a giant; it was as big as a room and was approached by walking inside it. Although the ENAIC was running tests by the time of Hopper's visit, she remained convinced that Aiken's decision to stick with an electromechanical device had been sound. Vacuum tubes were still problematic, and the pressure was on to quickly handle the ever more complex calculations required by the advent of guided missiles. This could not be done with the limited storage capacity of the Mark I, but needed the expansion to the full two-hundred-word storage of the Mark II.[88]

In a newspaper interview in August 1948, Hopper explained that she had literally grown up with the Mark II. It had taken two years to build, and when complete it had been shipped in twenty trailer trucks to Dahlgren to work on problems in the ballistics of guided missiles at the Naval Surface Weapons Center. The Mark II had thirteen thousand relays each with six contacts, a million feet of wiring, and a mass of cables, switches, and lights. It was made of Bakelite and steel and was built at Harvard in an old temporary building put up during World War I. It was warm in the summer of 1945; the windows were always open and the screens were not very good. One day the Mark II stopped when a relay failed. They finally found the cause of the failure: inside one of the relays, beaten to death by the contacts, was a moth. The operator carefully fished it out with tweezers, taped it in the logbook, and wrote under it "first actual bug found." A newspaper account of the incident, published in 1948, says nothing about Hopper inventing the term computer "bug"; indeed, it was clear that the term was already in use. The myth of her invention would appear later.[89] By 1992, however, even the *New York Times* had bought into the story, noting in its obituary of Grace Hopper that she was "known for coining the term 'bug' . . . to refer to mysterious computer failures."[90]

The bug incident did have one immediately useful purpose, however. From then on, whenever Aiken put his head through the door and asked if they were making numbers, if they were not, they would tell him they were debugging the computer, a term and a procedure they may have been the first to institutionalize. Something else also happened as a result of the bug episode. Somebody from the lab was down in Scully Square in Boston—a rather seedy area then, off limits to WAVES—and found a box of fake bedbugs in a corner magic store. Somehow, two or three days later, Mark I was full of bedbugs. Aiken ordered up all the vacuum cleaning equipment at Harvard and thoroughly vacuumed the computer. Unfortunately, that took all the dust out of the relays so they did not make contact any more. The clean machine would not work again for another couple of days.[91]

Until the Mark II went into operation at Dahlgren in 1948, their work of computing range tables had been done under contract by MIT with a mixture of old and new differential analyzers, IBM equipment, and human computers. The only problem Hopper could recall with the Mark II was with its switches. Like the Mark I, the Mark II had a big panel of switches to set the numbers for each problem. The crew went out to lunch one day while the machine was computing some shell trajectories. When they returned, the crew discovered to their horror that the shell trajectories had turned back on themselves and were bearing down on the Mark II. Desperate to figure out what had gone wrong, the crew checked and rechecked everything until they finally found out what had happened while they were away. The commanding admiral of the installation had come to the lab to show off his new computer to some visitors. Oblivious to everything, he demonstrated how the constants were entered, changing the switches and reversing the firing pattern. From then on, a lock was put on the glass door covering the switches.[92]

By November 1944, after only a few months of operating the Mark I for the navy, Aiken was already writing that "we are at present so much occupied with the problems submitted us in connection with the war effort that we cannot take the time to publish a suitable scientific article dealing with the calculator."[93] There was no time to look ahead, either. Hopper recalled that it was normal to be at the lab two or three days in a row when she had a problem running. Because the computer ran twenty-four hours a day, she would just grab a nap at her desk and never get home to bed. They all did it. Once in 1944 they had all been at the lab three days and three nights. Brendel was the duty officer and had been warned that a hurricane was coming and would be hitting full force by midnight. By the time the problem finished its run it was close to midnight and the storm was raging just as predicted, but nothing was going to stop Hopper from getting home for a hot bath. She, Brendel, Ruth Knowlton, and one of the enlisted men, little "Wiz White" as they called him, linked arms and fought their way home together. With water up to their knees, one person would hang onto a tree or a post while the other three strung out to grab the next anchor, laughing the whole time. That was just the sort of excitement Hopper sought, Brendel remembered, and the danger from downed wires probably made it just that much more of an adventure.[94]

There was very little time for social life during the war, and most evenings Hopper was much too tired to go out and have a beer and compare notes. She would just go home exhausted and fall into bed knowing she would have to be back at the lab at the crack of dawn the next day. There were some brief reprieves from the constant pressure though, particularly during rare lulls when they would go to Harvard Square for a proper lunch. On such occasions Hopper, who was a heavy drinker for quite a number of years, invariably drank Manhattans—more than one of them. She also recalled a trip on a tug out of Boston Harbor to welcome the carrier *Wasp,* limping home after being battered by kamikazes off Okinawa. That was the nearest Hopper ever came to sea duty. Occasionally, too, she would go over to Brendel's and Knowlton's apartment and pop corn.[95]

According to Brendel, Hopper was the only one who could win some free time for them from the commander. When she thought they had all been working so hard they were desperate for a break, she would arrange something. One July 4th she organized a picnic for the whole crew, officers, enlisted men, and civilians, at her family's place in Wolfeboro. They all piled into a school bus and drove up and spent the day swimming in Lake Wentworth, canoeing, and just generally having a good time. Hopper arranged to get excellent hot dogs from the New London submarine base, knowing that submariners had the best food. John, the youngest of Hopper's sister's sons, who was only three or four years old at the time, was fascinated with the bus. At one point he climbed in and, after playing with the lights, he honked the horn. Startled, Aiken, who had been leaning on the front of the bus, jumped and then scowled. Young John glanced at his Aunt Grace, certain that he was in deep trouble. To his surprise he found that she was grinning rather smugly. Apparently she, too, had enjoyed Aiken's discomfiture.[96]

Brendel also remembered a Christmas party, Christmas 1944, when the commander actually relaxed for a while and sat drinking with a group on the floor. He dared her to drink a water glass full of bourbon. She was dogged enough and angry enough with him that she did, and then walked home with Harry Goheen. "I wasn't drunk," Brendel insisted fifty years later, "I didn't pass out. I'll show you that picture. I don't know that you can tell."[97]

Aiken seemed to live at the lab permanently. He often went home late in the evening only to reappear after three or four hours' sleep. He also thought nothing of calling any one of his crew at any time, night or day. As Hopper explained over and over again to interviewers, "You were in the navy. You were on duty twenty-four hours a day. You were lucky if you got home to sleep. This wasn't just Aiken, this was the navy." All Aiken wanted was to see results coming out of the machine.[98]

The electronic ENIAC produced no numbers for the war effort. Intended to fill the army's pressing computation needs, the ENIAC was developed by John Mauchly, who was then an assistant professor of physics, and a brilliant young engineering graduate student, J. Presper Eckert. Hopper pointed out that Mauchly's original idea when he started work on the ENIAC, like Aiken's impulse to develop the Mark I, was to shorten the length of time and effort in the computations he needed for his own studies—in his case, for weather forecasting. Mauchly's project, too, would probably not have received funding without the threat of war. In spite of erroneous statements to the contrary in popular works on the history of computing, the ENIAC did not produce usable results until after the end of the war.[99]

The ENIAC was publicly introduced for the first time on 13 February 1946. Until then, it was a well-kept wartime secret, in part because it had been tested by running numbers for scientists involved in the atomic bomb program at Los Alamos. Built out of radio parts, the ENIAC had cost close to four hundred thousand dollars. It was eighty feet long and eight feet tall, weighed thirty tons, and with its eighteen thousand vacuum tubes it was a true electronic computer. It also had 70,000 resistors, 10,000 capacitors, and 1,500 relays. Its most astonishing feature was its speed of operation. If used to capacity, the ENIAC could perform more than ten million additions or subtractions of ten-figure numbers in five minutes. On the down side, its memory capacity was only twenty words and it was programmed in a cumbersome and time-consuming way by resetting some six thousand dials and switches. Aiken had not been interested in experimenting with electronics for his computer in part because of the notorious failure rate of vacuum tubes in smaller devices such as radios. Eckert and Mauchly found that by reducing the voltage slightly, they could prolong the life of the tubes, but nothing could be done about the enormous amount of heat they generated. This problem would not be resolved until computers moved to the next stage: the change from vacuum tubes to microchips. Meanwhile, the ENIAC had to rely on water cooling. Nevertheless, the ENIAC introduced the age of electronic computing, and its concepts eventually led to the UNIVAC I.[100]

Interviewed years later, Hopper liked to explain how it was that her work at Harvard during the war was really in advance of anything else then being done on computers. That was because at that time the ENIAC was not programmed. "It was put together with patch cords like punch card machinery,"[101] she said. In the ENIAC "you went from an adder to a storage to a multiplier, and so on and it was all done by plug wires," put together in a direct simulation of the problem to be solved. However, "the Mark I was programmed just the way we program computers today, step by step." To that extent, Hopper pointed out, "I had a slight head start on programming because I started in '44 on Mark I."[102]

With the ENIAC and the advent of electronic computing, some have looked back on the Mark I as a "technological dead end."[103] This ignores one of Aiken's most important contributions: the Mark I's programming system provided by punched tapes (today's software) was the first step toward fully automatic program execution and was much more like systems now in use than anything in the ENIAC or its contemporaries. The Mark I programmers created what were essentially the earliest digital computer programs: stored programs—including subroutines—only independent of the machine itself, stored on paper tape and in programmers' notebooks. By contrast, the ENIAC, designed for a specific task and not conceived as a universal machine, had an unwieldy programming system of external plugs that could take a day or more to set. In fact, very often just the setup time took much longer than the time it took to run the program. After a year of operation at the University of Pennsylvania, the ENIAC was moved to the army's Aberdeen Proving Ground where it continued to provide ballistics calculations similar to the work being done for the navy at Dahlgren by the Mark II.[104]

After the end of the war some of the same confusions attended the disestablishment of the Bureau of Ships Computation Project at Harvard as had dogged its establishment. In October 1945 the Bureau of Ordnance began negotiations with Harvard and with the Bureau of Ships to take over control of the Computation Lab. BuOrd already had a contract with Harvard for what it called "an improved relay calculator" (the Mark II), so it seemed desirable to consolidate control of computing. It was agreed that BuOrd would "administer the Harvard Computation Project as a computing service to the Bureaus, Offices, and Laboratories of the Navy Department in the same manner as it has been operated in the past by the Bureau of Ships." By November, officers attached to the Computation Lab, as well as to the Radiation Lab at MIT and Harvard's Radio Research Lab, were already being reassigned to the Boston branch of the Office of Research and Inventions. On the list to go were Arnold, Hopper, Goheen, Miller, Bloch, Campbell, and Brendel. Three weeks later, however, the orders for the Computation Lab officers were acknowledged to have been an error and were canceled. All officers reverted to duty at the Computation Lab, presumably until discharged from their wartime obligations.[105]

In December, a captain in the Office of Research and Inventions in Washington again wrote to the office's Boston branch regarding the disposition of Aiken's crew. "The actual direction of the Computation Project and its continuing officer personnel has apparently been taken over by BuOrd," he noted with some uncertainty. He therefore suggested that for administrative convenience the enlisted men, including Frank Verdonck, Delo Calvin, Hubert Livingston, John Hourihan, John Mahoney, and Durward White, while now coming under the control of the Bureau of Ordnance, should continue to remain on the payroll and leave roster of the Bureau of Ships. And so, apparently, the situation remained.[106]

For some time before the end of the war suggestions had been floated from various quarters about the desirability of establishing a peacetime navy computation center in the vicinity of Washington, D.C. Experience gained in the operation of the Harvard Computation Project suggested the breadth of the computational requirements of the Navy Department. To recap, these had involved metallurgy, ballistics, radio communication, radar, fire control, and pure mathematics, among other things. Most of the projects had originated with BuShips and BuOrd, with the NRL, the AMP, the Radiation Lab, the army air forces, Aberdeen Proving Ground, and the Underwater Sound Lab. Their solution had called on "all the techniques at the disposal of applied mathematicians."[107] "The most rapid progress in the application of modern methods of computation," it was argued, would be made in future "by carrying out all mathematical operations at a central laboratory where experience gained throughout the Navy Department as a whole can be brought to bear on each individual problem."[108] The chief item of equipment necessary would be an "Automatic Calculating Machine," one that would incorporate all the improvements in design and construction suggested by experience with the Mark I. Howard Aiken was asked to advise on the matter and recommendations were sought from other interested parties. A survey was circulated to the various navy scientific and research establishments to solicit projections of their future large-scale computing needs.[109]

Unfortunately for the navy, the idea of a computation center seems to have died, perhaps the victim of early postwar budget cuts. The closest the navy came to a supervisory authority for computer development was the Office of Naval Research, which functioned only to promote and help fund individual projects. Later the navy would pay dearly for this lack of centralized control of computing and Hopper would be one of those whose job it was to sort out some of the resulting confusion and inefficiencies.

In January 1946, Aiken returned to the inactive reserve and resumed his academic career at Harvard as full professor and Director of the Computation Lab now located in a brand-new two-story building of brick and glass inaugurated in December. Each of his staff reverted to civilian status and eventually left the lab, which now became a largely civilian organization for the first time since the Mark I had taken up residence in 1944. This posed problems of funding for Aiken because when his Mark II computer for the navy was completed, the navy no longer needed to finance the Mark I. Until then it had been operating under navy contract for twenty hours daily, the other four hours being set aside for Harvard use. With the navy out, Aiken secured a contract with the air force for 50 percent of his funding and with the Atomic Energy Commission for the other 50 percent.[110]

When the Mark I had begun full operation in the summer of 1944, Aiken was already planning its postwar use. He saw it as the first step in the establishment of a computation center at Harvard that would handle mathematical jobs for academic and commercial research laboratories. He had not foreseen, however, how important continued military and other government funding would be. After the war, when collaboration with government was no longer a patriotic duty, Harvard's distaste for government-sponsored, and especially military, research projects reasserted itself. In his annual report for 1946 Harvard President James B. Conant wrote that " . . . in time of peace I think it highly inadvisable for a university to undertake the type of work which was done during the war. . . . We can easily imagine a situation where substantial subsidies from Congress would result in a degree of control by Federal authorities which would be unfortunate indeed." Harvard, moreover, had a tradition of indifference toward what it viewed as the applied sciences and was not likely to support this type of research. Headlines such as "Highbrow Harvard Bows to a Robot Brain," which appeared after the war, cannot have helped.[111]

In August 1948 the *Boston Sunday Herald* announced the construction for the navy of the electronic Mark III in the Aiken Computation Lab. Each of Aiken's computers was smaller and faster than its predecessor, but the Mark III was his first electronic machine and had the first magnetic storage drum. Hopper recalled that sometime in 1946 the Computation Lab had fallen heir to four large square magnets shipped over from Germany. This was the beginning of all core memories, but they were not used for the Mark III because, as Hopper admitted, "we did not know enough about how to use them."[112] Instead Mark III used magnetic tape made of paper with a magnetic coating. Metal tape was not used until the UNIVAC in 1951, and Mylar tape was later still.[113] Claiming that the Mark III would "wade through forests of figures as easily as a mowing machine lays low a field of hay," the newspaper noted that many people believed its creator, Howard Aiken, would someday be compared with Thomas Edison as a contributor to scientific progress. Instead, of course, his name has been forgotten by all but a few in the field. The Mark III went to the air force.[114]

Once the initial postwar flurry of publicity subsided, little was heard of Aiken until quite recently with the appearance of two books about him by Harvard historian of science I. Bernard Cohen. Perhaps because the advent of electronic computing so quickly overtook the Mark I and Mark II, Aiken's contribution to computing was poorly understood. Even after he had completed the electronic Mark III and Mark IV, Aiken found that some of his contemporaries still viewed him as a conservative, especially when he abandoned machine design altogether in favor of program development, which seemed of only peripheral significance. A more persuasive argument has been made by Hopper, among others well qualified to judge, that Aiken was actually ahead of his time in recognizing the importance of software. This seems to have been generally overlooked, as have Aiken's many other postwar contributions to the new field in applied science: the science of computing.[115]

Aiken understood the need to program the growing number of computers, and at Harvard he introduced some of the first academic courses in computer science a decade before such courses existed in most universities. He also organized successful international conferences to encourage open discussion of computers and computing. The first of these, the Symposium of Large Scale Digital Calculating Machinery held in January 1947 at Harvard's new Computation Laboratory, was cosponsored by the Bureau of Ordnance. More than three hundred representatives of university, industrial, and government labs and research groups attended. Among the presenters were many of the big names in computing including, in addition to Aiken himself, Norbert Weiner, George Stibitz, Jay Forrester, Richard Courant, Wassily Leontief, John Mauchly, Herman Goldstine, and Richard H. Babbage, great-grandson of Charles Babbage. John von Neumann had to decline on the grounds of health, as did Warren Weaver of the Applied Mathematics Panel. A second, even larger and more international conference was held two years later, when postwar travel became easier again. As Aiken's deputy Hopper had played an important part in organizing and running both conferences.[116]

Harvard generally frowned on Aiken's postwar activities, however, including his close ties with industry, and ultimately the continual struggle for funding drove him to retire from the university at the minimum age in 1961. When he died suddenly at a conference in March 1973 at the age of seventy-three, Aiken left a generous bequest to Harvard. His generosity was not reciprocated. In spring 2000 the new Maxwell Dworkin computer sciences building was ceremonially inaugurated at the northeast corner of Harvard University's Holmes Field, formerly the site of the Aiken Computation Laboratory. The new building was a gift to the university from Bill Gates and his Microsoft associate and Harvard classmate Steven Ballmer. Instead of continuing to honor the name of Howard Hathaway Aiken, founder of Harvard's trailblazing computing program, the new center was named for the mothers of the two recent benefactors. A bronze plaque on the wall of the building is all that remains today to remind of Aiken's original inspiration. Recently a conference room at the computer center was named for Grace Hopper.[117]

None of Aiken's little band of scientists remained at Harvard for long after the war, dispersing instead to work in fledgling computer companies. Many of them went on to lifelong careers in the field to which Aiken had introduced them, making contributions that reflected his inspiration and rigorous training. Harry Goheen, a mathematician of some note, returned to the University of Delaware and was one of the original founders of the Association of Computing Machinery. Ed Berkeley, who had become chief research consultant for the Prudential Insurance Company, was the association secretary. Both Bob Campbell and Dick Bloch went to Raytheon to start up their computing project. As they scattered, Aiken's former crew took with them the essential skills they had learned under his leadership. This was one of the most significant measures of the impact of the Harvard Computation Lab: it had served as a training ground for future computing. "Howard Aiken was a good teacher," Hopper maintained. "He taught us in a rather curious way; he told us to go do something and then he kept an eye on us. He led us into the learning."[118]

Ruth Brendel returned to teaching mathematics at the University of Buffalo. The precipitous postwar demobilization with active forces shrinking from 12 million to 1.4 million in two years ensured her employability instead of putting her out of a job as it did many other women. In 1946 the university began a special intensive program in mathematics for returning servicemen and it desperately needed Brendel back to teach. Aiken refused to release her early, however, so the university went over his head and got permission from Washington for her discharge. According to Brendel, Aiken was so furious he would not assign her any work that last month. "I might as well have been a fly on the wall," she recalled, "because the commander didn't speak to me, he didn't give me any responsibility." She was quite relieved, therefore, to join the lonely executive officer, helping him with his research in Widener Library.[119]

Once back in Buffalo, Brendel stayed in the reserves, her wartime experience souring her on the commander and on computing, but not on the navy. She would have stayed in the reserves even longer but was forced to resign six years later, according to the regulations of the time, when she became pregnant with her first child. Like the men at the Computation Lab, Brendel, too, had been offered wonderful opportunities in computing at the end of the war. Unlike most of them, she did not go on in the new field, preferring to return to the teaching she loved.

Grace Hopper was an exception at the lab, remaining to work with Aiken. Although offered a full professorship to return to Vassar, she turned it down because, as she said, she liked computers better. Hopper loved teaching and she was good at it. But here she was on the cusp of something heady and new. She was making history. She was helping to create a whole new field. She had always been innovative, but now she was not just dreaming up new ways to teach old ideas, she was helping to create new ideas. So she remained at the Computation Lab as a research fellow in engineering systems and applied physics, with a three-year navy-funded contract. The death of her father in October 1947 affected her deeply, though, for a time dampening the enthusiasm of a new beginning. Walter Murray had worked almost until the day he died of lung cancer, probably the result of a lifetime of smoking. The funeral took place in New York City in the church where the family had been regular parishioners for a long time. Hopper had been very close to her father and missed his calm and always positive advice, but even his death did not stop her from smoking.[120]

Hopper had been promoted to lieutenant in 1946, and more than anything she had wanted to transfer to the regular navy as soon as that became possible with the Women's Armed Services Integration Act of 1948. But she was two years over the cutoff age and had to satisfy herself with staying in the naval reserve. During her final three years at Harvard, in addition to her regular work, she served with a reserve ordnance unit in Boston. She went to monthly meetings, went on two-week training duty every summer, and completed various correspondence courses, mostly in ballistics. Her unit was responsible for keeping current with the latest technical developments in case of deployment, which meant receiving instruction in new weapons systems including missiles, and in the new radars, and learning about changes in the structure and organization of the navy. Reserve officers in Hopper's unit were also shown the latest developments in rockets and solid fuels at the Indian Head rocket power plant in Maryland.

On temporary active duty in the summers Hopper was assigned variously to the Bureau of Ordnance, the Naval Research Laboratory, the Weapons Center at Dahlgren, and the Bureau of Personnel, where she listened to lectures and reviewed and critiqued navy computing projects. In addition, Hopper took courses at the Naval War College in Newport, Rhode Island, involving problems such as fueling times for a task force at sea, the most efficient area scouting plans for submarines, and the best use of forces to capture an island.[121]

During these immediate postwar years Hopper's name became known to the growing computer community, not just from the computing conferences, but also through a number of publications resulting from her wartime work at the lab. As Aiken noted, there had been little time to write for publication during the war, and security issues prevented the normal free exchange of scientific information. In 1946, with the lifting of restrictions, Aiken and Hopper coauthored three articles, "The Automatic Sequence Controlled Calculator" based on the manual of operations for the Mark I. All three articles appeared in the journal *Electrical Engineering*. The first article described the mechanism and dealt with its function of addition and subtraction. The second one covered multiplication and division, and the third concerned the preparation and planning of the sequence control tapes. The manual itself eventually became the first in a series of thirty-five volumes: the *Annals of the Computation Laboratory of Harvard University*. Published over the next sixteen years and consisting of detailed technical notes and mathematical results of the lab's operations, the *Annals* are an important part of Aiken's impressive legacy in computing.[122]

After the war, sooner or later according to Hopper, "practically everybody" visited the Harvard Computation Lab to see the Mark I. Before the end of the decade there were still only four or five computers in existence and they attracted a great deal of interest. The dribble of people coming through during the war had turned into a flood, more than two thousand visitors viewing the Mark I by the fall of 1946. These included scientists from the Soviet Union, China, France, Brazil, Mexico, Britain, Sweden, South Africa, Cuba, and The Netherlands. A number of people from MIT visited even more often than before, including Norbert Weiner.[123] He was due to have participated in Aiken's 1947 symposium but withdrew at the last moment after publishing an article in the *Atlantic Monthly* explaining his disgust with the bombing and poisoning of civilians in the recent war and disclosing his intention to withhold any future work that "may do damage in the hands of irresponsible militarists." More than likely this was another reason for Hopper's long-harbored animosity toward him.[124]

IBM's reaction to the Mark I was forever shaped by the legacy of Thomas Watson's intractable dislike for Howard Aiken. Indeed, one biographer wrote that "Watson's fury was vengeful and he despised Aiken more or less unremittingly for . . . twenty years." Watson never got anything out of his original investment in the Mark I, which may have exacerbated his feelings about Aiken. After the war, Watson renewed the contest by moving into the computer business himself. He hired his own PhDs such as Wallace Eckert, formerly of Columbia, and by 1948 IBM completed its own first general-purpose machine called the Selective Sequence Electronic Calculator, a blend of electronic and punch-card techniques. Hopper was justifiably scornful of the SSEC, referring to it as "that horrible mess." Like many others, however, Watson thought a couple of dozen computers would satisfy the nation's needs, and it was not until his son's influence was felt that IBM became actively engaged in the new industry.[125]

The Mark I had been the overture to modern computing, introducing many of the themes that are still important. And not all of the Mark I's postwar work was obsolescent; for another dozen years it continued to churn out answers twenty-four hours a day to mathematical problems in fields as varied as atomic physics for the Atomic Energy Commission, radio research, optics, electronics, and astronomy. Hopper had charge of its operation until 1 July 1948, and its base load problem was still working out tables of Bessel functions. It was scheduled to work out all orders of the functions through one hundred, and in August 1948 it was on function number fifty-four. In the two hundred years since Bessel defined his function, mathematicians had worked out only scattered values until the advent of the Mark I. Fourteen volumes of the tables had already been produced, which were useful in electronics, radar, and many other types of research. And yet, the production of these tables was a dead end, soon to be overtaken by the rapid progress in computing. Before too much more time passed it would be easier and quicker to run a problem solving the specific required function, rather than wading through a mass of tables to find the appropriate solution.

Hopper also used the Mark I to try out some ideas that indicated the potential of computing for commercial purposes. During the war she had gone home on leave at one point and told her father about the Mark I and its capabilities. He immediately saw the potential of computers in insurance for record keeping, computing premiums, and getting premium notices out. Whether Walter Murray ever talked to anyone in New York City about these developments Hopper never knew, but perhaps it was no coincidence that insurance companies were among the first to jump on the computer bandwagon after the war.[126]

In a novel attempt to use a computer for business data process-ing, Prudential Life Insurance Company sent some people to the Com-putation Lab in 1948. Using two digits to represent a character, they loaded the tapes with information from cards holding insurance data on all Prudential policyholders. The machine was able to process the data and compute premiums and dividends due, as well as interest on loans. Bills with the names and addresses of policyholders were printed out so fast that they could be made ready long before they needed to be mailed. "To the best of my knowledge," Hopper recalled, "that was the first time a data processing business program was ever written and run on a computer." The success of the experiment convinced Hopper of the future of commercial computing.[127]

Hopper could not remain at the Computation Lab after 1949. Since no one was appointed to the Harvard faculty for more than three years without being promoted or given tenure and—according to Hopper—no women were being promoted, she had to begin job hunting. She had no interest in returning to full-time teaching and was determined to stay in computing in spite of its unpredictable future.

In 1978 Hopper was the keynote speaker at a conference on the history of programming languages. At the end of her address one ques-tioner pointed out that there were very few references to the Mark I in computing literature. He wanted to know whether Hopper thought the Harvard group working on the Mark I should have been given more credit for the development of programming and programming languages. "Yes, they should be," she replied, "but that had occurred back in the old days before there was much in the way of publication." She then listed their many contributions, which were often overlooked. At the top she placed the development of the Mark III coding machine, which had been Aiken's concept. Next came the idea of putting subroutines together for the first time. "It now turns out," she noted, "that Aiken was totally correct in saying that the programs and the data should be in separate memories, and we're just discovering that all over again in order to pro-tect information. I think it's been very badly neglected." She also thought that very few people realized that the Mark II was a multiprocessor. Almost no one had looked at the logic of that system because it had been built out of relays in a great rush during the war. By then vacuum tubes and electronics were clearly the way to go, but Hopper believed that if people presently trying to build multiprocessors would look at the Mark II manual, they might find a lot to learn from its logic.[128]

This was not just the nostalgic rambling of an old woman. Hopper was able to continue to productively guide navy programming into the fourth decade of computing in part because she never lost sight of its beginnings. She had a way of zeroing in on the strengths and weaknesses of each development and remained ready to apply the strengths at any opportune time.

In the mid-1980s, Hopper looked back with great pleasure on her days at the Computation Lab. "The fun, the excitement, of that first computer is something that is almost impossible to convey to people today," she wrote. "Some of the jobs that were done were fantastic, they were gigantic—solutions of elaborate systems of partial differential equations, and other problems of that magnitude. . . . Today we can put all of the Mark I on one chip," she continued, "and that's a little embarrassing. The old *Manual of Operations* would be bigger than the computer nowadays."[129]

After she left Harvard, although she retained a great affection for him, Hopper had only occasional direct contact with Aiken, mostly at professional meetings and the like. She would have been very pleased by the two Cohen volumes—to one of which she contributed a chapter—that have finally restored the record of his achievements. And yet Hopper recalled that Aiken's greatest disappointment concerned his navy career. He had had one bad fitness report referring to insubordination (which sounds characteristic) and was never promoted to captain. "He should have made captain," Hopper said, with her usual loyalty.[130]

3

Women Enter the World of Technology
The UNIVAC Years: 1949–1967

I n the late 1940s even many involved in the design and construction of electronic computers thought their use was limited to providing mathematical solutions for scientific projects. A very few computers,
it was widely believed, would be sufficient to satisfy the world's need.
Originally, moreover, most computers were built at universities under
military defense contracts, like the Mark I, II, and III, the ENIAC, and
the new Whirlwind at MIT. Commercial development of computers was
in its infancy. Few investors saw computing as a developing market,
and capital was hard to come by.[1] The Association for Computing Machinery (ACM) had just been founded in 1947 and there were no journals, periodicals, or other institutional resources to nurture the new
industry. Information on computing still spread mainly by word of
mouth; how well informed people were depended a lot on who they
knew. For Hopper, her navy connections provided important access to
the developing field.

Hopper's predisposition to the practical application of mathematics had served her well at Harvard where—unlike some of her fellow
mathematicians engaged in war work—she found it easy to make the
adjustment away from a theoretical, academic approach. And yet, for
some time computer science still continued to suffer from professional
discrimination, a holdover from prewar prejudice against applied mathematics. In an interview in 1976, Hopper noted: "Some mathematicians
look down on computers because they're applications. They get very
snooty. But I have my PhD in math," she continued with characteristic
vigor, "so I turn my back on them." Leaving the secure world of academia
after five years at Harvard, Hopper risked everything to plunge into
the new business of computing.[2]

There were still opportunities for women in the workplace in the
immediate postwar years—even in an industry that later became as
male dominated as computing did—because many of the returning veterans took advantage of the G.I. Bill to go to college. In 1946 there were
over one million veterans enrolled in higher education, which was close

to half of the total number of students. Women in the computer field initially even had an advantage over men. Many of them were already experienced, having been drawn in on the ground floor during the war when the demand for mathematicians exceeded the available supply from the usual male sources. Although the gender-neutral environment of the pioneering days soon faded, Hopper's early training under Aiken gave her a decided edge. "Everybody knew everybody that was at Harvard," she explained, "we were the original group."[3]

After looking around and interviewing with practically everyone in the field, Hopper narrowed her choice. She could work either for John Mauchly and Presper Eckert, who had left the ENIAC and the Moore School in 1947 to set up their own Eckert-Mauchly Computer Corporation (EMCC) in Philadelphia, or for Howard Engstrom at Engineering Research Associates (ERA) based in St. Paul, Minnesota. She was drawn to ERA because she had known Engstrom since Yale and because of his navy connection. Hopper had also had an interview at IBM, "but that was back in the days when they still had an IBM flag and sang songs about it, and that was too much for me,"[4] she recalled.

In the end, Hopper joined Eckert-Mauchly. Her decision was based in part on her desire to remain close to family on the East Coast and in part on her belief that Mauchly's Universal Automatic Computer (UNIVAC) would be operating long before any computer produced by ERA. Interviewed thirty years later, Hopper noted with her usual self-deprecating humor that her decision was probably not all that important in the long run since the companies ended up together anyway when Remington Rand bought them both. Hopper remained with the UNIVAC Division through Eckert-Mauchly's acquisition by Remington Rand in 1950 and then through the merger creating Sperry Rand (later to become UNISYS) in 1955. She finally retired from the company in 1971.[5]

On 1 June 1949 Hopper joined EMCC as a senior mathematician at their new location on Ridge Avenue by the Schuylkill River. Although later to move to better facilities on Allegheny Avenue, the company was then in a big, old, two-story building, a former knitting mill with oil-soaked floors that was hot in summer and cold in winter.[6] There Hopper became a member of a small software group working directly for John Mauchly. Even while at Harvard, Hopper had been relatively uninterested in hardware, what she called the part of the computer "that you can kick." Instead, she focused quickly on methods to speed the writing of coding instructions to run individual programs. It was in this field that she made her major contributions, both to commercial computing and to the navy, and the next years saw her most innovative work for which she is best known in data processing circles.[7]

When they left the University of Pennsylvania, Eckert and Mauchly were convinced of the future of computing in business, government, the military, and research. They appreciated, also, that there would need to be substantial development before computers could handle the masses of data required for the solution of commercial and accounting problems as well as the ENIAC handled the solution of mathematical and scientific problems. Their objective was to create a truly universal electronic device that could deal with both different types of problems equally well.

When Hopper arrived in Philadelphia, EMCC had just finished building its first computer, BINAC, for Northrop Aircraft Corporation's secret Snark Missile project. BINAC was a binary automatic computer with a true stored program, and Hopper had to learn to program it. Because BINAC was programmed in octal—a mathematical system based on eight digits from 0 through 7—Hopper had to learn how to add, subtract, multiply, and divide in octal. At the time everyone was saying that the only way to write an efficient program was in octal. Hopper later said that she thought that because she was a mathematician she would have no problem with this new numerical system. Indeed, the only trouble came when she could not get her checkbook to reconcile. After a few months she turned to her brother in frustration and he found the problem: every now and then she had used octal when figuring her balance. Hopper realized that she could not work in octal all day and then live in a normal decimal world the rest of the time. Her answer was not that she should learn octal better, but that the computer should learn decimal. At this point the germ of an idea came to her to let the machine do the dirty work; she would instruct it in her own language.[8]

By the time Hopper appeared at EMCC some engineers were already leaving; BINAC had been built at a loss and the company was in serious financial difficulties. BINAC, though, had served a useful purpose as the model for the first mass-produced commercial computer, UNIVAC I, which was already under development for the National Bureau of Standards (NBS) for use by the Census Bureau. EMCC had won the Census Bureau contract by coming the closest to meeting their needs as set forth in a report on computing machines. The report, commissioned by the Bureau of Standards, had been written in 1946 by George Stibitz. During the war Stibitz had been a member of the NDRC's Applied Mathematics Panel, and after the war he was a consultant in applied mathematics at the University of Vermont. Stibitz's report had suggested that the Bureau of Standards itself might even manufacture an operating device. "The decision as to whether or not to have units manufactured by outside contractors may well be postponed until the [desired] form of the machine has been established," he added. The possibility of general-purpose computers built by commercial firms for sale on the open market was still a novel idea.[9]

The UNIVAC was a high-speed electronic digital computer that dealt with numerical data and that could also handle alphabetic characters. True to Eckert's and Mauchly's original intention, it was designed as a general-purpose machine for commercial as well as scientific use. An undated brochure from before the Remington Rand takeover of the UNIVAC demonstrates EMCC's selling points. "What's Your Problem?" the brochure asked. "Is it the *tedious record-keeping* and the *arduous figure-work* of commerce and industry? Or is it the *intricate mathematics* of science? Perhaps your problem is now considered *impossible* because of prohibitive costs associated with conventional methods of solution."[10] The UNIVAC System was developed by EMCC to solve these problems, the brochure assured its readers. It listed the unique qualities of its computer, including the fact that electrons worked fast (thousands of times faster than mechanical relays) and that the machine had automatic operation, low maintenance, and high reliability.

It was all highly experimental, though. Hopper liked to explain about those early days at EMCC that her group had a pact: if the UNIVAC failed, they would throw it out one side of the building where there was a junkyard and would themselves jump out the other side where there was a graveyard. Fortunately, no one had to jump because the UNIVAC I, completed in 1951, was a great technical success. However, the company was still not a financial success. In fact, the June 1948 contract signed by the Bureau of Standards to pay $169,600 for the census computer was well below what turned out to be the actual cost to EMCC. Other competing companies, such as Raytheon (for the EDVAC) and ERA (for a magnetic drum machine), were asking similar prices, and estimates for delivery time ranged from nine months after the demonstration of components to about two years. These prices were unrealistic in part because, in those early days, nobody realized how expensive computer maintenance would prove to be and how much software support would need to be provided. When Henry L. Straus, the wealthy businessman who had kept the UNIVAC enterprise afloat with substantial loans was killed in a plane crash in 1949, his widow sold the company to Remington Rand.[11]

By the time of the dedication of the census machine some three years later, informational material on the UNIVAC, now under Remington Rand management, noted that while the cost of the system varied according to the number of subsidiary components required, "the minimum cost of working installation is set at about $600,000."[12] Soon, the UNIVAC Division of Remington Rand was turning out a new computer almost every three months and testing them for sixty days before they were sent to the customer.

Eckert and Mauchly had realized that most commercial computer applications would require using proper names, addresses, and descriptive phrases. Therefore UNIVAC had to be an alpha-decimal device, capable of handling letters as well as numbers. This was accomplished by expanding the binary principle to accommodate all the characters found on the keyboard of a standard typewriter. It would no longer be necessary to assign numbers to represent the names of suppliers or customers, and the machine's ability to perform logical operations on alphabetic entries meant it could sort lists of names directly. Although still large—the UNIVAC I was fourteen and one-half feet long, seven and one-half feet wide, and eight feet high—it was much smaller than the Harvard Mark I and one thousand times faster.[13]

Enhanced speed was achieved by using magnetic tape instead of punch cards or paper tapes to introduce data to the computer and to receive results. The physical act of reading and recording on punch cards had been so slow that earlier machines had not been able to take maximum advantage of the speed of calculation made possible by electronics. Although even the ENIAC had been able to perform several thousand additions per second, the speed of obtaining solutions was restricted to the slow mechanical operation of loading data and punching out results.

The UNIVAC received data from reels of thin magnetic metal tape with information held in invisible magnetic dots instead of punched holes. Key-operated auxiliary devices called UNITYPERS prepared the tapes and could be used as either input or output, under the control of the machine. The UNIVAC could accommodate from four to eight tape units. The characters recorded on tape could be fed into the computer at a rate of ten thousand per second, the equivalent of reading all the characters on 7,500 punched cards in one minute. Results were recorded back onto the tape just as fast, enabling the whole operation to run at the speed of the electronic calculations. Another auxiliary device, the UNISERVO, was electromechanical. It converted the magnetic pulses on the tape to electrical pulses fed into the computer. When output from the computer was desired, the servo converted the electrical pulses back into magnetic pulses on tape. A UNIPRINTER, also an auxiliary device, had the ability to read the magnetic tape and automatically print out the information on it. UNIVAC I contained about 5,400 electronic tubes, about 25 miles of wiring, and many other electrical components such as switches, resistors, and capacitors. It also had a number of other innovative features including several memory devices such as acoustic delay lines. Its mercury storage tubes and magnetic cores enabled it to store over twelve thousand decimal digits or alphabetic characters, compared to the two hundred–decimal digit memory of the ENIAC.[14]

The first three UNIVAC machines to be completed went to the Census Bureau, the navy's David Taylor Model Basin, and the Army Map Service. At the dedication of the Census Bureau's machine, James H. Rand, president and chairman of the board of Remington Rand, called the UNIVAC "an important new tool for industrial mobilization, capable of improving the entire complex of our national production, distribution and manpower pattern." He had reason to be optimistic. After a period of rigorous acceptance testing, Census engineers and statisticians had estimated that at its present levels of performance the Census UNIVAC System would accomplish the work set out for it "at about one half the cost of doing it with any other tools which are available to us."[15]

The military connection with computing was also still essential: two of the first three machines went to the military. Informational material compiled for the Census machine dedication pointed out that the UNIVAC could "solve problems in Army, Navy and Air Force materiel control, logistical planning, mapping services and complicated supply operations faster and more efficiently than any other systems" then in existence. These logistical, supply, and personnel management issues would be the areas of most direct concern to Hopper during the remainder of her military service.[16]

Hopper had relatively little to do with Eckert, who was on the engineering side exclusively, designing hardware. She worked closely with John Mauchly, however, and admired him deeply, calling him "very broad-minded, very gentle, very alive, very interested, very forward looking." While Hopper knew that Eckert was a "very bright engineer," she always credited the brilliance of Mauchly's instruction code for making UNIVAC I the first machine that really did data processing. "The logic, the design, how the data flowed, how the instructions operated, and everything else was Mauchly's," Hopper said. He was also a wonderful boss whose leadership skills made the company an excellent place to work.[17]

It was all very informal at the UNIVAC Division. There was a large crowd in a big building, with lots of opportunity to exchange information and ideas. Although hardware and software were developed in separate departments, it was nevertheless easy for Hopper and her group to get answers about the computer design from the engineering side of the house. Typically, if a problem occurred while running a test routine, the engineers blamed the software and the programmers blamed the hardware. Early hardware designers were slow to foresee that the difficulty of programming their devices meant an escalating shortage of skilled programmers for the fast-growing number of new computers. Hopper addressed the problem between engineers and programmers in her usual way. She bought a small china figurine with green suit and red hat, and took a photograph of it placed inside the computer. The next time there was a complaint about the software, she took out the photo and showed the engineers the gremlin in the hardware.[18]

At first Hopper found that the atmosphere at EMCC was not that different from Harvard. This was especially true as she herself persuaded some of the Harvard crew to follow her to Philadelphia. She also managed to hire one of the naval officers she had known, as soon as he got out of the navy. Together she and her small, loosely organized group struggled with the pioneering concepts and techniques of a new field. They tested and refined the UNIVAC I—and later the UNIVAC II—while developing automatic programming routines. In those days Hopper always took home a briefcase bulging with papers. At one point she wryly claimed to work 168-hour weeks because, as she said, "my mind keeps right on figuring these problems, even when I'm asleep." Her tools were paper and pencil. She seldom got time on the machine and dreamed of having a briefcase-size computer to take home at night.[19]

Between 1951 and 1955, forty-six of the first generation UNIVAC computers were delivered to a wide range of businesses, which generated a pressing need for programming support. Hopper selected her team not by checking their test scores but by looking for enthusiastic, independent, innovative, and action-oriented people. She created her own questionnaire to present to them to help her identify those qualities. Some of the group she assembled came from the ranks of recent college graduates, some came over from engineering, and some, like Hopper, were former math professors. All appeared gripped by the enthusiasm and sense of adventure that characterized a Hopper workplace. Hopper's connections with the Moore School, where she began to teach evening classes on computing, also proved a fertile source of recruits. She prided herself on the inclusiveness of EMCC, ascribing the diverse workforce to John Mauchly's freedom from bias—including gender bias. He would employ anyone who was qualified, and Hopper's department soon became known as the United Nations for its Chinese, Japanese, Hungarian, Indian, Filipino, and other workers.[20]

At the University of Pennsylvania her reputation for hiring foreigners, African Americans, and women meant that she received many otherwise hard-to-place applicants. Once they started programming at UNIVAC, employees found another reason to stay: the boss was a real team player. Whenever she was interviewed, Hopper always gave credit to the whole team for whatever was accomplished. While maintaining a reputation for outspokenness, she was astute in internal company politics, realizing she could get much more done if her people were happy. Later in life she prided herself on all the young people she had trained who had gone on to carve out successful careers and assume leadership positions. "I just beat them all over the head, and made them grow up," she said, explaining the success of her mentoring style.[21]

Hopper always maintained that she never saw any prejudice against women in computing. This she ascribed to their early entrance into the field during the war. At EMCC, certainly, Hopper had once again landed in an organization that was "singularly unprejudiced [against women]," flexible, and willing to employ anyone who was qualified.[22] Her personal good fortune, though, seems to have permanently affected her view of the profession. She insisted, for example, that programming was never cast as a man's job and pointed out that secretaries regularly graduated to programming, which they had picked up on the job. If she ever wavered in this opinion—which may have been valid in the early days but which became progressively less so as more men entered the field—she never did so publicly. This raises the question of what part the media played in defining science and technology as a man's world, thus helping to make it so. An article featuring Hopper's work in the *UNIVAC Newsletter* of March 1967 ran under the headline: "Grace Hopper Mixes Insight, Foresight; Has Important Role in 'Man's World.'" This completely contradicted her perception of reality. "It's becoming less unusual these days to see a woman invade a man's sacrosanct world of technology," the article began. And it continued: ". . . Univac's Dr. Grace Hopper is evidence of the role women can play in today's complex business world."[23]

Hopper's views notwithstanding, by the 1970s computing as a profession was overwhelmingly dominated by men. In 1968, for example, women formed only 8.73 percent of the computer science workforce in industry. They fared better working in government computing jobs but even there they still represented only 18.63 percent of the workforce. In the period 1971–1972, men gained 86.5 percent of degrees in computing in the United States. Twenty years later, near the end of Hopper's life, women still earned only 28.7 percent of the degrees awarded in the field. As in other aspects of her life, Hopper was a committed publicist for what she believed ought to be, sometimes overlooking what actually was.[24]

In later years Hopper pointed out that when she joined Eckert-Mauchly, Frances E. (Betty) Holberton was already there as a programmer. During the war Holberton was one of those hundreds of women who had been recruited from colleges across the country to help the war effort by working as "computers" on ballistics firing tables at Aberdeen. There she was chosen to be one of six women to work on ENIAC. With little instruction and no manual to follow, they had to figure out how to program problems into the machine and make it produce the correct solutions. Guided by block diagrams, wiring schematics, and consultations with engineers, their tasks involved a typical wartime mix of mathematics and technology. In fact, Holberton and the five other women were doing pioneering work comparable to that of Bloch, Campbell, and Hopper at Harvard, and they were responsible to a considerable degree for the success of the ENIAC project. A number of them, including Holberton, moved to EMCC with Eckert and Mauchly and went on to distinguished careers as programmers.[25]

Hopper particularly acknowledged her debt to Holberton: "a very, very brilliant woman," who "taught me how to use flow charts [for computer programs] and everything under the sun."[26] She also credits Holberton with being the first person to use a computer to write a program: her "Sort-Merge Generator." This was a "tremendous piece of work," according to Hopper, since nothing like it had ever been done before, and Hopper regretted that Holberton never received due credit.[27] For Hopper herself it was far different. After working closely with Mauchly and Holberton to develop an instruction code for UNIVAC, she began the work that was to make her justly famous: her role in the invention of the compiler and her part in the creation of COBOL.

Hopper's gamble to move into industry paid off as the 1950s saw dynamic developments in computing with rapid changes in hardware, increasing interest in software, and a growing differentiation between the two. As it moved out of academic laboratories, however, computing became subject to the competitive forces of the marketplace. Hopper took her place in the vanguard of this growth, quick to pick up on the latest changes and at times responding, at times leading. While little in her Vassar or her Harvard Computation Lab experience would suggest an aptitude for the rough world of business, she was eminently pragmatic and a persuasive salesperson, using those skills to the full for the next thirty years, both in industry and finally once more in the navy.

Hopper was one of the original visionaries to recognize that computers could serve as the prime vehicle for their own programming. She was a key player in conceiving, developing, and implementing the whole concept of compilers. In 1951 she started working on a compiler—a group, or library, of subroutines with a set of instructions telling the computer how to select from them and assemble a program. Many computation jobs used the same short sets of instructions, or subroutines, even for problems having very different objectives and results; yet for each job the programmer had to write in pages and pages of duplicate code. This was a tedious, time-consuming, and error-prone procedure. The subroutines might be used for solving certain classes of equations or for extracting roots, and they were logically identical no matter what program they were inserted into. Hopper's first step, therefore, was to design a tape with a three-letter call sign for each subset of instructions. Then all the programmer had to do was enter the appropriate call sign and the computer would retrieve the instructions from its library of instruction tapes. What had previously taken a month of programming time the computer could now accomplish in five minutes.

Hopper had brought with her from Harvard a whole notebook of subroutines and was looking for a way to link them. Once completed, her compiler told the computer how to do that, greatly simplifying program writing and avoiding many of the errors that occurred from copying. While Hopper did not invent the word "bug" to signify a computer error, she did come up with the term compiler. To her this followed logically from the notion of a library of subroutines. When people went to libraries and assembled information from various books, they were compiling something. Therefore the computer could be said to be compiling when it selected and assembled a number of subroutines.[28]

Hopper had another motivation for creating compilers. As soon as computers began coming off the assembly line, it meant that a program would work on different machines of the same model. As Hopper put it, "The transfer of data and instructions to a sister computer requires no human intervention save that of transporting tapes." This made it economically efficient to write good programs to use on multiple machines.[29] As more and more computers were produced, programming became a bottleneck. It took a long time to write programs and it would take more and more skilled programmers to keep up with the growing demand. Eventually software surpassed hardware as the driving force of the computer revolution.

After each new development she introduced, Hopper was scrupulous in acknowledging the debt she owed to everyone who had gone before her. In a long paper titled "Automatic Programming, Present Status and Future Trends," which she gave in England in 1958, she noted that subroutines had been a part of computer operations since the Mark I but that during the war there had been no time to organize or systematize their use. This had been done first by the group working on the EDSAC in England, which had provided the first real step in automatic coding. That same group also published one of the first works in this field, "Preparation of Programs for an Electronic Digital Computer," by Wheeler, Wilkes, and Gill. According to Hopper that work provided "a strong thrust in the direction of building routines to assist the coder." Hopper herself had been most influenced by John Mauchly's Short Order Code and by Betty Holberton's Sort-Merge Generator. Mauchly's code operated on the BINAC in 1949 and, although it was written in algebraic format and had no letters, it helped Hopper realize the possibility of using some kind of a code other than machine code.[30]

Hopper also mentioned as a step in this direction a routine developed in 1952–53 at MIT so that the Whirlwind I binary computer could be used by students during summer sessions. Soon, there was a proliferation of similar pseudocodes, as they were called. Pseudocodes used a symbolism other than the instruction code for presenting the information defining a problem to the computers. These pseudocodes could be used to indicate which subroutines were desired from the library. They were interpretive in the sense that they looked at each statement, went to the called-for subroutine and executed it, and then went back to the next statement. They did not create an actual program. Mauchly's Short Code interpreter, developed further and adapted for the UNIVAC I by 1952, and Speed Coding for the IBM 701 developed in 1953, were of this type.[31]

While she was working on her first compiler, Hopper hit on a technique suggested to her by the basketball games she had played as an undergraduate in college. Under the old rules for women they were not allowed to move with the ball so they had to pass it forward and then race ahead to receive the next pass. Remembering this showed Hopper a way of making forward jumps to a part of the program that had not yet been written. She put a little section at the end of the memory called the "neutral corner" to temporarily hold forward jumps until the right part of the operation had been reached. Hopper's ability to visualize operations in physical terms and to reduce complex procedures to simple component parts were key to her success in programming.[32] The next step was made possible, as Hopper recognized, by the new computing system of the UNIVAC I. Here the input-output equipment was under the control of the central computer and the multiple input-output units could be used as secondary storage. The pseudocode and interpretive routine completed a problem in a single pass. Now it would be possible to use a compiler to break the process into two passes, creating a computer-coded problem as a byproduct.[33]

Working on this idea between October 1951 and May 1952, Hopper created the first compiler, the A-0 (A for Algebraic). She had written every instruction herself, by hand, and she reported on it at the Association for Computing Machinery's annual meeting at the Mellon Institute in Pittsburgh that May. Her "basic argument was that we were using subroutines which were checked out and known to work; we were putting them together with an automatic program which had been pretty well checked out too, and that only left the programmer the possibility of making major mistakes in logic." Convinced that people would be very excited by the notion of an easier way to write programs, Hopper took two hundred copies of her talk to Pittsburgh and put them out at the back of the room for people to pick up. Half of them were still there when it was time to leave. This was just the beginning of Hopper's lifelong battle against the apparently ingrained human resistance to change.[34]

A version of Hopper's ACM talk was published as an article, "The Education of a Computer," which has become a classic. It was the first work in America on automatic programming, outlining a compiling system enabling computers to write their own programs from key instructions. The A-0 was not what would later be called a compiler, nor was it what would later be called a language. Hopper referred to it merely as "a series of specifications." Her objective had been to find a way to get the computer to put subroutines together to produce a program, and she had done it. Given a call word, the computer would pull a desired subroutine and the subroutines would be piled up one after the other. This let people write a mathematical program quickly for one-time execution to get a quick answer.[35]

Hopper's premise had been simple. Looking to the future she saw the time, not far off, when only professional programmers would have to understand the number system and the code representing operations. The primary concern of the user, she wrote, would not be "how many additions per second or how many pulses per inch, but rather a broader question, how long between question and answer; not how many bits per tube or how many revolutions per minute, but how many problems per day, how many bills per hour." The user's concern was that the data should be received at a reasonable rate and that it could be shown to be correct. Therefore Hopper saw that it was not the computation itself that was hard to plan, but rather the flow of data. And here there were so many variables that programmers had great difficulty trying to find the optimum balance between input, computation, and output. Hopper's conclusion was simple: "Properly instructed, the computer can optimize more effectively than a programmer." [36]

Mathematicians and engineers would no longer have to be programmers as well. They could consult the catalog of available subroutines and select those that would convey their problem to the computer. The UNIVAC then, "on the basis of information supplied by the mathematician, under the control of a 'compiling routine' created by a professional programmer, using subroutines and its own instruction code, produces a program." The program would guide the computer through the computation on the input data and would produce the desired results. [37]

Hopper's idea for a compiler then took the process a step further. She proposed that the compiler itself could look up the subroutine and copy it directly into the program. The program could then run as a unit and could itself be saved in the library as a more advanced subroutine. "Stated bluntly," Hopper concluded, "the compiling routine is the programmer and performs all those services necessary to the production of a finished program." [38]

When she introduced this notion, people told Hopper that computers could only do arithmetic and it was obvious that they could not write programs; only an expert in writing machine code could do that. Never one to be stopped by opposition, Hopper said that soon compiling routines of all sorts would be devised, including those to handle commercial rather than mathematical programs. She further claimed that she could make a computer do anything she could completely define. This announcement was met with great skepticism, but of course she was right. [39] Hopper foresaw no end to the education of her computer. She told her colleagues that at present the UNIVAC had "a well grounded mathematical education fully equivalent to that of a college sophomore." Moreover, the computer neither forgot nor made mistakes. It was making good progress in its undergraduate studies and was well on the way to graduation. "It is inevitable," Hopper wrote, "that it will present itself as a candidate for a graduate degree." [40]

That same year Hopper became the director of automatic programming development at the UNIVAC Division. As she recalled years later, her group had expanded to about twenty-five members and yet had no official title, so she just began to use the name Automatic Programming Department on all her memos. Eventually, she explained, since she was obviously heading the group, they just made her director. By 1959 the group had swollen to sixty. By then Betty Holberton had transferred to the Applied Mathematics Laboratory at the navy's David Taylor Model Basin. She was there between 1953 and 1956 in order to be closer to Washington where her husband worked. Later, she moved on to the National Bureau of Standards.[41]

In the meantime, the number of computers was growing rapidly in the United States and abroad, just as Hopper had expected, and they were beginning to be used for a variety of different purposes. Defense needs, and particularly the demands of the navy, remained a major influence on the development of computing. Eugene Smith, who had been navy liaison with the Computation Lab for the Bureau of Ships, continued with the bureau as a civilian after the war, urging the navy to expand its computer use, especially in shipyards. In fact, navy funding and support added significantly to the expansion of computing. Hopper pointed out that it was Mina Rees at the Office of Naval Research (ONR) who "was very largely responsible for turning up the money after the end of the war to continue the work on computers." During the war Rees had sponsored many of the navy's computer contracts—including those with the Harvard Computation Lab. Rees and Gene Smith knew each other well, and Hopper worked closely with them both.[42]

Beginning in 1951, Gene Smith and Mina Rees sponsored a series of seminars in Washington, D.C., to gather the latest information on coding, or automatic programming, as it was just beginning to be called. The field was finally gaining some cohesion, and people began to exchange information and techniques. The next symposium was held three years later at the ONR. Hopper was convinced of the need for open discussion to stimulate professional development. She was very active in support of the navy seminars, helping with their organization and acting as master of ceremonies. By 1951 engineers had accepted the computer, but as Betty Holberton pointed out, many in the business world were still very skeptical. They had questions such as, "How do I know the data is on the magnetic tape?" And "What is the legal implication of data on a magnetic tape?" There was obviously still a great deal to figure out and a great deal of educating to be done.[43]

In England, a computer was designed and built for the Lyons Tea Company, where it dealt with inventory and payroll. In the United States, during the presidential election of 1952, a UNIVAC I bought by the A. C. Nielsen Company astonished everyone when it correctly predicted Dwight Eisenhower's landslide victory with only 7 percent of the votes counted. Of course, nobody believed it could be right until many more of the returns were in. U.S. Steel used a UNIVAC to do its entire payroll, including group incentive pay. The Metropolitan Life Insurance Company used a UNIVAC to compute premium notices for all its policy makers and for data files and payroll. In fact, the insurance business, which might be presumed to be conservative, seemed to be among the most receptive to the use of the new technology. In this expansive atmosphere computer companies proliferated, many not lasting very long. IBM, too, finally moved away from its punch-card machines and started production of computers for business use.[44]

Although there was always a scramble among computer companies for government contracts, once clients such as Metropolitan Life, Prudential, Aetna, the big banks, and some manufacturing companies such as U.S. Steel, Westinghouse, and DuPont began to show profits from computer data processing, the pool of potential users increased enormously. Everybody began to join the computer revolution. The arguments in its favor were compelling. An article in a management magazine in 1953 explained that State Farm Mutual Automobile Insurance Company was studying the applicability of the UNIVAC to its business. State Farm spent approximately eighty man-hours a week calculating and printing weekly reports for its operating divisions and preparing year-to-date figures. According to the article, UNIVAC could complete and check the calculations in fifteen seconds. It would take an additional thirty seconds to print out the findings.[45]

With the expansion of computing and the spread of computers to the private sector, Hopper and others understood that the key to selling them was going to be to make them easier to program. The next step after that would be to make them able to communicate with each other. The early compiler had been a first effort at simplification, but more was needed. Since it would be impossible to teach everyone how to write computer code, there would have to be an interface that would accept what Hopper called "people-oriented" data that the computer itself could then translate into machine code. Hopper's thrust was always to simplify and to demystify. She reserved some of her most cutting remarks for those who insisted that only an expert in writing machine code could run a machine; she had no time for programmers who saw themselves as high priests standing between computers and the public.[46]

In the early days of computing there had been no such thing as a programming language; there were only assembly codes and each was completely different, being written for completely different machines. Each of the few existing computers was autonomous, and because they did not need to communicate with each other there was no need for a common language nor any interest in it. The idea of a portable program did not emerge for quite a while. But because of her navy service Hopper recognized earlier than many the value of imposing some form of standardized code. Each navy computer had its own assembly code, and men sent to that installation had to be trained in that code. When— normally after two years—they were transferred to another installation with its own assembly code, they had to learn that one too. This was not only a waste of time, but caused errors when operators inevitably mixed up the codes. Since the programmers were portable, it seemed to make sense to Hopper that they should be trained once in a standard method of coding and documentation techniques, and then take that method with them and apply it wherever they were stationed.[47]

Building on the success or her A-0 compiler, Hopper developed ever more sophisticated versions to program mathematical problems. At the same time, people at MIT were working on a formula translator, the ancestor of FORTRAN, a language still in use today. Hopper's next major development, the A-2, was the first compiler that had a sort of pseudolanguage that was not machine language, but neither was it English yet. The A-2 compiler was designed primarily for use in mathematical problem solving. The A-2 operations manual of 1953 described the compiler as "a programming system for UNIVAC which produces, as its output, the complete coding necessary for the solution of a specific problem. If the problem has been correctly described to the compiler the coding will be correct and checked (by UNIVAC) and the program tape may be immediately run *without any debugging.*"[48]

At first nobody would believe how much time a compiler could save. A programmer at DuPont got caught one night with a routine for some mathematical project due for management the next day. There was no way he could write the routine in time so in desperation he turned to the A-2 compiler that had been languishing unused for months. It worked, he completed the routine, and he got a promotion and a raise. That was the first commercial use of the A-2, and after that, Hopper recalled with pleasure, "everybody started to use the compiler. It's a wonderful thing what a raise will do." Armed with this example, she urged many trainee programmers to take advantage of her compiler. She told John L. "Jack" Jones, whom the air force sent to UNIVAC for training, that if he learned her program he'd get a commission. He studied hard, recognizing the use of the compiler, and eventually the air force sent him to MIT to get his master's degree. By 1979 he was vice president of Southern Railway.[49]

In the meantime Hopper persuaded Nora Moser at the Army Map Service to give the A-2 a try. She did, which took great guts according to Hopper, and she made it work very successfully. The Mathematical Computation Branch of the air force used it and made helpful suggestions for its improvement. They also sponsored UNIVAC automatic programming workshops at the Pentagon where Hopper and others from Remington Rand, as well as army, navy, and air force representatives, made presentations on the A-2 and its uses.[50] Betty Holberton tried it out at the David Taylor Model Basin. Years later she described the experience. "We attempted to get programmers to use Grace Hopper's A-0 and B-0 and FORTRAN, and when one person would try it, the word would get around: the compiler was too slow; it had bugs; the object code was too slow. And we had to start an open shop and train engineers from other laboratories before we got any takers. . . . The professional programmer, "she concluded, "was afraid of job security."[51]

Hopper got support from the navy for her compiler, including from Gene Smith, and from there it was taken up by the Census Bureau and New York University. Little by little the compiler spread to those who wanted to find a faster and easier way of writing programs. Hopper kept many of the testimonial letters that said, in her words, "Yeah, we used the compiler, and we find it useful, and it saved us some time."[52]

By the time the AT-3, or MATH-MATIC, compiler was ready in 1956, Hopper believed her team had got it right from the very start. MATH-MATIC, one of the early mathematical languages, was capable of accepting English verbs and mathematical symbols. Given its commercial name by the UNIVAC Division's marketing department, the complier was designed to compete with IBM's FORTRAN (FORmula TRANslation), also developed in 1956 for use on scientific and mathematical problems.

Hopper always made perfectly clear that FORTRAN was the first of what she called with emphasis, *true* programming languages. She thought her own MATH-MATIC was superior, although FORTRAN, too, accepted English verbs and mathematical symbols. But she also made the point that these later developments would have been impossible without the generators and the compilers, the tools with which to implement the languages. MATH-MATIC was later overwhelmed by the number of IBM computers on the market.[53]

In 1955 the government rented an IBM computer to automate social security records, then numbering close to 120 million. The UNIVAC on which Hopper worked that same year was contained in a 9-by-15-foot cabinet and consisted of 200 miles of wiring, 5,000 vacuum tubes, and 975,000 parts. By that time there were several hundred giant computers in use around the country, and Remington Rand, IBM, and RCA were turning out six or seven more each month. Remington Rand sold mostly to east coast companies including U.S. Steel and Westinghouse in Pittsburgh, Carborundum in Buffalo, and DuPont in Wilmington. In addition to their business applications, the giant computers were also used to predict the weather, in the SAGE air defense system, and for guiding Nike missiles.[54]

Yet Hopper knew from her navy contacts and her summer reserve service that most of the people doing data processing for the navy—for example, those she worked with at the computer center in Mechanicsburg, Pennsylvania—were totally untrained in the use of symbols. As she characterized it, "They wouldn't know a cosine if they met one walking down the street in broad daylight." She believed people either loved symbols or hated them, and non-symbol-oriented data processors were increasingly rebelling against the use of symbols.[55]

It was obvious that there was a growing need for a new type of compiling routine, one to prepare data processing programs rather than mathematical programs. A major stumbling block was that mathematics dealt with decimal or binary numbers, which had a fixed length and type of decimal notation, whereas there was no common vocabulary in business and commercial systems. Just as difficult, business data-processing problems involved alphabetic as well as numeric quantities. It soon became clear that the only common symbolic terminology used in business was the English language. It was therefore decided to select thirty or so verbs for a data-processing pseudocode.[56]

Continuing her efforts to expand the variety of tasks the computer could be taught to handle and determined to make data processing accessible for business purposes and to word-oriented people, Hopper began work on an English language compiler. She reasoned that the computer could be made to translate letters of the alphabet into machine code. Hopper did not claim to have originated this idea. In an article published in May 1953 she explained that the British mathematician Alan Turing had forecast programming a computer to put together programs for itself. According to Hopper, Turing showed in a paper published around 1936 "that if a computing machine is able to modify its own instructions, it can solve any problems capable of numerical solution."[57]

In addition to the mathematical A-series, Hopper now proposed creating a plain English compiler—the B-series. In 1953 she presented a report to management proposing that mathematical problems should be written in mathematical notation and business problems should be written in English. She stated that she and her department could supply compilers to translate each to machine code. At the time, however, no one thought computer programs could be written in English, and Hopper got no funding for her project. It was a startling concept to think of communicating with a computer in English. It seemed perfectly obvious that a computer could not understand English and in frustration Hopper just "kept screaming" that of course she did not expect it to understand anything, ever. All she was going to do was to "match bit patterns."[58]

Failing to get institutional support, Hopper continued working on building a data processing compiler on her own. "When you have a good idea," she loved to tell audiences, "and you've tried it and you know it's going to work, go ahead and do it—because it's much easier to apologize afterwards than it is to get permission."[59]

Even John Mauchly was not very enthusiastic about using English since he was a symbols person. Hopper, although she loved symbols, placed herself firmly on the data-processing side in the interests of making computer use accessible to as many people as possible. Still in search of company funding, by January 1955 Hopper was ready to launch a new attack. On 31 January she submitted a report to management titled "The Preliminary Definition of a Data Processing Compiler." Following good engineering practice, she had already built a little pilot model compiler that would take only twenty statements, but it was sufficient to demonstrate that her idea would work. With top management gathered around in the machine room, Hopper ran a demonstration English-language program through the pilot compiler to prove that it could produce a machine-coded program. This first minicompiler was a pricing and inventory file that read:

> Input Inventory File A; Price File B; Output Priced Inventory File C. Compare Product #A With Product #B. If Greater, Go To Operation 10; If Equal Go To Operation 5; Otherwise Go To Operation 2. Transfer A To D; Write Item D; Jump To Operation 8. Rewind B; Close Out File C And D; Stop.[60]

Similar language would later be used in COBOL (Common Business-Oriented Language), which Hopper helped to create.

Afraid that one demonstration would not convince management to provide her with the biggest budget she had yet requested, Hopper had written the same instructions in French and also in German. Each of the following sentences was equally acceptable: "READ-ITEM A; IF END OF DATA GO TO OPERATION 14. LISEZ-PAQUET A; SI FIN DE DONNES ALLEZ EN OPERATION 14. LESE-POSTEN A; WENN ENDE GEHE ZU OPERATION 14."[61] Running this for management was probably a mistake. Twenty-three years later Hopper vividly recalled what happened next. "That hit the fan!! It was absolutely obvious that a respectable American computer, built in Philadelphia, Pennsylvania, could not possibly understand French and German! And it took us four months to say no, no, no, no! We wouldn't think of programming it in anything but English." What had been to the programmers just a substitution of bit patterns, to management appeared to be a risky move into foreign languages.[62]

When she finally got her funding, Hopper and her group created the B-0 compiler (B for Business), a language suitable for business data processing and one that was also easy to use. The B-0 later became known (thanks again to the marketing department) as FLOW-MATIC. By the end of 1956 the FLOW-MATIC compiler could translate instructions written in a limited vocabulary of English sentences—the FLOW-MATIC pseudocode—into a computer-coded program ready to run on the UNIVAC I or II. It was not that easy, though, as unexpected problems cropped up. For example, they had to find a way to deal with spelling errors. If someone wrote in "compair" instead of "compare," the computer stopped. The solution was to make the computer state that it could not locate that verb and ask for a correction. If the same error occurred again, the computer typed out: "You wrote compair, did you mean compare, if so, hit the start bar."[63] It was also difficult dealing with a computer that had only a one-thousand-word memory. In later years when Hopper heard programmers complaining about having to deal with only 64K, she would remind them that that was "a heckuva lot more memory" than she had had. One thousand twelve-character words were only 12K and yet all of FLOW-MATIC and MATH-MATIC fitted in those memories.[64]

FLOW-MATIC was a big breakthrough. Apart from a slight difference in terminology, compilers from then on followed the pattern it established. Hopper was always somewhat disappointed that all of her initial language was not adopted. For example, she preferred two words, "compare" and "test," to the "if" statement that came into common use, and she always maintained that her term "jump" was "a little nicer" than "go to." But making programming nicer was not really Hopper's concern: her passion was making it easier. Over and over again, her interviews reinforce that this was always on her mind. "We figured we would make it easy for people," was her frequent refrain, and at that she was extremely successful.[65]

Before the FLOW-MATIC was ready to market, it had to be extensively tested to determine training time, operating time, and overall usefulness. Four installations agreed to try it out on real problems, among them the air force's Air Materiel Command in Dayton, Ohio. A number of people with different backgrounds were selected for training at Air Materiel Command, including some with no computer experience. In just two weeks they all successfully learned how to write programs using FLOW-MATIC. FLOW-MATIC was then used on real problems, and careful track was kept of the whole operation, especially the time expended from defining the problem to debugging the resulting program. By the end of the project it had been determined that the use of FLOW-MATIC "supplied a four to one improvement over manual techniques."[66]

Next, Hopper and her team produced subroutines for a variety of non-UNIVAC-family computers to prove the independence of the system from any particular machine. They had already demonstrated that the system was even independent of the FLOW-MATIC English pseudocode by modifying the compiler to accept and reply in German and then in French. The desire to use German had one long-term effect on programming languages. Because only imperative sentences in German placed the verb at the beginning of the sentence, all the verbs chosen for FLOW-MATIC were in the imperative form, and so they remain. The possibility of substitution also meant, as Hopper pointed out, that FLOW-MATIC was really a code and not a true language. From the point of view of simplicity and speed, Hopper did not think this discipline was a bad thing. She sometimes said that modern programming had lost touch with some of the beauties of the early simplicity. "We can make a simpler language if we stick to the format of a code of some kind and the exact definition provided by a code," she noted. The FLOW-MATIC compiler had proved that it answered the need for more rapid coding techniques and that it could be widely used.[67]

Although Hopper's research and development group got their first plain-language compiler up and running, there was still no demand for it so they had to go out and market it themselves. As a result, Hopper developed formidable skill at what she called the "marketing game." She later referred to introducing the compiler as the biggest selling job she had ever been through. She had the support of Martin Simmons at U.S. Steel, who was a convert, and also of Walt Carlson, who finally pushed it in a big way at DuPont. Westinghouse began to use FLOW-MATIC, and Jack Jones introduced Hopper to Joe Cunningham, who worked at the Pentagon, and through him she got air force support. Her compiler was accepted at Wright-Patterson Air Force Base and, more important, the air force began to make noises that they would like all their computers to respond to English. Hopper managed to interest Norman Ream at Lockheed, and he was so impressed he threw out some IBM equipment and bought UNIVAC equipment instead. IBM sent someone to Lockheed to tell the company what a mistake it had made, but Lockheed made the switch to UNIVAC anyway.[68]

One of Hopper's best ideas was outlined in an internal office memo defining a "layette" for a computer. Hopper had the notion that they were delivering a computer so they also had to deliver a layette to go with it—the compiler. Somebody—Hopper could not remember who—had called the layette "software," and the name stuck. When she could not persuade management in her own company to believe in the efficacy of her compiler, she just went out and sold it directly to their customers. "Make it easy. Make it slide in," was her marketing advice.[69]

Pushing full steam ahead as always, Hopper was frustrated at how slow the progress seemed, and in spite of her success it was irritating that it was easier to convince customers of the utility of her compiler than it was to persuade her own organization. Some of the opposition at UNIVAC came from a young man who was working on building up a tremendous library of input-output routines, which Hopper thought was just "nuts." Her FLOW-MATIC system made it unnecessary to write the input-output because the compiler knew how to write the whole thing. It was particularly galling to Hopper that there was a tendency in the company to prefer the young man's system—an interpretive technique—to hers because he was the first person to graduate from Harvard with a degree in computer science. Hopper's mentor Howard Aiken was now turning out professionals who were competing with his original wartime protégés.

Still, Hopper had confidence that her compiler was a superior system because as subroutines were added to the pseudocode, the end result was a written program. The interpretive system, however, was the more popular at the time, even though it produced no program but only built up an ever larger and more unwieldy library of subroutines.

Never one to abandon her convictions, Hopper stuck with her program and she was soon proved right when customers began to fall off from using interpreters.[70] Interviewed in Dallas in spring 1959 on a visit to Southwestern Methodist University's UNIVAC, Hopper was asked about her FLOW-MATIC system. "This is just common sense," Hopper responded, "I think from this point of view it took a woman to do it."[71]

Once Hopper had gone out and got the customers on her side, they put pressure on her bosses, who then came around too. Above them, at headquarters in New York, top management was still unconvinced. But with such powerful backing from customers, Hopper finally got her way and the money came flowing in to develop the project. "Not the proper way to behave I don't suppose," Hopper reflected smugly years later, but it worked, and she gained experience selling an idea and influencing people through networks and contacts.[72]

A measure of Hopper's accomplishment was given in June 1978 at the ACM History of Programming Languages Conference in Los Angeles. Hopper was the keynote speaker. She was introduced by Jean E. Sammet, another outstanding woman in the field who designed and developed IBM's COBOL compiler in the 1960s. Sammet drew loud applause by noting that "Grace Hopper did more than any other single individual to sell the concepts of the higher level languages from both a technical and an administrative viewpoint. . . . Furthermore she did this," Sammet continued, "when these comments and thoughts were often falling on deaf ears, and she had to battle her way through normal company funding authorization chains, and to convince the *users* that the systems she was developing would really help them."[73]

In her many interviews in later years Hopper was scornful of those who had scoffed at the idea of communicating with computers in English. This may well reflect the bitterness of some of the criticism she had had to endure at the time. One of her favorite targets was Herb Grosch, a computer pundit who went around saying that the only way to program a computer was in binary code. He was a man of some influence at the time and he made a lot of noise telling everyone that it would be inefficient to write programs in English. Hopper's response was to demonstrate that it was not the English that made it inefficient or efficient, it was the quality of the compiler. "That was an awful battle trying to tell that to people," Hopper recalled. "It wasn't the language that gave you a bad program—it was the compiler." To that very day, Hopper insisted, the UNIVAC compiler had produced much more effective code than IBM did.[74]

These were still very informal days when jobs were only loosely defined, and a considerable part of Hopper's responsibility ended up involving customer service. UNIVAC computers were delivered with a few minimal routines such as Holberton's Sort-Merge Generator and Mauchly's short-order code, but that was all. Customers had to send their employees to UNIVAC to be trained to use the computers. Another group actually trained the customers, but Hopper's group ran informational seminars for them. They also visited installations to help customers get the computing started.

Howard Aiken, who had, after all, begun his work designing an automatic calculator to save him from tedious calculations, no doubt approved the direction of Hopper's career. By this time he himself was moving away from designing hardware, and at the second symposium on large-scale digital devices that he organized at Harvard in 1949 he had already begun advising participants to go into programming. Like her mentor, Hopper claimed that her key motivation was sloth. "I'm lazy as all get out," she said. "I never want to do anything over again." Yet the significance of her system was clear. FLOW-MATIC could cope with the problem of coding. Now with the ability to code rapidly and without errors, Hopper saw that there would be an acceleration in research programs concerning data retrieval, language translation, and the many other problems awaiting computer solution.[75]

Pseudocodes and the compilers that converted them into machine code had appeared in answer to the need to produce debugged routines more rapidly and economically. MATH-MATIC was being used widely by 1956, and by 1958 all navy shipyards, by then using UNIVAC IIs, had shifted entirely to FLOW-MATIC. FORTRAN, introduced in 1957, had made rapid progress in the scientific and engineering environment that was used to symbols. Data-processing languages progressed more slowly. The early compilers were slow and cumbersome and programmers viewed them as a threat to their specialized knowledge. Nevertheless, data-processing languages did begin to proliferate as IBM came up with Commercial Translator (COMTRAN) and Honeywell developed FACT.

Neither Hopper at UNIVAC nor her opposite numbers at IBM, RCA, Sylvania, Burroughs, and other commercial companies, nor navy and air force representatives, thought a multitude of languages was a good idea, but they could not work together to develop one language without coming up against antitrust laws. They also needed to be sure that whoever sponsored the quest for a universal language would be seen to be completely neutral as far as manufacturers were concerned and yet would have the stature to command attention. They realized that the only way to get around these problems was to have university or government sponsorship. Preliminary meetings of industry, academic, and military representatives were held under the auspices of the University of Pennsylvania, but the university was unwilling to undertake any long-term sponsorship of a group to create a single uniform computer language. The air force declined as the junior service, and the army representative at the talks said he did not know enough about computing to make any commitment. Eugene Smith, who had both the expertise and the interest, had to decline on behalf of the navy for lack of funds.

Following Smith's suggestion, the group asked the Department of Defense (DoD) to institutionalize continued meetings. Air force Col. Charles Phillips, the deputy comptroller for automatic data processing (ADP), agreed. In 1958 Phillips convened a meeting at the Pentagon including representatives from every government agency that had computers, all the computer manufacturers, and all of the biggest computer users. Hopper helped him compile the list of invitees and named herself the representative of the UNIVAC Division of Remington Rand. At this historic meeting it was agreed that there should be a common language for programming data processing programs and that the language should be English. A steering committee was set up that formed an executive committee calling itself CODASYL, the Committee (or sometimes, Conference) on Data Systems Languages. Three task forces were established, the Short-, Intermediate-, and Long-Range Committees. There were also a number of subcommittees. Nominal DoD sponsorship—they never got a penny from Defense according to Hopper—kept the whole thing free from legal challenge.[76]

Under the initial chairmanship of Colonel Phillips, Hopper and Robert W. Bemer of IBM were chosen as special advisors to the executive committee of CODASYL. The original executive committee was composed of other top people in the field, including Gene Smith and Norman Ream, all of whom Hopper knew well. More importantly for Hopper, they were almost all UNIVAC users. Her influence at CODASYL was based largely on these professional connections. Joe Cunningham, her original air force contact, succeeded Phillips as chair, yielding in turn to Hopper's former student, Jack Jones, who by then was high in the ranks of Southern Railway. Hopper was at the core of the move to standardize data processing languages from the very beginning, a respected member of a small group that established the forms and procedures defining developments from then on.[77]

The Short-Range Committee of CODAYSL was the only one of the three main committees that every really functioned. It had been tasked with studying the situation and creating an interim common business language that might stop the gap for a year or two. The intent, apparently, was to halt language proliferation until the Intermediate-Range Committee could produce a really good common language. Including the chairman, the committee had nine members, three of them women. These women, Mary K. Hawes of Burroughs, Betty Holberton of the navy, and Jean Sammet of Sylvania (later IBM), played a significant role in the evolution of a standard business language for computers. They too, like Hopper, were pioneers in the field and attained positions of importance. Examples such as this led Hopper to continue to believe (long after it was no longer true) that in computing women were on an equal footing with men.[78]

The Short-Range Committee and subcommittees considered as models for their common language UNIVAC's FLOW-MATIC (1958), IBM's COMTRAN (1959), and AIMACO (Air Materiel Command, 1959), developed by the air force with much help from Jack Jones and some from Grace Hopper's group. What emerged in 1960 was the first version of COBOL, Common Business Oriented Language, which was frequently updated but not replaced. The Intermediate-Range Committee's work had been preempted, unintentionally, by the Short-Range Committee, although it did go on to do some other useful work. The bulk of COBOL, including the format, was based on Hopper's 1958 FLOW-MATIC manual. FLOW-MATIC had the advantage of being the only business data-processing high-level language in use prior to the introduction of COBOL. The navy was quick to demand COBOL, accepting it officially in 1960, and other organizations began to implement it as well. IBM dithered for quite a while, hoping to sell customers on COMTRAN, but they too eventually had to yield to COBOL. While COBOL—soon the most widely used programming language for mainframe computers—had been generated by a committee, Hopper's compiler was at its heart. "The influence of her work and her thoughts was high," Jean Sammet observed, even though she had not had any direct participation in the Short-Range Committee itself.[79]

It was a great day for Hopper and for the rest of her group when they ran the first COBOL program. First they ran it on UNIVAC II and then the next day they took it over to RCA and ran it on the RCA 501 machine, proving that one data-processing language could be run on different machines produced by different manufacturers.[80]

Within a year of its creation, however, rumors surfaced that CO-BOL was dead. Such rumors reappeared regularly from then on, but the first time it badly depressed some COBOL advocates, particularly Howard Bromberg, formerly a Hopper associate at UNIVAC who had switched to RCA. Driving past a stonemason's one day, Bromberg stopped and bought a white marble gravestone with a reclining lamb on top. He got a reduced price because the lamb's ears were chipped. Bromberg had the mason carve the word COBOL on the front and had the gravestone crated up and sent to Colonel Phillips at the Pentagon. Hopper loved to tell the tale of the trouble Phillips had getting the tombstone—which he had not ordered and was not expecting—through Pentagon security. He had it installed in his office as long as he was there and then eventually took it home. The gravestone story circulated quickly and did wonders for raising the moral of COBOL enthusiasts. When they celebrated COBOL's twentieth anniversary, everyone wore pins with a picture of the tombstone.[81]

COBOL survived, in part, because the manufacturers, over time and for economic reasons, had to drop their own efforts at languages and accept COBOL. They had no choice but to support COBOL in order to get business. The Department of Defense also pressured users on behalf of COBOL because DoD really wanted a single language. Betty Holberton served on the COBOL development committee and was very much involved in its creation. In 1978 she explained why she thought COBOL had been successfully implemented. She began by describing some of the strengths of the language itself. "But in the end," she concluded, "I'd like to say that Grace Hopper's continued effort to inform management was very important because, in my opinion, the option of using compilers, left to the user, might easily have made it go down the drain because they resist change."[82]

Over the years techniques were developed to build compilers that were faster and produced highly efficient object code, or machine language. Then variations of languages began to appear and were implemented partly because of competition among their creators and partly because of the programmers' desire for what Hopper referred to as "bells and whistles." Once again it appeared as though the very energy of the industry would lead to massive confusion. However, the United States of America Standards Institute (USASI) took the matter in hand and established standards for FORTRAN (1966) and then COBOL (1968). In 1967 the air force documented a standard JOVIAL (Jules Own Version of the International Algorithmic Language). These standard languages were defined, evaluated, standardized, and approved by volunteers from throughout the data-processing community. The criteria they had to satisfy, as Hopper explained, was that they had to be "commonly acceptable, competitive, maintainable, open to extension, and above all useful."[83]

Meanwhile the Eckert-Mauchly partnership had broken up after eighteen years. John Mauchly left Remington Rand in 1959 to form his own company, Mauchly Associates. Later, returning to his original interest, he formed Dynatrend, a systems consulting company specializing in weather forecasting. He died of heart problems in 1980. Eckert became director of engineering for the UNIVAC Division, staying on through the various changes to become vice president and technical advisor for computing systems at Sperry Rand in 1963. That same year the first UNIVAC I, which had been moved to the Census building in Suitland, Maryland, in 1952, was finally retired after twelve-and-a-half years and presented to the Smithsonian Institution.[84]

Outside of her navy work, COBOL was Hopper's chief claim to fame. Just as Howard Aiken's mentees spread out to work in industry and advance what they had learned from him, so Hopper's protégés, too, spread her work and her reputation. Apart from the death of her mother in 1960, which was a great sadness, Hopper's life at this time was very satisfying. In August 1961, she was promoted and appointed director of research in systems and programming for the Remington Rand Division of Sperry Rand. Her new assignment gave her responsibility for broad-scale systems and programming research for all Remington Rand divisions.[85] Then in June 1964 Hopper was appointed senior staff scientist at the UNIVAC Division and traveled widely representing UNIVAC interests in Europe and Japan, as well as around the United States and Canada. When she was home, she lived at 2301 Rittenhouse Claridge in Rittenhouse Square, where she had a pleasant, good-sized apartment. By the time she left in 1967, however, the area was becoming rather seedy and plagued by drugs.[86]

Hopper had thoroughly enjoyed the "wild" early years of computing, when nobody believed what could be done and anything might happen. Gradually, however, the industry began to settle down. Very few of the small computing firms survived the 1960s and ultimately even UNIVAC was overtaken by IBM. Hopper saw quite clearly that the problem was one of salesmanship. IBM already had an experienced and aggressive sales force selling punch-card equipment and it was easy enough to divert them to computer sales. UNIVAC, on the other hand, struggled to set up systems support. By the time Remington Rand tried to convert typewriter salesmen to selling computers they had already lost the competitive edge. The lack of support for Hopper's initiatives was typical of the company's poor marketing and unwillingness to invest heavily enough in software. Hopper never had much time for IBM, however. She saw that its corporate persona discouraged individual recognition, and anyone who seemed to shine too much was quickly forced out of the limelight. The firm was also particularly secretive and, unlike other organizations, according to Hopper censored all its employees' conference papers. Although she never mentioned it in interviews, she may also have disliked the way IBM used attractive young women, recent college graduates with degrees in mathematics, to act as systems service representatives. While this certainly brought women into the field, it was a dead-end job at the lowest level. It was the young women's communications and customer relations skills that IBM tapped into, and the job was never intended as a first step in a meaningful professional career. Hundreds of women were employed this way in the 1950s and into the 1960s. Hopper would have seen this as women settling for a lot less than they were capable of.[87]

Hopper expressed her general scorn for IBM by criticizing its huge three-story IBM computer—the SSEC—that was on display in the lobby of their New York City office. She called it a monstrosity that was approached by climbing up and down flights of stairs inside it. According to Hopper the computer never was any good because IBM "as usual took something from everybody." The result was "a total mishmash of every idea anybody had had." The machine had electronic circuits, relay circuits, step counters, and several tape units. It used punched paper tape and magnetic tape, but since no one could get everything to work at one time, it was an "impressive gadget," according to Hopper, with no real function.[88]

In addition to her CODASYL work, Hopper's work at UNIVAC was varied and demanding. Among her other duties she directed, coordinated, and actively participated in research into basic theories and techniques of automatic systems design in order to stimulate her company's development efforts. This research involved business, university, and governmental activities to determine their long-range requirements for information-processing systems. She also worked on basic theories and techniques of creating, recording, retrieving, processing, and transmitting information, and developed new and advanced concepts in systems design and information processing for such future computer fields as medical science, language translation, simulation processes, and the theory of decision making and strategy.[89]

As if this were not enough to keep anyone busy, Hopper was also responsible for supervising UNIVAC Division's contributions to the development, support, and use of the University of Pennsylvania Computation Center. She cooperated with the Wharton School at the University of Pennsylvania to analyze future business trends in the utilization of business systems to "determine and advise concerning potentially profitable areas for new developments." Hopper always had a keen nose for business, her own as well as her company's, and she was never happier than when she was earning money from a number of sources at once. When she turned 60 and was still working full time, she was ecstatic at the thought of drawing social security on top of a full paycheck.[90]

Still, she was concerned about her future. She wrote in her Vassar class report for 1966 that she knew she could stay on at UNIVAC until she was sixty-five but that she was already scouting around for jobs after that. She considered the civil service, where a number of her early computing colleagues worked and where she could stay on until she was seventy. Or she could move into consulting or work as a contract employee. "I will do almost anything to stay with the computers," she told her classmates. "The field is still critically shorthanded. Of course," she continued, "I hope the price will come down some day so I can have a computer of my own!"[91]

For all her inventiveness, constant stretching of what she demanded from computers, and the anthropomorphic language she used to describe their functioning, Hopper was hard-eyed in her appreciation of their limitations. A computer "can do anything but ask intelligent questions," she told an industry newsletter in 1967. "Man alone can do that. If a man can't define a problem, the computer can't do it."[92] When asked what she was most proud of in her life, she usually said it was "all the young people I've trained over the years—that's more important than writing the first compiler."[93]

At fifty, Hopper had been described as "a slight, fragile-seeming woman with blue eyes and gray hair and rather gaily dressed."[94] Of course, she was anything but fragile. By the time she was sixty, her hair was completely white and her face was a mass of wrinkles. Skirts were getting shorter and shorter then, and although Hopper recalled wearing shifts that showed the knees when she was in college, by the time she turned sixty she said she liked her skirts to cover her knees. It was probably at this time, too, that Hopper began to get a reputation for being "feisty," especially for her strong, no-nonsense opinions about data processing. She also admitted to being an extremely annoying

employee because she would not do anything that she did not understand. That was a euphemism, of course, to explain that she would not
follow stupid or unnecessary directions. It was an approach she extended to everything she touched.[95]

While Hopper had carved out a career for herself in computing,
her brother, too, was very successful. He started out working for Banker's
Trust Company, staying with the firm for twenty-five years and attain-
ing the position of chief economist. Since he had always wanted to teach,
Roger took early retirement from Banker's Trust, accepting an appointment as associate dean and adjunct professor of finance at Columbia
University Graduate School of Business. Later he became the S. Sloan
Colt Professor of Banking and Finance, a chair endowed for him by
Bankers' Trust. Roger, described by a colleague as one of the most intelligent and public-spirited people he had ever known, had a wonderful blend of business and educational wisdom. Like his sister he was
an inspiring teacher who loved to expound on a wealth of subjects, his
hands weaving a web of ideas as he spoke. In 1976 Roger moved back
to Wolfeboro to live year-round. Until then, he and his family had a
luxurious penthouse apartment on West 95th Street, directly across
the road from where he had grown up. His mother continued to live in
an apartment a few blocks away, and they would all gather at church
on Sunday mornings.[96]

During all her years working for UNIVAC Hopper remained active in the naval reserve. She would later say of her civilian career in
industry that whenever she hit a brick wall in computing the navy
would send her on some assignment, some training duty usually, that
would open up for her the key to whatever had been holding her back.
She also said of the navy that it was a continuing thread throughout
her civilian career because from the A-0 on, it was always the navy
that gave her the best response to her work.[97]

Grace, Roger, and Mary Murray. Ca. 1918.
Courtesy William T. Westcote.

Grace Murray. Ca. 1924.
Courtesy Mary Murray Westcote Collection.

Lt. (jg) Grace Murray Hopper. 1944.
Courtesy Mary Murray Westcote Collection.

Computation Lab staff portrait in front of Mark I. August 1944. Top: Bissell, Calvin, Verdonck, Livingston, White. Bottom: Bloch, Arnold, Aiken, Hopper, Campbell.
Grace Murray Hopper Collection, Archives Center, National Museum of American History, Behring Center, Smithsonian Institution.

Lieutenant Hopper and Specialist White examining Mark I sequence
mechanism. 1944.
*Grace Murray Hopper Collection, Archives Center, National Museum of American
History, Behring Center, Smithsonian Institution.*

IBM Automatic Sequence Controlled Calculator (Harvard Mark I).
Courtesy IBM Archives.

Lt. Grace M. Hopper, USNR. 1946.
Courtesy Mary Murray Westcote Collection.

Grace M. Hopper. Ca. 1955.
Courtesy Mary Murray Westcote Collection.

Grace M. Hopper and the UNIVAC. Ca. 1962.
Courtesy Unisys Corporation.

Adm. Elmo Zumwalt, CNO,
presents certificate of promotion
to Captain to Cdr. Grace M.
Hopper. August 1973.
National Archives Photograph No.
428-N-1157763.

Capt. Grace M. Hopper at
Stonehenge, England. 1973.
Courtesy Mary Murray Westcote.

Capt. Grace M. Hopper, Director, Navy Programming Languages Section, in her Pentagon office. 1975.
National Archives Photograph No. 428-N-1166531.

Capt. Grace M. Hopper. June 1980.
National Archives Photograph No. 428-KN-30487.

Capt. Grace M. Hopper takes oath of office from Secretary of the Navy John Lehman during promotion from Captain to Commodore. President Ronald Reagan stands at left. December 1983.
Official U.S. Navy photograph from the Collections of the Naval Historical Center.

Cdre. Grace M. Hopper with Nanoseconds at Bloomsburg
University Commencement. December 1984.
Courtesy Bloomsburg University.

Cdre. Grace M. Hopper during groundbreaking ceremonies for the Grace Murray Hopper Navy Regional Data Automation Center, NAS North Island, San Diego, CA. Rear Adm. Paul Sutherland, CO NAVDAC, stands to Hopper's left. September 1985.
Official U.S. Navy photograph from the Collections of the Naval Historical Center.

Grace Murray Hopper Service Center (Regional Data Automation Center), NAS San Diego, CA. 2002.
Official U.S. Navy photograph.

USS *Hopper* (DDG-70) at sea. 1998.
DoD, Defense Visual Information Center, March ARB, CA.

4

A *WAVE* Ordnance Officer?
Naval Reserve Duty Philadelphia: 1949–1966

I t was hardly surprising that the navy had an early advantage in postwar computing. After the war many of those who had pioneered the Mark I and the cryptologic devices at CSAW remained in the vanguard of computer developments and influenced the navy's progress in the field. Mina Rees at ONR was eager to "keep the navy in touch with the progress being made, and enable the navy to benefit from what we anticipated would be spectacular achievements in the new technology." Until the advent of the National Science Foundation in 1950, ONR was almost alone in providing federal funding for computer research.[1]

In the 1950s the navy held a substantial stake in much of the large-scale electronic computing going on in the United States. Howard Aiken's Mark II and Mark III were being used for ballistics calculations, while the Whirlwind I computer at MIT, begun under navy contract in 1944, later was sponsored in part by ONR. There was also a navy logistics computer—the ONR relay computer—at George Washington University, in Washington, D.C., designed to maintain inventory controls for electronic spare parts. The Atlas code-breaking computer had replaced the wartime bombes at CSAW's Nebraska Avenue site, and a RAYDAC computer was at the Naval Ordnance Test Station at Inyokern, north of Los Angeles, in California. Delivered to California in July 1952, the Raytheon-built general-purpose RAYDAC was used chiefly for missile data reduction. Bob Campbell and Dick Bloch were among those who had worked on its design. They had both joined Raytheon after the war to establish its computer project, which at one point was staffed almost completely by Harvard Computation Lab alumni.[2]

The navy, when it needed additional computer time, made arrangements with the UNIVAC Division of Remington Rand in Philadelphia to use its computers. A navy team would move in to the UNIVAC Division's plant and work on a new computer during its six-week testing phase. When the computer was shipped out to the customer, the navy team would move on to the next machine.[3] The navy continued to lead the way in innovative computer use when in 1956 it established a project office to develop the Naval Tactical Data System (NTDS), a computerized shipboard battle management system. The Armed Forces Security Agency, later the National Security Agency, the secretive electronic surveillance and code-making and -breaking organization, also became a major sponsor of computing. It had been formed by pooling the cryptologic resources of the Army Security Agency and the navy's CSAW.[4]

Navy influence also permeated commercial computing. The postwar era saw the emergence of private computer companies, many of them founded by men who got their start in wartime navy computing. Notable among these, of course, was Howard Engstrom. At the end of hostilities, he and Lt. Cdr. William C. Norris, formerly a Westinghouse engineer and also at CSAW, left the navy to form their own computer company, Engineering Research Associates, in St. Paul, Minnesota. They were soon joined by a number of other former CSAW engineers. Not wanting to lose such intellectual capital, the navy actively aided in the establishment of ERA and maintained a close relationship by means of contracts from ONR and BuShips. The Naval Computing Machine Lab even relocated from Dayton to St. Paul to work closely with ERA on its new digital computers.[5] "It was the navy that helped them find the money [to do all that]," Hopper said later. "I was there when they had them go ahead."[6]

Eventually, ERA failed financially and, like EMCC, was bought out by Remington Rand. Because ERA was located so far away, the two divisions had little to do with each other. Only later were they merged to create the UNIVAC Division of Remington Rand. Although Norris left ERA and formed Control Data Corporation, the whole heart of UNIVAC, on into the 1960s, was drawn from the original group at CSAW. By 1968 the president of UNIVAC was a former CSAW lieutenant and several of the vice presidents had served there also.[7] In peacetime, UNIVAC took up the mantle of both Harvard and CSAW as a prime training ground for computer personnel. Groups like those sent from Prudential and groups from John Hancock took the early training courses at UNIVAC and then went out and spread their expertise to other groups. Hopper was always running into people all across the country who told her, "You don't remember me, but I heard you lecture in 1950." Or, "You taught me about computers in 1953."[8]

Thus Grace Hopper was a member of a relatively small cadre of navy-trained computer engineers who formed the core of the field after the war and who greatly influenced its development. People were portable and they took their skills with them to wherever the opportunities seemed best. Former Lt. Cdr. Ed Berkeley, the navy liaison to the Computation Lab, joined The Prudential Insurance Company after the war. In 1947 he had helped found the Association for Computing Machinery, in part as a result of Howard Aiken's Computing Conference held at Harvard that year. Gene Smith, as already noted, went from the navy to the National Bureau of Standards, from where he encouraged the commercial development of computers, particularly the UNIVAC. John H. Curtiss, also a mathematician and former naval officer, joined the NBS, where he too promoted computerized systems. Years later, reflecting on the significance of military sponsorship, Grace Hopper often claimed that there would not have been a computer industry without that early navy support. Surely there would have been, but doubtless it would have developed more slowly.[9]

Interest in digital computing was not exclusive to the navy, of course. During World War II the U.S. Army had sponsored the ENIAC at the University of Pennsylvania, and, not long after, the Census Bureau had provided funding for Eckert's and Mauchly's UNIVAC I. But it was the air force that took up computing in a big way after the war, especially to deal with the high speeds of postwar aircraft and missiles. In 1950, the air force took over MIT's navy Whirlwind project to form the basis of its Semi-Automatic Ground Environment, or SAGE, air defense system. The first SAGE sites were operational in 1958, each site supported by two, 175-ton Whirlwind-based IBM computers. After the war the air force also took over sponsorship of Howard Aiken's Mark III and Mark IV computers under development at the Harvard Computation Lab.[10]

Wartime work on radar at MIT's Radiation Laboratory also spun off some important developments in early computers. A large number of the scientists at the Radiation Lab were Bell Telephone Company engineers on military leave. Bell Labs had been involved in the computer field before the war with George Stibitz's complex calculator and other machines, but Hopper was convinced that the concepts of electronic computing were communicated to Bell Labs by the men working at MIT. It was they, she thought, and not people like Stibitz, whose practical knowledge of electronics gave Bell Labs a head start in the field after the war.[11]

During her eighteen years with the UNIVAC Division, living and working in Philadelphia, Hopper also continued to serve the navy. She was assigned to the Fourth Naval District in the Philadelphia Navy Yard, where she was an ordnance officer with Volunteer Ordnance Unit 4-3. Although the presence of women both in the military and in engineering was no longer novel, "mention of a WAVE ordnance officer will still cause startled glances," according to the Fourth Naval District news bulletin. [12]

The commanding officer of her unit, who had been at the Franklin Institute before the war, returned to work there afterward. Practically the whole unit, according to Hopper, was made up of Bell engineers who had been in radar and electronics during the war. These men brought back with them to Bell Labs in Pennsylvania an acceptance of the concepts of computing. When development got under way, there was an audience receptive to the new ideas. For Hopper this remained one of the defining differences between war and peacetime. Those engaged in war work realized they were living in a new world. They were conditioned to accept new ideas and after the war they continued to embrace change, helping to encourage new developments. Later, Hopper thought, people closed their minds again and reverted once more to the usual resistance to change. [13]

Hopper's annual two weeks of active duty training were spent undertaking computing tasks for the navy. Programmers, or coders as they were still often known in the early 1950s, were in short supply and Hopper's expertise was in demand. In the first years after her arrival in Philadelphia, for example, and still a lieutenant, Hopper was frequently assigned to the Naval Proving Ground in Dahlgren, to work on the Mark II. In 1950 she spent two weeks at Dahlgren coding "a large problem for the Aiken Relay Calculator" as the navy now called the Mark II. Already, her computing services were described as "important" to the Navy, and it was regretted that she did not have more time to give to the reserves. [14]

Eventually, Hopper's influence permeated much of navy computing. The 1950s and 1960s saw a rapid expansion in the uses of computers, and in the early Cold War era both the newly independent air force and the navy sought to exploit every technological advantage. Hopper played a part in the extension of computing to different navy tasks, working as a consultant on many classified projects. These assignments required her to learn new fields of application such as flutter and fuselage analysis, electronics and radar, accounting systems, and logistical problems, including those involving explosives. Electronic brains provided the intelligence for ordnance equipment from mines and torpedoes to missiles and fire-control gear, and computers were also increasingly used in engineering research, design, and application. Pending work on her navy desk in early 1953 included, among other things, a logistics problem, plans for a weekend visit to a naval activity, plans for training, and a memorandum on personnel requirements caused by the labor shortage. Where Hopper's influence was greatest was in writing programs for logistics, personnel, and inventory and stock control.[15]

While computer terminology was still fluid in the 1940s, Hopper's navy assignments were often misidentified as work on calculators. By 1952 navy vocabulary had come to grips with the new technology and Hopper's fitness reports routinely described her as an expert in automatic or electronic digital computers. By then, in addition to her regular duties with Ordnance Company 4-3 in Philadelphia, her responsibilities had extended to frequent work on logistics for the Bureau of Personnel. With the Korean War, shortages of labor made her services more necessary than ever and loosened congressional purse strings to pay for military expansion. In May 1952, Hopper completed a program for quality control in logistics and logistics planning for the Bureau of Ordnance.[16]

Curiously, in later interviews when Hopper spoke freely of her experiences in World War II she never mentioned the Korean War nor how it affected her duties or even the computing projects she was assigned. She was equally silent about the Vietnam War even though she gave one of her major oral history interviews in 1968 just as the war was gearing up, another in 1972 at its height, and another in 1976 just after it ended. Nor did she make any mention of the social and political upheavals at home. Even her extensive comments on the Second World War were nonpolitical. She did not question or analyze the war so much as describe the conditions under which she was working and the intense patriotism that motivated her and her colleagues. How much her military training had to do with this silence on the later conflicts and how much was the result of her own inclination it is impossible to tell. But from her interviews one would hardly know there had ever been conflicts in Korea and Vietnam.

Meanwhile, even as she began to make a name for herself in the larger navy world beyond her reserve unit, Hopper did not neglect the more mundane side of her reserve obligation. Her enthusiasm for the navy, for which she later gained such fame, was already strongly manifest. Her superiors noted that she not only led her Philadelphia unit in attendance, but that she also regularly recruited new members. This was true in spite of the fact that her activities were restricted to what was, according to her superior officer, "permissible for WAVES." There was still a two-tier system in the navy: WAVES were second-class citizens and remained so for at least another twenty years, until the end of their separate status (and name) in 1972. Thereafter, navy women still had to overcome barriers holding them back from sea duty and combat. Nevertheless, Hopper's fitness reports from this era invariably described her as outstanding in interest and ability, and she was usually "particularly" recommended for promotion. Her dedication paid off and in 1952 she was promoted to lieutenant commander.[17]

The UNIVAC Division proved to be a most understanding employer with regard to Hopper's reserve obligation. It may have been gratifying to learn of Hopper that "this Wave officer rates higher than the male officers in the unit, of corresponding rank and length of service, in value to the Naval Service,"[18] but praise was accompanied by additional, and increasing, navy demands on her time. In 1953 the Bureau of Ordnance addressed a letter to Remington Rand requesting that newly promoted Lieutenant Commander Hopper be allowed time off to give a series of talks on digital computers to reserve officers throughout Ohio. Worse still, the request was made "with the understanding that no funds are presently available for this purpose." Prudently, Capt. H. R. Wright, the author of the letter, thanked Remington "both for your cooperation in the past and for your consideration of this request." Hopper gave her talks and Remington Rand picked up the tab.[19]

Why was it willing to do so? Perhaps in large part because the navy was one of its most valuable customers and all indications were that this would continue to be true. By 1952 Remington Rand had taken over both the EMCC and ERA and continued their navy contracts. Still, confidence in computing was not universal; many naval officers strongly resisted the new technology that seemed mired in the "mist of magic," as one navy bulletin put it. Grace Hopper, supreme pragmatist and effective public speaker, bridged the gap between the civilian producers and the military users of computer technology, benefiting both sides and enhancing her own reputation at the same time. She soon became one of the navy's most requested speakers, a position she maintained for the next thirty-three years, reluctantly relinquishing it only when she could no longer travel.[20]

Among the tasks assigned to Hopper during her reserve service was to write a program for a rocket trajectory and a program for a turbine problem. She was also tasked to provide information on new storage devices and to write specifications for projected computers. She also had to write manuals for completed computers. In this latter task she had had the best of training in producing the Mark I manual under the tutelage of Howard Aiken. Aiken had taught her to write with great clarity no matter how complex or technical the subject.

Hopper remembered this instruction with gratitude and always tried to maintain Aiken's demanding standards in her own writing.[21]

As if she did not have enough to do between a full-time job in a rising industry and her reserve commitments, Hopper also continued to take courses helpful to her navy career. In April 1953, for example, she completed a course in field economic mobilization at the Industrial College of the Armed Forces. Later that year she successfully passed a BuOrd course on the fundamentals of guided missiles. The following year she took Naval War College correspondence courses in logistics, navy regulations, and operational planning and staff organization.[22]

By 1954, Hopper's superiors referred to her as an "outstanding authority in the fields of computer design and automatic programming of digital computers." She gave lectures to BuShips officers on a wide range of subjects including the application of UNIVAC to engineering, statistical, and business problems, and on advanced programming techniques. She also reported on recent developments in automatic coding for electronic digital computers, for which she was well qualified by her own work on compilers. Her A-2 compiler, the first to be used extensively, came out the following year. In addition, she was assigned to report on the development of small-scale electronic digital computers.[23]

Following each of these assignments, Hopper received outstanding commendation in her fitness reports for her expertise in the field of electronic computer design and programming, "both operational and engineering wise." The praise may have been pro forma for the navy, but her area of expertise was not. By 1956 she was described in the new terms she helped to define, as a highly experienced systems analyst.[24] The following year, having been promoted to the rank of commander, her fitness report positively glowed. Grace Hopper was an "outstanding officer" whose value to the navy could not be "measured by normal standards." She was seen as a leader in the field of development of automatic programming and one of the very few people in the entire country who understand this new vital field." During a two-week tour at the Philadelphia Naval Shipyard, Hopper had rapidly analyzed the difficulties experienced in the installation of a computer for the facility. Zeroing in on the flaws in the intended system, she made specific recommendations for its improvement. She also initiated a measure to solicit additional recommendations from the resident computing staff, deeply impressing the shipyard commander.[25]

In part, of course, Hopper's success was because of her expertise in a still little-known specialty. In a 1953 article coauthored with John Mauchly, she had pointed out the shortage of trained programmers, a shortage that would not soon be rectified because of the ever-increasing rate at which new computers were coming into use. Successive commanders of the Philadelphia Naval Shipyard knew that the U.S. Navy was "extremely fortunate to have CDR Hopper as part of its reserve component," as one recorded in March 1959, because there were still few people at all familiar with methods to automatically program computer systems.[26]

Hopper was not working alone to computerize the navy, of course. There were others, too, struggling with the primitive conditions, many feeling their way, without her training and background. One of the early and still lesser-known navy programs to be automated was a classified intelligence operation at the Naval Research Laboratory (NRL). In the summer of 1959, the Countermeasures Branch of the Radio Division of NRL hired Karl Gustafson, then a young graduate student, as a summer intern to computerize a direction-finding task. Most of the staff of the Radio Division were engineers and World War II radar experts, but they knew no computing. Neither Gustafson nor his equally young electrical engineer supervisor thought they knew much about computers either, but they had taken a few courses and were learning and so they were given the job.[27]

Position fixing by high-frequency direction finding (HFDF) had been used with considerable success by the U.S. Navy in World War II, particularly to locate German U-boats in the Battle of the Atlantic. HFDF technology promised equally impressive results against the Soviet navy in the Cold War. A high-frequency direction finder works by reading the direction of arrival of high-frequency waves from a distant transmitter. When two or more direction finders receive a bearing, the location of the transmitter can be determined by triangulation. High-frequency waves can travel thousands of miles when they bounce off the ionosphere and return to earth in a series of skips. This phenomenon makes the location of even the most distant transmitters susceptible of discovery. Conversely, a direction finder can ascertain its own location by triangulating emissions received from a number of known transmitters. The military value of this technology is obvious, particularly for navies that, having no land lines, must rely heavily on radio. Gustafson's assignment was to computerize the direction-finding operation that was monitoring Soviet submarines worldwide from their radio transmissions.[28]

Electronic direction finding also had other potential uses by the early 1960s, among them to keep track of American planes flying over alien territory, to track the new electronic intelligence satellites, friendly and enemy, and to detect various other forms of emissions—for example, from nuclear testing. What direction finding was actually used for during those years is still largely classified, but Gustafson wrote an account of the computing tasks he was assigned when he returned to the NRL full time in 1960. He spent the next four years writing programs to speed the operation and improve the accuracy of HFDF. It had taken World War II operators several minutes to plot a location by hand on a table-size chart. The new objective was to reduce the time to thirty seconds with the result appearing on a computer printout.[29]

HFDF was particularly suitable for automation because of the large number of variables affecting its speed of operation and its accuracy. Both speed and accuracy could be dramatically improved with electronic processing of the input from many different receiving stations (a dozen or more were required for good coverage of an ocean-size area), as well as input regarding weather, geography, ionospheric distortion, and human error.

Until 1962 most of Gustafson's systems design had to be done on a desk-size Litton Industries vacuum tube computer with program and data entry by means of punched paper tapes and a magnetic drum memory with only 4,096 locations—at that time the only general-purpose machine available to the Countermeasures Branch. The primitive nature of the technology and the memory limitations meant that Gustafson spent what he referred to as "huge amounts of time devising computational schemes" to avoid time-consuming multiplication and division as well as "endless hours devising tricky loops" to save memory locations.[30] This heavy investment in time for what would now be called software development reflects part of the great expense to the navy of creating systems for specialized work.

The NRL did have the use of more powerful computers than the LGP-30 in the early 1960s—for example, the room-size NAREC—and they were also linked to computers at Remington Rand/UNIVAC for electronic and radar work. But most of the direction-finding programming was accomplished on the LGP-30. After systems design was complete, hardware had to be contracted for and built. According to Gustafson, IBM bid $26 million for the NRL direction-finding contract in 1962 and Burroughs won the award with a bid of $13 million.[31]

Direction finding was an important, real-time tactical operation. It depended on a high percentage of uptime and adaptability, accomplished by a system that allowed for easy expansion or replacement of individual units. The Burroughs machine provided that. Although the impetus was on military effectiveness, the result was also to keep down costs by providing for the replacement of modules. After 1962, hardware advances including core memory, card and magnetic tape input and output, and transistorized memory added greatly to processing speed. When applied to direction finding, this greatly enhanced the speed of position fixing. Direction finding was typical of the sort of specialized challenge facing much navy computing. It was addressed by bringing on board experts to create unique systems. There were many such tasks of navy computing that required special, nonstandard systems, particularly those that involved scientific research and technological development. This fact soon caused problems for a service forced to begin thinking in terms of standard systems.[32]

During these years navy computing evolved with little central direction, each shore activity developing its own capabilities as best it could. In response to a navywide effort to consolidate support services, initiated by the secretary of the navy in 1962, the Fourth Naval District undertook a study of all management advisory services. That October, the study group published its findings. Among the areas of concern in the report was the need to furnish "immediate and competent advice to top and middle management officials on central data processing capabilities." The Ships Parts Control Center and the Ordnance Supply Office apparently had personnel who were "computer oriented," but neither formal nor effective informal lines of communication were found to exist with the Naval Supply Depot (NSD). This led the study group to conclude that there existed a "lack of appreciation for the proper application of modern machine techniques to Naval Supply Depot problems." In their opinion this could result in a "failure to recognize the areas of fruitful application [of computing] to NSD operations."[33]

About this same time the air force recorded its own difficulties with some of the same issues of communications and standardization that dogged the navy. In a speech at a UNIVAC Scientific Exchange conference in August 1958, Col. E. R. Miller of the air force Air Materiel Command noted the "lack of a common communication media between our Headquarters management personnel, our Depot operating management, and our computer programming group, particularly during the development of EDPE [electronic data processing equipment] systems." This the colonel ascribed in large part to the ignorance of management about computing. He was also concerned with "the difficulty of coding instructions for intricate equipment needed to produce the proper data processing." According to the colonel, this led to each piece of equipment having its own specific code, with little standardization and no possibility of skills being transferred when personnel were reassigned.[34]

These were exactly the sorts of problems for which Hopper's talents were suited. During these years of reserve duty she was in constant demand to explain the growing number of uses of computing and to design systems for integrating computers into the myriad functions of the navy. Not all supply issues concerned widgets and canned beans. The Mechanicsburg, Pennsylvania, complex, which was struggling with automation, among other things supplied the navy with missiles and nuclear materials.[35]

A recent history of the WAVES describes Grace Hopper as "redoubtable." Certainly one of the reasons for this was her seemingly limitless energy. In addition to engaging in demanding, creative work in the daytime and to maintaining a second career as a navy reservist at night and on weekends, Hopper also taught courses in business and industrial applications of computers to evening classes of up to forty students at a time at the Moore School. At least she did not need to prepare for her classes, since she was fully confident that her lectures addressed the latest developments in the field. Hopper enjoyed teaching immensely and found the electronic engineers, computer scientists, and business school students lively and challenging. She also gave of her time and energy to professional organizations and scientific associations. She had joined the Association for Computing Machinery soon after its establishment and served from 1952 to 1956 on the ACM Nomenclature Committee and from 1956 to 1958 as an ACM Council member. She also served on the editorial board and later as the ACM representative to the Mathematical Sciences Division of the National Research Council.[36]

Some time in 1960 Hopper's navy superiors began a campaign to secure her promotion to captain. At first they were circumspect in their efforts, merely stating that Hopper should be promoted when eligible even though they knew that was impossible under the current regulations because "there is only one Wave Captain authorized." Only one woman in the entire navy could hold the rank of captain, and that person was the Assistant Chief of Naval Personnel (Women), the unwieldy title given to the highest-ranking WAVE. The cap on promotions had been set by Congress in the 1948 Women's Armed Services Integration Act and would not be removed until 1967.[37] The year after the cap was lifted, six women were promoted to captain, all of them in the regular naval service, not the reserves. There were no women admirals until 1972. Meanwhile, in 1964 Hopper's promotion was being "most strongly recommended . . . in the event that higher grades are opened to women." This mantra was repeated annually until Hopper secured promotion to captain in 1973, fourteen years after her promotion to commander.[38]

By 1963, Hopper had fulfilled several reserve assignments in both the Bureau of Ordnance and the Bureau of Ships. But when the Bureau of Personnel asked for her help, she almost overwhelmed them. The saga began with a 24 April letter to Commander Hopper from Rear Adm. C. K. Duncan, BuPers Assistant Chief for Plans. He noted that Hopper had, on numerous occasions, served with the Bureaus of Ordnance and Ships, and he explained that BuPers, too, had problems. "We need guidance," wrote the admiral, "and advice, in the general adaptation of automatic data processing to personnel management." He tried to woo Hopper with flattery, observing that he felt sure their problems would be "of particular interest to one with your experience and capabilities." The admiral then politely suggested to the commander: "Should you find it possible to accept orders for two weeks active duty for training with BuPers we would be happy to issue them." And finally, as accommodating as he could possibly be, he closed by assuring her that "the timing of this duty can be adjusted to fit your personal plans."[39]

Presumably having received an affirmative answer from Hopper, the Director of the Plans Division, Capt. D. J. Carrison, wrote to her in June to confirm their arrangements. Noting that they were "approaching the point where our horse and buggy methods of planning are producing diminishing returns," Capt. Carrison laid out an agenda to maximize the benefit of Hopper's two-week stint with them. He hoped that two days of orientation and familiarization with the setup of the bureau would suffice. To that end he explained their organizational structure, which consisted of assistant bureau chiefs with horizontal responsibilities for all personnel functions, such as plans, personnel control, and education and training. In addition, there were project managers, or "czars," with vertical responsibility in one field, such as Polaris under Vice Adm. William F. Raborn and surface missile systems under Rear Adm. Eli T. Reich. It looked as though there would be a need for other project managers too, possibly for antisubmarine warfare, for naval tactical data systems (NTDS), for operations control centers, and more. It was clear to many in the bureau, the captain continued, that some sort of reorganization along vertical lines would be necessary, but without abandoning horizontal supervision in some areas such as performance, morale, training, and planning.[40]

"Please don't get the idea that we are asking you to come in and reorganize the Bureau," Capt. Carrison hastened to reassure Hopper, "because we are planning to get a management consultant firm to give us assistance in this after you have completed your tour with us." But he wanted her to know that they were flexible, ready for change, and "receptive to any suggestions" she might make. In the meantime, in order to prepare for her visit, the bureau had borrowed three officer students from the operations analysis course in Monterey who were familiar with automatic data processing methods and capabilities. They were getting a six-week tour of all aspects of the bureau so that they could make a preliminary report to Hopper when she came on board. This should prove helpful to her, Capt. Carrison concluded, because they "speak the language . . . of computer processes."[41]

Apparently Hopper's tour at the Bureau of Personnel was a success. "Little do you know what a revolution you have wrought," wrote Capt. W. R. McQuilkin from BuPers in August. "I have been so busy trying to catch up with the avalanche which your 'pearls of wisdom' launched that I haven't had a moment in which to properly thank you. . . . Permit me to quote your parting remark," he continued: 'I don't feel I have done anything but ask questions.'. . . I shudder to think what might have happened if you had supplied answers," he concluded.[42]

As a direct result of Hopper's visit, the bureau established an Operations Analysis Division—reporting directly to Admiral Duncan—with billets for six operational and systems analysts, three of them to be lieutenant commanders, and one a supergrade (GS-16) civilian. But who was going to hire these specialists? "Of course at the moment there is still just me on the receiving end of all this and I need help," admitted Capt. McQuilkin. "If my memory serves me correctly," he went on persuasively, "you did say that in case of dire emergency you might spare the Bureau of Naval Personnel a wee bit more of your precious time." The dire emergency had arrived, he assured her, and asked whether she would be willing to help him interview a list of candidates for the position in operations research. "I am anxiously awaiting your reply," he closed, adding—perhaps as an irresistible clincher—that Admiral Duncan and Captain Carrison both sent their personal regards.[43]

Evidently, Hopper did help Capt. McQuilkin with his interviewing. At least, she spent three days in October working on a special project in the bureau's Plans Division.[44] It is worth quoting at some length Hopper's fitness report for that August, written by Admiral Duncan. "Commander Hopper's preeminence in pioneering and developing automatic data processing equipment is well known in the electronic computer industry," began Admiral Duncan. He continued:

> As manager of the Research Division of UNIVAC Corporation she brought to BuPers a wealth of experience in the problems of organizing "Big Business" to most effectively make use of automatic data processing equipment. Her erudite questions served as a catalyst to bring into focus the BuPers shortcomings in its organizational ability to effectively use computers. As a direct result of her two weeks of active duty training, BuPers is now forming an Operations Research/Systems Analysis Division whose primary purpose is to fill the gap between management and the effective use of the Bureau's automatic data processing equipment. Through the use of operations research techniques as applicable to personnel problems it is conceived that simulations of the Navy's strength versus requirements can be projected in order to give management alternative solutions to personnel problems. Singular credit belongs to Commander Hopper for defining requirements of operations research systems analysis and for further identifying the disciplines which qualify an individual in these new fields.[45]

By 1964, Hopper's fame had spread so widely in the navy that she did not have to apply for routine two-week training duties, as did most officers. "Cognizant activities in the Navy, aware of her eminence in the profession, actively solicit her service and advice," wrote her commanding officer with proprietary pride. "They invite her again and again," he concluded.[46] She was particularly sought after to advise on the makeup of navy computer installations. She spent her two weeks' active duty in 1965 at BuPers in Washington. In December 1966 she was on two-week temporary active duty as a curriculum advisor at the Machine Accountants' "A" School at the U.S. Naval Training Center in Bainbridge, Maryland.[47] Indeed, she also wrote the curriculum and learning objectives for the navy's new Programmers "C" School due to begin the following spring. Her most valuable contributions to the curriculum were in the areas of teleprocessing and high-level language.[48]

More than just technical skills, valuable though they were, accounted for Hopper's long and successful naval career. She was quintessentially a team player and so was well suited to military life. In 1965, and again in 1966, her Reserve Research Company, the number changed to 4-13, won recognition as the top among the eleven research companies in the Fourth Naval District. Hopper's Officer's File is full of letters of commendation for her contribution to the unit's activities, such as serving on the Senior Advisory Board. Just as at Vassar, Hopper more than pulled her weight with regard to additional duties. According to her commanding officer her "tact and understanding with her associates left little to be desired," and her "enthusiasm, dedication and loyalty to the Naval Service" were described as "boundless."[49]

The high praise Hopper received in her fitness reports reflected more than the standard hyperbole common in bureaucratic structures. Her reviewers made it clear that they followed her civilian career by frequent reference to the external honors and awards she continued to pile up. In 1964, for example, her fitness report drew attention to Hopper's selection for the "Woman of the Year," by the Society of Women Engineers. That same year she was also given the Armed Forces Service Ribbon. The following year her fitness report noted that she was the only woman Fellow of the Institute of Electrical and Electronic Engineers.[50] Of equal significance was the field she was in. In June 1966 President Johnson sent a memorandum to the heads of all federal departments and agencies calling for improved management of automation in the government. He pointed out that "the electronic computer is having a greater impact on what government does and how it does it than any other product of modern technology."[51] Management problems created by the rapid and often haphazard growth of computing in the government had just begun to attract serious notice. From then on, automatic data processing in the government was to become the subject of Congressional investigations and legislation, Presidential messages, and innumerable directives and regulations. Navy computing was not immune from such scrutiny and was subject to increasing efforts at control, but it appeared that Hopper would not be around for this next phase.

Finally, the years had caught up with her. By her own account, late in 1966 Hopper received a letter from the Chief of Naval Personnel telling her that she had served 23 years, which was over twenty. "I knew that," she loved to tell interviewers. The letter also informed her that she was about to turn sixty. "I knew that too," said Hopper.[52] The final paragraph of the letter asked her to apply for retirement, which she reluctantly did, effective 31 December 1966. Her final fitness report stated simply that Commander Hopper was "an outstanding officer in all respects and a wonderful person. Our best wishes go with her on her retirement."[53] "It was the saddest day of my life," recalled Hopper.[54]

5

I'm in the Reserve, Retired, and on Active Duty
The Pentagon Years: 1967–1977

On 1 August 1967, seven months after she was put on the Naval Reserve retired list with the rank of commander, the navy recalled Hopper to active duty for a special assignment in Washington. "I'm in the reserve, retired, and on active duty," she quipped.[1] Her temporary appointment was to last six months; instead, she stayed nineteen years. At first she took a military leave of absence from the UNIVAC Division, renewing it annually as the navy annually renewed her active duty appointment. Finally, in 1971, she retired from UNIVAC at the mandatory age of sixty-five but continued in the navy.

Hopper had been brought to the Pentagon by Norman J. Ream, formerly of Lockheed, who had been made special assistant to the secretary of the navy and tasked to impose order on the navy's automatic data processing. Hopper knew Ream well, of course, from the CODASYL committee among other things, and Ream was very familiar with Hopper's role in the creation of COBOL. According to one close observer, Ream was an impressive individual who was treated with deference by those around him. He both respected and trusted Hopper. She had direct access to him and worked very closely with him for the remainder of his navy stint.[2]

Hopper was recalled to the navy department to standardize computer programming languages for all navy computers not part of weapons systems. However, because what she produced was in the public domain, it reached a much wider circle than just one service. She ended up standardizing COBOL for the entire Department of Defense and influenced a whole industry.

The navy had participated in the development of specifications for COBOL since 1959. When it became apparent in 1967 that COBOL would be approved as the national standard, Ream turned to Hopper to head an effort to enhance the use of Standard COBOL in the navy and to develop procedures for validating compliance with the forthcoming standard. She was made director of the Navy Programming Languages Group in Ream's office. In the fall of 1968 her group was transferred to the Office of Information Systems Planning and Development under the assistant secretary of the navy for financial management (ASN[FM]). In this position, which lasted until 1970, Hopper was responsible for implementing the use of Standard COBOL navywide. This involved standardizing the numerous different and incompatible versions of COBOL that had been proliferating almost unchecked to accommodate the different types and generations of hardware and the different tasks undertaken at different activities.[3]

Each hardware vendor had implemented COBOL on its own machines in a unique fashion. Each picked the features of COBOL it liked, lopped off features it did not like, and invented new features of its own. A COBOL program written for a UNIVAC computer, say, would not run on an IBM or an RCA, and the navy bought computers from all the different vendors because none was churning them out fast enough to meet the navy's needs. In the beginning, COBOL had looked very good coming right out of CODASYL. The experiment of running the same COBOL program on an RCA and then on a UNIVAC had been very encouraging, but that did not last long. The vendors "got innovative" and put their own little features onto COBOL according to Dick Fredette, who later worked closely with Hopper. Because both the navy department and the entire Department of Defense had such a variety of computers of different generations, there was a growing need for a single program that would work on them all. Without a uniform language there was no portability; programs had to be revised and rewritten every time they were transferred from one machine to another and across generations.[4]

The expansion of the navy in response to the Vietnam War, and the consequent increasing demand for computerized systems, had made a restructuring of navy computing essential, particularly when it was seen that the navy's operational supply and logistics activities, when automated, had a measurable impact on warfighting capabilities. One system, for example, the UADPS-SP, made a very significant contribution to supplying the Vietnam War, which was just heating up when Hopper got to Washington. By dramatically reducing labor requirements it accounted for substantial savings. In 1967 the Naval Supply Center Oakland, applying this automated system, used less than half the personnel it had used in 1952 during the Korean War to manage approximately twice the logistics workload.[5]

The strains of the war, however, also brought to light the inefficiencies and duplication of effort caused by lack of coordination in the navy's automated systems. This was not solely a navy issue. Ever since the passage of the National Security Act of 1947 and the creation of the Department of Defense, the navy had had two masters and, therefore, dual concerns. It had to serve its own interests while also complying with orders, regulations, and guidelines from the Department of Defense. This was certainly true in the field of technology. In addition to the DoD, the navy also had another layer of bureaucratic oversight with which to comply: the federal government. And, of course military computing depended for its hardware and much of its software on commercial companies, adding one more relationship to manage. For the next ten years Hopper's efforts to standardize navy computer languages involved taking into account, and as far as possible complying with, the demands of these three external constituencies while at the same time satisfying the best interests of her own service.

In the years before Hopper's recall to the navy, the collecting, processing, and exchange of data had expanded enormously in a broad range of federal, state, and local governments, in the military, in industry, and among the public. In addition to DoD concerns, congress, the Bureau of Budget (soon to be the Office of Management and Budget), other federal agencies, and computer producers and users had all become increasingly aware of the need to facilitate the interchange of data. That meant eliminating or minimizing variations in data being exchanged. Throughout the 1960s and 1970s the DoD was still the nation's primary user of computers so the navy was in a good position to spearhead much of this effort and Grace Hopper was often the tip of the spear.

Striding through the Pentagon in her customary single-minded fashion, Hopper quickly adjusted to navy routine. When she had worked in the private sector, she always felt that the best response she received regarding her innovative ideas came from the navy, so she was not surprised to be called back. For a woman, however, Hopper's recall was unusual. Overall the number of navy women actually decreased during the Vietnam War, and women were restricted, as before, to less than a third of the enlisted ratings. Most WAVES continued to fill clerical, health service, and administrative positions. While the status of women in the navy had not changed much, the changes in computing since Hopper left active duty in 1945 were profound. From a couple of pioneering but highly specialized cryptographic and computational operations during the war, computing had spread to almost every phase of naval operations.[6]

In 1955 there were still only several hundred computers in use in America. The launch of Sputnik in 1957, however, and the widespread sense of falling behind the Soviets in science galvanized the nation to train applied mathematicians, especially in digital computing. Courses in digital computing began to appear in math and engineering departments in academic institutions across the country.[7] The number of computer installations in the United States increased dramatically from 15 in 1950 to over 40,000 by 1968. According to the American Federation of Information Processing Societies, the dollar value of such installations grew from $1 million in 1950 to more than $7.8 billion by 1966.[8] The navy mirrored this trend. By 1968 it had over 760 general-purpose computers, an increase of over 100 percent in three years. It employed over 18,000 people in the field and continued to support the development of pioneering hardware and software. But the growth had been haphazard, as Hopper had discovered while still in Philadelphia.[9]

The Department of Defense launched its first major attempt to combat the proliferation of incompatible systems in December 1964 with a directive to standardize data elements and codes throughout the DoD. The directive argued that any "increase in the effectiveness and efficiency of the defense effort rests largely on improving the interchange of information."[10] Congressional interest in the widespread and increasing use of automatic data processing throughout the government dated from about the same time as DoD interest with the passage in 1965 of Public Law 89-306, known as the Brooks Bill. The Brooks Bill split responsibility for establishing and maintaining federal information processing standards among the National Bureau of Standards, the Office of Management and Budget (OMB), and the General Services Administration (GSA). The result of these initiatives was not just to establish automatic data processing budget ceilings for all federal departments and agencies, including the DoD, but also to impose stringent controls on the development of new management information systems (MIS) and to establish detailed equipment validation procedures for the purchase of new ADP equipment.[11]

In response, in December 1965, a DoD standardization program was established that assigned responsibility to the air force to oversee standardization of computers and information processing departmentwide. The air force's mandate covered, among other things, the standardization of terminology, methods of problem description, character codes, and programming languages. The objective was to develop standards for all the services that would provide "maximum compatibility among Defense information processing systems in the acquisition, use, and interchange of equipment, information, programs and personnel."[12]

Until that time the navy had had no formal ADP management program, only general policy guidance from the secretary of the navy. Gradually, however, individual commands had begun to formalize ADP management responsibilities and had tried to develop standardized systems of like activities. Under Ream, and in compliance with DoD requirements, the navy began replacing unique programs with standard systems wherever feasible and converting nonstandard to standard programming languages, as well as moving into third-generation computers. In 1968 Ream placed responsibility for conversion to standard languages squarely on the navy itself and not, as had been previous practice, on the vendors.[13] A few weeks after Hopper reported to Ream, he wrote the chief of naval operations (CNO) that conversion would not be considered complete "until all programs are written in COBOL, with a compiler compatible with the full USA Standards Institute (USASI) standard."[14] This was Hopper's challenge.

Although the name soon changed from the USASI to the American National Standards Institute (ANSI), the principle of compatibility with national standards remained the same and governed Hopper's entire remaining time in the navy. The COBOL standard was approved by ANSI in August 1968 and adopted as a DoD standard in November of that year. Each of the military services was urged to work with industry to further develop ADP standards responsive to DoD requirements and to encourage industry use of those standards. DoD activities were also directed to "make optimum use of the facilities of industry groups in the development of standardization documents having a present or potential DoD use." Always short of funds—as she had been at UNIVAC, too—Hopper became extremely adept at pursuing this particular approach.[15]

Initially, navy computers had been programmed primarily in the various manufacturers' assembly languages or machine codes. This resulted in massive reprogramming and translation efforts whenever there was a change in computers whenever or the simulation of the old computer environment on the new machines was required. The former case was expensive and delayed implementation and the latter case deprived the system of the higher speeds and enhanced processing capabilities of the new hardware. For programmers, though, the constant need to upgrade and reprogram meant stable employment. For them, standardization looked like unemployment.

Of the three main languages used by the U.S. government at the time, FORTRAN (handled by the army) was for scientific applications and JOVIAL (handled by the air force) was used for command and control.

COBOL (handled by the navy) was used for managerial and administrative systems. The navy had also developed a high-level language compiler for tactical data system applications, the Compiler Monitor System number two (CMS-2), which was developed from a 1960 version of JOVIAL. In general, navy tactical data systems and later those embedded in weapons systems were planned, developed, installed, maintained, and administered separately from nontactical systems. They experienced many of the same problems as nontactical systems, particularly with regard to standardization.

A June 1971 memorandum for the undersecretary of the navy noted that the new AN/UYK-7 computer (made by UNIVAC) was central to the operations of four new classes of ships. Therefore, it was necessary to turn to a large number of contractors and subcontractors, including UNIVAC, Litton, Hughes, RCA, Raytheon, Lockheed, and Computer Service Corporation, to implement the system. The navy's control over the methods and software techniques used by those contractors was "very weak," according to the memo. Most contracts gave the contractors responsibility for the design, implementation, and delivery of operating combat systems, including weapons, sensors, and command and control. Therefore, the report concluded, "the navy is in a poor position to enforce the necessary standardization to ensure compatibility, control interface requirements, and to minimize support costs once the new ships are introduced into the fleet."[16]

But three-quarters of the navy's work was ashore and required straightforward data processing. Hopper's main concern, therefore, was with COBOL, used for inventory, payroll, personnel, and other management information systems. A very high percentage of navy programming was done in COBOL and there were millions of lines of COBOL code to deal with. It was even used for administrative functions on small shipboard computers when they first came in.[17] It would obviously take years to convert existing nonstandard programs. The navy is "a great, big, old, traditional thing," Hopper told an interviewer in 1969, "and when you push it you generate friction; it gives off squeaks and squeals. But we'll keep at it, and apply a little grease here and there. We told them to proceed with all deliberate speed," she elaborated, "which in the navy means get there as fast as you can but don't burn out the boilers on the way."[18]

This focus on COBOL for MIS gave Hopper a difficult and wide-ranging job. Business or logistics data processing was different from scientific data processing, which primarily involved computation. Scientific applications were usually much smaller and more flexible than business applications. They were more receptive to innovation and were often able to adopt a new concept as soon as it became available. Business data processing, on the other hand, was tied to moving or manipulating large masses of data. Navy logistics and business-type data systems were not only large, but involved multicommand users. New approaches took time, effort, and training to implement. According to one navy observer, it was not necessarily bad to be a bit slow. He warned against "being in the vanguard of implementing a new technology for business data processing . . . because the delay allows companies in industry to encounter the problems first." By the time DOD procurement rules had been complied with, someone else should already have worked out the start-up problems inevitable in any new system. All this was a warning, however, that implementing the new Standard COBOL would be neither easy nor fast. [19]

"When I went back to the navy I asked for eight people and they gave me four," Hopper noted in an interview for the British magazine *Dataweek.* "I had no tapes, no computer and no staff. They just said 'do it'—the usual navy technique." [20] Hopper assembled and trained a little group of highly qualified technicians to assist in the development of COBOL audit routines and other tools for implementing Standard COBOL. The way she got suitable personnel to work for her was easier than putting together her UNIVAC team because she did not have to worry about salary and other incentives. She just grabbed the brightest of the bunch from the navy ADP school. In addition to a civilian secretary, Norma Gealt, Hopper's crew consisted of two enlisted data processors, first class, and a GS-15, Richard Fredette, whose job description was "digital computer systems administrator." [21]

Fredette had graduated from college in 1956, having gone through the Naval Reserve Officers Training Corps (NROTC). He served four years in communications in the navy, but when he got out he had no idea what to do about a career. At that time computers were almost unknown—he had barely heard of them himself—but he did hear that programmers were needed, so he took a test and got a job as a civilian programmer with the army. Then for a while he worked in private industry; his background was in economics so he had gone into business computing. By the time Hopper was pulled out of retirement Fredette had been brought in from the field to look at COBOL and see how the navy could make the best use of it and if it could possibly be standardized. He was doing some research in the Navy Yard library one day when Hopper came in and they got talking. Fredette told her what he was working on, and she started to help. "I sat there enthralled,"

Fredette recalled. "From that point on," he remembered, "I was captured by her, as was everybody who knew her." The bond was set. Hopper got him assigned to her group and he remained her indispensable deputy for most of the next two decades.[22]

It took Hopper's group almost two years of constant effort to persuade the navy to make mandatory the use of Standard COBOL, even though the DoD in the meantime adopted the standard. Still, this was considered fast for the normally glacial pace of government change and it was accomplished only because of the wholehearted support of Norman Ream.[23]

As Fredette later recalled, it had also taken some fancy politicking by Hopper. "The Navy, like many people," Hopper observed, "is allergic to change."[24] Not only had Hopper and her group faced the normal objections raised to any change, they also had to sell their proposal to diverse navy constituencies. At the time, as was often true, relations between the secretary of the navy (SECNAV) and the chief of naval operations were not particularly cordial. Anything proposed by one side could expect to be vetoed by the other. Hopper got around this difficulty by getting Fredette, representing her own SECNAV side, to write the proposal for Standard COBOL jointly with a representative from the CNO side. Then Hopper "trekked" the draft to everybody ahead of time, getting suggestions and additions. With their own words in the proposal nobody could disapprove the final version when it came around again. "So it worked," concluded Hopper; "nasty female tricks." In July 1969 the Naval Material Command specified COBOL as the standard higher-level digital computer programming language for systems commanders.[25]

To get ideas accepted and implemented, Hopper would explain to her staff, just "go to the guy that has to make a decision and find out what he's aiming for, and then sell him what he wants." She became adept at identifying important decision makers and then persuading them that the new ideas she proposed would be to their advantage and would save them time and money. First, though, it was necessary to do the homework, "see what the score is." After that Hopper saw it as a question of marketing; selling ideas was just like selling anything else and relied mostly on persuasion.[26]

For the next eight years Hopper undertook development of COBOL certifiers to check navy COBOL compilers for compatibility and standards. She understood that if there was to be a standard, there had to be a way to test for conformance to it or it would be meaningless. As she put it, "if you're going to have compilers, you ought to have a way of telling whether the compiler meets the standards." Until Hopper arrived, nothing of the sort had been attempted. She brought some FORTRAN test routines with her from UNIVAC, but she did not have any for COBOL so she took the FORTRAN routines to Betty Holberton, who was then working at the National Bureau of Standards. Together they started to build a set of test routines for COBOL, developed further by the young sailors working in the Programming Languages Group.[27]

Hopper made up for her lack of equipment and facilities by persuading major manufacturers such as Honeywell, RCA, and UNIVAC to let her use their computers at no cost to the government to evaluate compilers and COBOL efficiency. She began at the cooperating manufacturers by running routines against compilers and then repeated the procedure at major users such as U.S. Steel. The degree of compliance with ANSI Standard COBOL was reported to the navy's Automatic Data Processing Equipment Selection Office (ADPESO) for use in evaluating proposals from the manufacturers. In October 1969 the first hardware vendor was instructed in the use and application of the navy COBOL audit routines. Instructions were given to eight other vendors between October 1969 and July 1970 to improve the interface with navy programs. Hopper then worked on a system for validating programs and for applying Standard COBOL navywide.

With almost no budget, staff, or equipment, how did Hopper pull off such a feat? The answer has to lie in her sharp business sense and her powers of persuasion. She could not give away navy assets so instead she traded her validation routines to the manufacturers for the use of their facilities to evaluate the programs. She even persuaded the manufacturers to print the new navy program manuals in exchange for an official navy letter of thanks and the promise of program updates. That was how the navy seal ended up on a manual that cost UNIVAC one hundred thousand dollars to produce. At the same time Hopper was making progress with her objective to get the navy using Standard COBOL as soon as possible. It was hardly coincidental, too, that Hopper had an especially close relationship with UNIVAC: she was still technically employed by them and only on loan to the navy.[28]

With her background in the commercial sector it was natural for Hopper to favor customary commercial practices even when working on navy projects. She was an early and persuasive advocate for cooperation with industry and led the way in demonstrating how effective such teamwork could be. "Marketing is not necessarily aggression," she informed an interviewer. "Avoid the confrontations . . . infiltrate."[29]

In a long memorandum she wrote soon after joining the Navy Programming Languages Group, Hopper made the case for her job.

Called "Standardization of High Level Programming Languages," the memo began by explaining that the world of computers was governed by a never-ending cyclical progression. As more and more powerful computers were built, this led inevitably to more sophisticated software that in turn called for more programmers, the combination leading to rising software costs. As well as the cost of programming new problems, updating and maintaining systems also required continuing support. "Thus," according to Hopper, "the magnitude of the software task is not only large but continually growing."[30]

The best solution to this problem, Hopper noted, was to reuse programs. However, programs could be moved from one computer to another, of different generations, and of different manufacturers, only if they were written in a high-level language. At that time that meant they should be in ALGOL (Algorithmic Language), COBOL, FORTRAN, or JOVIAL. And still, they could be transferred only if the high-level language and its corresponding compiler had been standardized. A major concern was to avoid machine-dependent or vendor-unique features in programming languages. The same rules applied to programmers. They could be easily transferred from one installation to another, without delay for retraining, only if the programming languages, the documentation, and the compilers were common and standard. Hopper thus demonstrated that cutting expenses by the mobility of both programs and programmers depended on the use of standard high-level programming languages.[31]

For the manager of a facility, however, it was not enough just to adopt a standard programming language. Managers had to be aware, Hopper warned, that they would have to exercise tight control of the installation and the use of the language. All the normal management functions were necessary for the effective use of software. In Hopper's words this entailed "direction, monitoring, provision for training and evaluation of programmers, provisions for maintenance, development, and extension of the language and its satellite packages, and establishment and enforcement of local standards." Hopper's job was to aid the manager in those tasks by providing technical assistance in the use of computer systems. Her group was working on a package of programming tools designed to facilitate Standard COBOL. The package itself was entirely written in Standard COBOL and included comprehensive, navy-standard compiler evaluation routines.[32]

Hopper blamed the problems with COBOL—in industry as in the navy—on the fact that in their haste to develop languages they had all overlooked how they would be implemented. No one thought to check that the compilers would properly implement the language so that they would give the same answers on different computers. "A language isn't very useful if you get different answers on different computers," Hopper pointed out. "At least it isn't to an organization like the navy which at any given moment has at least one of every kind of computer." Her solution was to build a set of programs that would validate a COBOL compiler. They compared the execution of the compiler against the standard, monitoring the actions of the compiler. Hopper's set of COBOL validation routines was the first such set to use software to check software. It was designed to prove, in her words, "whether or not a compiler did in fact correctly implement the standards."[33]

Having created test routines, the next task for Hopper's group was to ensure that the compilers used by navy facilities implemented Standard COBOL. The navy's audit routines (NAVAUDIT-C)—the "C" was for COBOL—were modular so that any facility could be evaluated separately. The reports produced by running the compiler evaluation routine noted any deviation from the standard, whether by addition or omission, and documented any incorrectly implemented elements. Because of the large number of programs written, and still being written at the time, by nonstandard compilers, Hopper's group had created a preprocessor: NAVPREPILE-C. When run, it provided a comprehensive set of checks—for example, of syntax errors, nonstandard statements, and problems requiring debugging. Checking for such problems before submitting the program to the compiler was expected to save time and reduce the number of recompilations.[34]

Hopper's group also created a translator (NAVTRANS-C) to convert "old" COBOL statements into ANSI Standard COBOL statements, substantially reducing reprogramming needs. The routine would also detect and flag any unique extensions and nonstandard statements. One of the most egregious yet widespread of these, as Hopper explained to *Computer Weekly,* was the "if" statement beloved by all programmers. Since this statement was found to be a major source of errors, its use was severely cut back, creating considerable irritation among programmers. To soothe them, Hopper developed a translator that changed any form of COBOL into Standard COBOL, making it so easy to use that resistance seemed pointless. The translator was so effective that it was quickly adopted by the army as well.[35]

Soon, because of Hopper's success, other agencies were forced to follow the navy's example and develop federal standards. This effort was led by the National Bureau of Standards, pressured by the success of the navy's validation routines, which the NBS itself ought to have produced. It was not until October 1969 that the NBS came out with a draft of the *Handbook for Data Standardization,* and it was not widely circulated for comment until the following year. Seriously lagging in this field, the NBS later turned to Hopper's Programming Languages Group to create FORTRAN test routines for them.[36]

In 1969, Hopper's contribution to the creation of COBOL won recognition from her peers. "The first 'Computer Sciences Man of the Year' is a woman," announced *Dataweek* that June. The Data Processing Management Association (DPMA) had introduced the award to recognize and honor "distinguished service in the field of computer sciences and information processes," and Grace Hopper was the very first recipient. The *Dataweek* article explained that Hopper was on special military leave from UNIVAC, to which she would shortly return. The magazine could not resist quoting Hopper's reaction to the award—that it really meant "Person of the Year"—and wondered if there was just a hint of feminism in her remark. "After all," Commander Hopper had told them with obvious irony, "I am technically an officer and a gentleman in the U.S. Navy by Act of Congress, and I even try to let ladies go through a door before I do."[37] Another interviewer that same week went away with the opposite impression of Hopper, noting that she was clearly not a feminist because she had not been offended by the word "man" in the award, taking it to mean "mankind."

Hopper's working life, stretching from the 1930s to the 1980s, spanned an era that saw great changes in how women were perceived and what jobs were open to them. When she achieved prominence in computing, and when she rose in the ranks of the navy, she outpaced a gender-appropriate vocabulary. To Hopper, however, such concerns were a matter for amused tolerance. She knew they had to change. Just a year before the DPMA award—although by then she had worked in computing for twenty-four years—Hopper still described herself as a mathematician. "I've been called an engineer, a programmer, a systems analyst, and everything under the sun," she told an interviewer, "but I still think my basic training is mathematics. . . . Titles for programmers and things hadn't been developed; they didn't exist." She continued, "At one point we were called systems engineers, programming engineers. It was the feeling in the early days of personnel departments, feeling around to get titles for these bugs that they had." At Eckert-Mauchly, Hopper had been listed as senior mathematician, a title she believed had been created because "it sounded impressive enough to match the salary."[38]

Such a lack of concern about formal titles apparently came natu-rally to Hopper. What was important to her was that she be allowed to do the job. Many women who came after her would find this attitude hard to accept, but it was common among her generation of women scientists.[39]

In fall 1970 there was another effort to direct the development of navy ADP with a major reorganization. The assistant secretary of the navy for financial management now became the navy's senior ADP policy official, replacing the special assistant to the secretary of the navy. All ADP administrative functions were transferred to the Program Plan-ning Office under the CNO. That gave the admiral heading the Infor-mation Systems Division (OP-91) in the Program Planning Office the coordinating authority for all automatic data processing matters for the navy. OP-91 was also charged with providing policy support on ADP matters to the ASN(FM). From then on, all correspondence on ADP matters was to be directed to OP-91 by way of the CNO. Rear Adm. Roger E. Spreen was appointed OP-91, becoming Hopper's new boss. Spreen did not have much background in ADP, but he was very well liked and respected and considered a good leader. He allowed his people considerable individual freedom to innovate, which went down well with Hopper.[40]

The Information Systems Division was composed of six branches, one of which was the Technical Support Branch (OP-916). Hopper's Programming Languages Group became the Navy Programming Lan-guages Section (NPLS) (OP-916D) of the Technical Support Branch. Her title became ADP programs officer.[41]

Among the other functions now assigned to OP-91 were three that closely affected Hopper's work with COBOL. One was to direct the effi-cient development of management information systems, most of which relied on COBOL. Another was to exercise CNO command responsi-bilities for the Naval Command Systems Support Activity (NAVCOSSACT) and the Automatic Data Processing Equipment Se-lection Office. Hopper worked very closely with both these groups, par-ticularly with NAVCOSSACT in its role as maintainer of computer programs. And finally, OP-91 was tasked to "exercise effective direc-tion, and coordination where appropriate, of information systems analy-sis, design, and programming efforts within the Navy."[42] When turnover briefings were organized for Admiral Spreen's arrival, section heads were invited to participate. Hopper was the only one requested by name to brief him on her functional area.

The mission of Hopper's immediate boss, OP-916, head of the Technical Support Branch, included the development of machine-independent languages and the administration of the navy department standards program and the navy department software program. Among other functions, OP-916 was to act (or delegate someone to act) as navy department principal representative to organizations, both public and private, dealing with programming languages, standardization, and other technical matters. This mandate included participation on federal, national, and international committees. Hopper and her crew represented the navy on many such committees.[43]

While at times it must have seemed as though progress in standardization was very slow, Hopper's efforts were noticed and appreciated. In November 1970, the ASN(FM) wrote a memorandum for the CNO recommending that Hopper be continued on active duty for another year. In the memo he described Hopper's contributions to the navy's efforts in the standardization, application, and use of high-level programming languages, and in the development of languages for data description and operating systems interfaces. This work, he noted, had resulted in "substantial savings" to the navy. He requested Hopper's continuation in the navy because "no other officers possess her particular qualifications and she is a recognized expert on computer technology and one of the country's foremost computer languages authorities." Additionally, the memo extolled the favorable publicity brought to the navy by her numerous appearances before professional groups and her international recognition and awards. While such letters were usually boilerplate, there was nothing standard about the navy keeping on a sixty-four-year-old woman and sounding as though it really needed her.[44]

Hopper was also widely respected by professionals in her own field. In 1970, she was awarded the seventh annual Harry Goode Memorial Award, presented to her by the American Federation of Information Processing Societies at the annual National Computer Conference in Houston, Texas. The award had been established in 1964 to encourage and honor outstanding contributions to the information processing field, and Howard Aiken had been the recipient that first year. Hopper was honored for her "pioneering work and leadership in the development of computer software, and for her impact and influence on the computing profession and her fellow colleagues." She was also recognized for her "pioneering work and leadership in the development of important concepts for mathematical and business compilers, and for her contributions to the development and acceptance of

English-language problem-oriented programming." Finally, the award commended Hopper for her "outstanding work and continued efforts in the education and training of men and women for careers in computer science and data processing."[45]

The biographical section of the Harry Goode award made particular mention of the time and energies Hopper had "continually given" to professional organizations and scientific associations. "Commander Grace Murray Hopper," it concluded, as a scientist, author, researcher, and educator had maintained "a level of competence, performance, and integrity which commands the highest respect, and for which the computing profession is greatly indebted."[46]

Hopper's immediate boss, head of the Technical Support Branch, made sure to forward the press release of Hopper's award to Admiral Spreen with a note reminding him that this was the award mentioned during the previous day's briefing. Her navy superiors were certainly aware, just as they had been in Philadelphia, of Hopper's national reputation and the benefits this conferred on the naval service. Aware, too, was at least one congressman, Jack Brooks of Texas, sponsor of the Brooks Bill, who wrote a note addressing her as "Dear Grace," to offer his congratulations. He was a great fan of Hopper's for all she had done to establish common standards for computing. She was to spend another sixteen years enhancing that reputation.[47]

By December 1970, as well as continuing their COBOL work, Hopper's group was also beginning to look into standardizing navy FORTRAN. Hopper received a letter that same month from the Office of Computing Activities at the University of Dayton in Ohio. The assistant director wanted to know whether they could have copies of her software to test commercial compilers from a number of vendors and, in addition, whether she had a FORTRAN test program available. Hopper's response demonstrates her antibureaucratic attitude as well as her commitment to the sharing of information in order to improve the field. She told the assistant director that her group had tested compilers for Burroughs, CDC, GE, IBM, NCR, and UNIVAC under the navy Audit Routines but that she had not yet received official permission to release the results. She was sure that if he contacted the companies directly they would share the information with him. If not, she told him to send her a tape that she would return with the latest audit routines. Then he could ask each company to run them! "As to FORTRAN," she wrote, "we have a set of test routines, not yet official, and not yet integrated into our program management system. However, if you will send us a 7-track tape, we will be glad to send them to you."

Hopper forwarded a copy of this letter to her boss with a note saying that she had "temporized on this while I dream up a policy paper or something. Have a nice weekend, Grace."[48]

Cooperation was not just a one-way street, and Hopper's openness was rewarded by a generally very good relationship with industry. In January 1971, the USM Corporation of Boston lent the NPLS what NPLS called a "not-so-mini mini-computer" for use in testing FORTRAN audit routines. The SPIRAS-65 system had 16K bytes of storage, a teletype, and punched paper tape. The software accompanying it included a basic operating system, an assembler, and FORTRAN IV, as well as various utility routines. Obviously such gestures would be repaid many times by the help gained in producing programs acceptable to the navy.[49]

By this time Hopper's group had produced a manual for training and reference: *Fundamentals of COBOL*. Over twelve thousand copies had been sold by August 1971, and it was then in its second printing. Priced at $3.25, the manual represented a substantial saving to all government installations over commercial texts that ranged from $7.50 to $15.00. Still in the planning stage was a catalog and index of sample statements illustrating the correct use of statements in Standard COBOL, as well as a collection of programming tips (called NAVTIPS-C). Finally, as soon as there was time, Hopper intended to produce instructor and student training guides.[50]

Part of Hopper's job was to persuade managers to support the use of the implementation tools she was providing. She had already had practice of this sort with her compilers, and she was very good at it. One of her standard stories was that twenty years after the Wright brothers first flew an airplane, jet planes had not yet been thought of. It was then twenty-five years since the Mark I at Harvard, and she had no idea what the "jet" of computers would be. But she was sure that there would be one. The trick was to plan for change, to assume that change would come, and in unexpected forms. The wise manager would be prepared for successive generations of computers evolving through time. It was not likely that computers of future generations would accept the same machine instructions, but they could be expected to accept high-level languages, although perhaps after automatic translation.

Hopper's solution was not to decree that henceforth all computers must be alike. This would prevent the development of a future "jet" computer. What she advocated instead was mandating the use of standard high-level languages. It cost much less to convert standard languages into new versions as they came out than it cost to convert assembly language into standard high-level language. Although the use of COBOL both in everyday work and during conversion would bring substantial savings eventually, Hopper saw that there were still two "stumbling blocks" in the way. The first was the problem of converting the huge mass of data used by the navy, and the second was the problem of converting programmers to the use of Standard COBOL. This was the challenge to managers and would take time and care to overcome. "Management must decide and enforce that new programs be written in COBOL," Hopper stated bluntly. "Programs subject to change or major maintenance must be rewritten in COBOL, and a plan must be made, implemented, and monitored for re-writing the remaining programs in COBOL."[51] How worthwhile would this effort be? Hopper had the answer to that, too. The real savings, she said, would come from "savings of scarce programmer time, the mobility of programs and programmers, and the freedom to progress readily to the computers of the future." For a sales pitch, that proved pretty persuasive.[52]

Arriving at the Pentagon at 7:00 AM, Hopper would hurry to her office next to the computer room, staying until her day finished sometime between 4:30 and 6:00 PM. It was so dark in the sub-subbasement where her group was located, with no windows, that when the electricity blew, which it did periodically, it was impossible to see. One day Hopper appeared for work decked out in a miner's hat and light. She loved that sort of practical joke.[53]

Hopper had always been impatient with bureaucracy, an approach made clear by the clock in her office that ran counterclockwise and the Jolly Roger that flew over her desk. The rest of the equipment her crew had "liberated" from nearby offices when assigned to stand watch at night. As always with Hopper, she set the tone for a congenial workplace where humor and jokes were the norm. They all referred to their office deep in the bowels of the Pentagon, for example, as "the Penal Colony."[54] This sort of banter, as at the Harvard Computation Lab, helped relieve an otherwise intense workplace. A tremendous amount of dedication was demanded of the group because computer time was scarce and provided to them only on a time-available basis. This required the enlisted technical specialists to be immediately available twenty-four hours a day, including weekends, to take advantage of any unpredictable lull or slack in computer schedules at the several facilities providing service. The NPLS used an average of twenty hours a week of computer time, which they had to divide among three computer facilities, two in the Pentagon and one in the nearby Bureau of Naval Personnel.

They also traveled extensively in support of the job—often, too, at short notice. To ease the burden as much as she could, Hopper would always volunteer to work on Christmas Eve and Christmas Day so that her colleagues could be home with their families.[55]

In spite of the difficult demands on her staff, Hopper had the knack of arousing a deep personal loyalty in them. George N. Baird, a data processor first class (DP1), one of the original enlisted technicians in the "six-month task group" organized in August 1967, had requested an extension of duty in his present billet in October 1970. He was making the request, he wrote, so that he could continue his work in the navy's "important effort" to standardize and promote the use of high-level computer programming languages. "My current assignment in this activity has given me a high feeling of accomplishment and personal satisfaction," he continued. "Further, I feel that the training and creative experience acquired in performing my duty uniquely qualify me to make many additional essential contributions to the objectives of my unit."[56]

Apparently Baird was granted an extension because he was still with the group almost five years later when he was due to be released from active duty. Hopper and her boss were hoping to have Baird converted to civil service status so he could continue with the NPLS as a civilian, and in that they were successful. He did stay on for a while before transferring to the National Bureau of Standards.[57]

Hopper trained her young crew so well that after they finished their navy tours they got good jobs in civilian data processing. Arnold Johnson was another of the original navy crew. He went right from being an enlisted man in the navy to a GS-12 at the NBS. Dick Fredette and Norma Gealt also stayed with Hopper from the time she returned to active duty until her retirement. She was very good to work for. She set high goals for her crew and then let them run and accomplish them any way they wanted. Hopper often told people she would come back to haunt anyone who claimed as justification for a particular procedure that it had always been done that way. She was quick to eliminate obsolete and redundant practices and those adding no value to the product. To encourage innovation and risk taking, she always advised: "Go ahead and do it, you can always apologize later." Another of her most-often repeated and well-known adages was a paraphrase of Benjamin Franklin: "A ship in port is safe, but that's not what ships are for. DARE and DO."[58]

While it is true that as a naval officer Hopper was shorebound, whenever she could she spent her rare hours of relaxation out on the water.

When stationed at the Pentagon, she even tried to get a license as a small boat coxswain. She badly wanted a navy license to pilot small boats but apparently she never succeeded in getting one, perhaps because that would be treading on enlisted territory. Still, whenever she had time she went to Annapolis and took out a whaleboat or some other small craft.[59]

Hopper's early work with CODASYL, the committee producing the first version of COBOL in 1960, and her work on the American National Standards Institute's committee to standardize the many versions of COBOL that quickly followed, had given her a unique perspective on how to eliminate language discrepancies.[60] She was still faced with the thorny issue of debugging, however, which arose persistently in the transition to Standard COBOL. Ever the realist, Hopper acknowledged that it was impossible to debug any program completely. "You can always find a bug five years later," she cheerfully affirmed. Nor did she underestimate the difficulty of her assignment, figuring that conversion to Standard COBOL would take at least three to five years.[61]

A major difficulty facing all those responsible for computing was the shortage of programmers. In the late 1960s, although it was already changing into a predominantly man's field, computing still offered opportunities for women, particularly as it was a young industry with few established traditions and initially less gender prejudice than other businesses. This was true also in the navy, where of the nine women captains, three had come from the electronic data processing field. At the end of the decade about one-third of all programmers in America were women, and still there was a shortage. Training was often inadequate, with little in the way of enforceable standards in commercial programming schools. Of constant concern to Hopper during these years was to see to the training of personnel so that they could implement her standardized programs.[62]

Money, too, was always a factor in determining change. Hopper was expected to produce portable programs because the navy did not want to pay for conversion. Yet implementing standardization had costs too. Nevertheless, the navy was the first organization—military or civilian—to mandate a standard computer language, as far as Hopper was aware. She and her group certainly felt like trailblazers. As they worked on the original test routines, other standard routines had seemed to evolve naturally, such as the flowcharter known as FLOBOL (NAVFLOCHART-C). FLOBOL was designed to automatically generate program flowcharts from COBOL source input programs, which relieved the programmer of the tedious job of writing the flowcharts. FLOBOL was available to all government agencies on request and had been selected for use by the army as well. The system was maintained by the NPLS.[63]

The importance of the cost-saving work of NPLS was obvious in the GSA notice announcing FLOBOL. A recent survey had revealed to the GSA that many installations were renting various different commercial software programs for flowcharting at considerable cost to the government. The announcement drew attention to the availability of the navy's FLOBOL software program, which had been implemented in many installations and could probably be used to reduce expenses in many more. Agencies using commercial flowcharting programs were directed to contact the NPLS, where FLOBOL was available free of charge.[64]

But the GSA in the 1970s seemed to have a particular problem grasping the realities of ADP development. A month after the above announcement was issued, the assistant commissioner for automated data management services at the GSA questioned the utility and the cost effectiveness of FLOBOL. He expressed his reservations in a letter to Admiral Spreen, one of the major points of which seemed to be that the GSA already had its own flowcharting package, produced a few years earlier, which it had made available to other government agencies. The assistant commissioner believed that if sufficient low-cost commercial flowcharting packages were also available, it was unnecessary to invest in FLOBOL in the future.[65]

Admiral Spreen asked Hopper to draft a reply for his signature, which she did with gusto. The GSA letter, she informed Admiral Spreen, "provides an excellent opportunity to once more present the details of the justification for the use of standard high level languages and the navy efforts in this enterprise."[66] Hopper's explanation was thorough and masterly. It also demonstrated the very close links between her early work at UNIVAC and all her later work for the navy—a relationship that proved to be of benefit to both parties. FLOBOL had a long history, according to Hopper, and she was going to spell it out. The first flowcharter, by her account, was designed, developed, and written in FLOW-MATIC—the direct ancestor of COBOL—for use on the UNIVAC I in 1956. In 1960, when the first COBOL compiler became operational on the UNIVAC II, the flowcharter was lifted into the COBOL in that unit. In 1966, the flowcharter was rewritten in UNIVAC III COBOL by a programmer at the Charleston Naval Shipyard and distributed to all of the shipyards that used UNIVAC IIIs. By that time, according to

Hopper, the cost of design and development had been completely recouped by both UNIVAC and the navy. Later, FLOBOL was transferred to the Navy Programming Languages Section. NPLS prepared a translator from old, nonstandard COBOL to American National Standard COBOL in order to translate and salvage existing FLOBOL programs.

Having laid the groundwork for the emergence of FLOBOL, Hopper then moved on to defend its cost effectiveness. She noted that FLOBOL maintenance and improvement costs as new COBOL modules were developed were minimal, totaling less than five thousand dollars a year, or twenty dollars a year for each of the more than 250 installations that used the flowcharter. The distribution costs were also low. User installations forwarded a tape to NPLS. The COBOL package was copied on the user tape and returned. Since eight tapes could be copied simultaneously on the IBM 7090, the copying costs were one eighth of $150, or $18.75 per copy. Return mailing of the tapes cost less than two dollars per tape. In sum, development, maintenance, and distribution costs were less than twenty-five dollars per year in each navy installation where FLOBOL was used.[67]

Finally, Hopper explained some of the excellent qualities of FLOBOL. It operated on all computers having a Standard COBOL compiler, including some for which there was no commercial flowcharter available, and it would run with no additional development costs on all future computers implementing the Standard COBOL. This was an important consideration because at that time there was already movement into the third generation of computers. Her final paragraph explains the philosophy that drove her efforts during the whole of her second active duty tour:

> The savings accruing to the government by the production of generally useful routines in standard high-level languages is indeed substantial. The Navy will continue to vigorously pursue such clear cost-reduction programs. The results will be made available to all government installations in the expectation that the Navy will ultimately receive reciprocal benefits.

Hopper ended on a masterly note: "Your support in issuing Special Notice No. 5 regarding the availability of FLOBOL is appreciated."[68] She calmly pretended not to appreciate that the GSA letter had intended to signal deep reservations about FLOBOL, not support. Hopper's covering brief for Admiral Spreen also revealed much about the way she operated and why she aroused such admiration. She explained that all of the prices quoted in her letter had been based on maximums; for example, commercial prices for use of IBM 7090 time ranged from three hundred dollars to six hundred dollars an hour, and she had used the higher figure to price the fifteen minutes needed to copy eight tapes. She had also not included oven foil in the price of shipping. Since some parcel post traveled by air, the use of foil was necessary because of the increased power of radar and because of "detection devices for bombs and explosives." At present, Hopper concluded, "no Navy stock rooms stock the foil so I supply it personally." No reply from the GSA was in the files.[69]

The uses of digital computing were still so little understood outside a relatively small circle of practitioners that in spring 1971 the Department of Defense Computer Institute (DoDCI) ran a series of one-week orientation seminars for flag and general officers and civilians with a grade of GS-16 and above. Courses were designed "to acquaint military officers and civilian executives of all DoD components with the fundamentals of digital computers, their capabilities, limitations, applications, and techniques."[70]

As part of this educational effort, during the next several years Hopper and her staff traveled the nation making presentations of their work. In June 1971, for example, Hopper, Fredette, and Baird presented their audit routines, translator, and program checking and debug routine to the International Monetary Fund. One or other of them also represented the navy on every important committee working on programming languages. Among many other committees she sat on, Hopper was appointed by Admiral Spreen to represent the navy on the group with the longest name: the ADP Policy Committee Ad Hoc Group on Implementation Policy for the DoD COBOL Validation Routines. She also continued on the Executive Council Committee of CODASYL—a position for which she had been specifically requested by the chair, her old friend Jack Jones. In addition, she was the ACM representative to the National Science Foundation and served on the DPMA's scholarship committee.

Dick Fredette sat on both the American National COBOL Standard Maintenance Committee and the ANSI COBOL Audit Routines Committee. DP1 George Baird also represented the NPLS at the COBOL Maintenance Committee meetings, the Federal Information Processing Standard–COBOL committee, the DoD Technical Interpretation Panel COBOL, and the CODASYL PLC committee. David R. Eaton, another enlisted technical specialist, also a data processor first class, sat on the American National Standard–FORTRAN committee, reporting back to the NPLS on all developments. After a meeting in New York in June, for example, Eaton noted that progress continued to be good in the development of the new FORTRAN standard. The committee did not want to invalidate existing FORTRAN programs when rewriting the standard, and its members were mostly making changes in arrangement. When the new ANSI Standard FORTRAN was published in 1972, NPLS had a FORTRAN validation routine tested and ready for simultaneous release.[71]

During all those years in Washington Hopper regularly taught one night a week. It had been so important to her to maintain this contact with young people that she made continued teaching a condition of her move to Washington, where from 1971 onward she held a class in management science at George Washington University. She devoted another night to her colleagues in the Department of Defense computer industry. In addition, at least once a week, and often more, she had an out-of-town speaking engagement. As she became better known, she was invited to give talks on navy computing to local computer clubs, academic programs, symposia, and conferences. In 1972 she mentioned having given talks at 175 colleges and schools. When she traveled she sent postcards from all over the country, and later the world, to her grandnephews and -nieces, always signing off: "Hastily, Grace."[72]

When Hopper was recalled to active duty, it was before resistance to the Vietnam War had reached its peak. In the course of the next few years, however, as opposition heated up, there was concern about whether she should travel in uniform. This bothered her deeply, as she loved the navy and was very proud of her service, but devotion did not blind her to a keen sense of the ridiculous. She loved to tell audiences how she was frequently mistaken for a crossing guard or an elevator operator. When she told one man who asked her what she was that she was a naval officer, he replied that she must be the oldest they had! At airports, to her great amusement, she was often taken for a stewardess.[73] Typical of her increasingly rigorous schedule was that for 30 September 1970. In the morning Hopper spoke at the annual meeting of the Association of American Railroads, Systems Division, in Atlanta, Georgia. Late that same day she addressed a dinner meeting of the Cleveland, Ohio, chapter of the Data Processing Managers Association. These meetings and other activities of the NPLS were listed in weekly reports submitted to the Technical Support Branch. Many of Hopper's presentations on the list were followed with the notation "nctg," which signified that they were made at no cost to the government. Generally, whatever organization invited her to talk covered expenses. In addition, she was usually paid an honorarium of several hundred dollars. She never kept any of the money, sending it all to the Navy Relief Society.[74]

It was for these presentations that Hopper devised a way to demonstrate visually the significance of increasing the speed of computer operations. The Mark I in 1944 required 333 milliseconds to do an addition. By 1951, UNIVAC I, representing the first generation of commercial computers, required 282 microseconds for the same operation—a thousand-fold increase in speed. In 1958 a second generation of computers began using a new discovery—the transistor—that made possible faster, cheaper, and more dependable machines. In 1964, the CDC 6600 computer reduced the addition time to 300 nanoseconds, another 1,000 percent increase in speed.

The third generation of computer hardware was introduced in 1966. These were computers built around silicon chips, but they still depended on the compilers pioneered by Hopper and her staff at UNIVAC. Hopper's first thought to explain this progress in speed was to clarify the concept of a nanosecond. She had the works department cut up some copper wire in 11.78-inch lengths, which was the distance light or electricity traveled in a billionth of a second—a nanosecond. Armed with these nanoseconds and comparing them to a 984-foot long coil of wire representing a microsecond, she could convince any audience of the savings generated by improved processing speeds. Eventually, she gave out so many nanoseconds that the cost of the copper wire became prohibitive. Instead, she had her staff stripping the plastic coating off electrical wires, which they then cut into nanosecond lengths. Later, with the development of computers operating in picoseconds, Hopper saved cafeteria pepper packets, each grain of which represented a picosecond. Few who saw this demonstration could ever forget it.[75]

Nevertheless, Hopper found it a great struggle to get her audiences to embrace change, in spite of her enthusiasm and her innovative teaching techniques. "The young people are honest," she recalled. "They have just learned something. They have just gained command of it and I come along and tell them they are going to learn something different. They fight it right from the word go. They have formed a habit of mind," she continued, "and a way and it's comfortable and they ain't about to change.... Some young people," she concluded in a moment of uncharacteristic pessimism, "are worse than some of the people who survived the war years." Increasingly, she directed her efforts to reach these young people; more and more of her talks were at student chapters of the ACM or other undergraduate computer organizations.[76]

As well as traveling themselves, members of the Navy Programming Languages Section also received frequent visits from those wishing to share in the results of their work. A representative from the National Bureau of Standards visited early in 1971 to discuss the work being done by the Navy Department on the DoD COBOL audit routines. He was interested in establishing better communication links between his group and NPLS. That summer, two representatives from the Army Computer Systems Support and Evaluation Command met with Hopper, Fredette, and Baird in their Pentagon office. The army had decided to tell all its COBOL installations to use FLOBOL. NPLS agreed to continue to distribute tapes, on request, to the army installations and to receive "bug" reports.[77]

Sometimes, too, the NPLS was the recipient of generosity. In a memorandum to the Chief, U.S. Army Strategy and Tactics Analysis Group, drafted by Dick Fredette, Admiral Spreen expressed gratitude for a FORTRAN translator the army had just given the navy. The translator would be very helpful to many navy installations needing to update older FORTRAN programs to a newer version, especially in preparation for future systems conversions. "We in the navy," wrote Admiral Spreen, "heartily endorse an increased level of sharing and exchange of ideas and services among the military and other government activities. Permitting us to expand the use of your translator is an excellent example of stretching the taxpayer's dollar just a bit further." On the bottom of the draft for Admiral Spreen's signature Fredette explained the motive for the letter: "The translator will be useful to the navy—and we thought it might help to encourage additional exchanges of this type by giving this one proper recognition."[78]

While there were still those who resisted standardization, many in the navy appreciated Hopper's work. In June, the Bureau of Medicine and Surgery (BuMed) announced "with considerable satisfaction" that it had just accepted the ANSI COBOL compiler developed by NPLS for the UNIVAC 418 computer. The BuMed chief, addressing himself to the CNO, wrote that his bureau wished "to express its appreciation for the excellent assistance rendered by Commander Grace Hopper (OP-916D), and her staff during the planning and evaluation stages of the UNIVAC 418 COBOL compiler. The Navy COBOL audit routines," he continued, "and assistance provided by Commander Hopper in their use contributed immensely to the success of the project."[79]

In the course of this work Hopper had, as always, negotiated an agreement that would ensure the further dissemination of her software. The Bureau of Medicine and Surgery was providing Hopper with all the documentation for the UNIVAC compiler for subsequent distribution throughout the federal government. This would increase the effectiveness of current installations and prolong the useful life of government-owned UNIVAC 418 computers. The Naval Medical Data Services Center also agreed to continue to provide test time as required for compiler maintenance and to provide such ADP services as systems tape duplication for distribution to other installations. Hopper had set in motion a practice that, like a pebble thrown into a pond, sent its waves out to the far reaches of the government. "The importance of the availability of an ANSI standard and the Navy audit routines cannot be overemphasized," concluded the BuMed chief.[80]

Also in June, the National Association for State Information Systems, representing the fifty state governments, requested that NPLS share with it the results of NPLS's COBOL compiler validations. ADPESO had obtained written approval to do this from IBM, RCA, CDC, and others. Hopper urged Admiral Spreen to agree because "it is important to enlist as much outside support as possible in the standards area, resulting in greater pressure on the vendors to respond to those standards the Navy seeks." Hopper knew her work had ramifications beyond the navy department, large as it was, because the navy was a major customer for computer manufacturers. In addition, leading industrial corporations frequently followed the navy's example in their own purchases. Hopper repeatedly showed herself to be very astute when it came to pressuring her former colleagues in commercial computing.[81]

In an August 1971 meeting all the hard work of the NPLS to date was vindicated. The office of the secretary of defense announced the status of its negotiations with the General Services Administration, Office of Management and Budget, and National Bureau of Standards regarding the general use of the DoD COBOL validation routines in the federal automatic data processing community. Each of the offices agreed that the DoD validation routines, which had been developed and were being maintained by the navy, should be used by all federal agencies to verify COBOL compilers. This meant, of course, that no vendor who was not in compliance could sell to DoD. The air force had yielded to the NPLS the responsibility for developing, promulgating, and maintaining the COBOL audit routines to be used by all DoD components. To accomplish this goal Hopper and her group worked closely with the air force in the Pentagon and with the office of the assistant secretary of defense (comptroller) in overall charge of DoD computing.[82]

Part of the secret of Hopper's success was that she had created a whole set of validation routines in-house with her own small but very talented group of enlisted specialists, supervised by Dick Fredette. The air force had gone to a vendor for a set of COBOL routines that had some good features but was not as complete as that created by the NPLS. By adding in the best features of the air force routines, Hopper's group had created a winning product. There must have been quite a party at the NPLS when the news arrived.[83]

Hopper's continuation on active duty for another year was due to be reviewed by the January 1972 Continuation Board. Two months earlier, Admiral Spreen had addressed a memorandum to the ASN(FM), in which he called her continuation "essential, especially during the next year when she will be implementing the COBOL Compiler Validation System for all the Services as requested by OSD [office of the secretary of defense]."[84] Hopper's contributions to the navy since returning to active duty had been substantial, the admiral continued, particularly in money saved, both current and future, by the implementation of her innovative standardization plans. The heart of his letter conveys Hopper's achievement:

> The entire data processing industry is in debt to her and to the Navy for effectively bringing about the standardization of COBOL through the implementation of the COBOL Compiler Validation System in Navy procurements. This action led the majority of vendors to produce compatible COBOL compilers for the first time, advancing the industry and the Navy toward the uninhibited exchange of computer programs and program libraries. In addition to continuing her work in standardizing COBOL, Commander Hopper is planning similar efforts in the next year for FORTRAN, data management systems and other related areas.

Spreen ended his recommendation by recognizing Hopper's many appearances before professional and academic audiences, which "has also brought great credit and attention to the Navy's accomplishments in data processing. Commander Hopper's unmatched talents," he concluded, "long and rich experience, her forward thinking, high intelligence and world-wide reputation makes her totally unique and irreplaceable to the Navy."[85] Hopper got the continuation.

Still, in spite of very general appreciation of her efforts, the greatest hurdle Hopper had to overcome in order to accomplish her mission in the navy was the same hurdle she had met in business: overcoming resistance to change. Her schedule of speeches intensified as she criss-crossed the country spreading the message of standardization of programming languages. On 14 February 1972 she spoke in San Diego, California, and the next day in Phoenix, Arizona. On 16 February she addressed the Association of Computer Manufacturers at Fort Huachuca, Arizona, and she ended the four-day trip talking to the DPMA in Tucson on the seventeenth. She was at it again the following week, lecturing in Oklahoma City on the twenty-first; in Houston, Texas, on the twenty-second; in Arlington, Texas, on the twenty-third; in Melbourne, Florida, on the twenty-fourth; and in Montgomery, Alabama, on the twenty-fifth. In some ways, Hopper felt, more people listened to her outside the navy.[86]

Interviewed in 1972, Hopper described something of the mentality she was up against in her own service. For the past three years there had been a group of people in the navy department who advocated putting an online minicomputer on board ships for administrative purposes. Another group of people opposed this idea, and for three years they had been sending memos back and forth debating the feasibility, the cost, and the use of the project. Hopper finally tired of the game and asked the admiral to add up the cost in time and money spent on the correspondence. She told him it would be much cheaper just to buy a computer and put it on board ship and find out whether it was worth it. The admiral agreed that this was a good idea and gave the requisite order that it be done. There were some advantages to military service after all.[87]

The disadvantages of trying to push change through a large bureaucracy were obvious too. All proposals for change were circulated around the navy to affected offices, which then had a chance to respond. It was not at all unusual for the responses to be contradictory. The commander-in-chief, Atlantic Fleet, objected to a proposed instruction regarding navy department computer program documentation standards because he thought standards should be made mandatory. The reply from OP-916 was that the new wording in fact made the standards "more mandatory" than they had been before, because the waiver procedures, and therefore the "escape clause," had been removed. The next response, from the chief of the Bureau of Personnel proposed that the new standards be made "less mandatory" and be promulgated "as a guide." OP-916 countered that "the proposed standards allow selection of the proper type and extent of documentation based on requirements and local command prerogatives." The issue of local command prerogatives, often referred to in the navy at that time as the "Right of Command," was to play a major role in the ongoing debate about how far standardization could or should be taken in the navy. The "Right of Command" would prove an impediment to standardization perhaps as significant as the more pedestrian resistance to change.[88]

Another significant comment on the proposed standards came from the chief of naval material, who wrote to support the practice of keeping separate standards for "tactical/weapons/combat digital computers." The response from the head of OP-916 was prophetic. He wrote that the new standards had achieved a high degree of credibility and acceptance, and "until the two worlds (tactical and MIS) and their standards come closer together through more intensive negotiation, which will take time," he did not recommend inclusion of tactical standards under OP-916 instructions. He also mentioned political implications to the merger—namely, that it would link tactical with management systems so that an attack on either one would tend to drag in the other, which to some extent is what happened as a result of a 1975 GAO report.[89]

By April 1972 Hopper's Programming Languages Standards Section was not much larger than her original staff had been. In addition to Dick Fredette (OP-916D1) and Norma Gealt, of course, she had five enlisted data processors working for her, including George Baird, who was still there, and David Eaton from the original team. Yet in less than five years after her return to the navy, she and her little group had already made their mark. That June, the Salt Lake City Chapter of the DPMA decided that in order to express their appreciation for the work done and to give encouragement to the navy programmers who had created the COBOL validation routines, they would sponsor one of them as a member of DPMA for a year. David Eaton was chosen for the honor.[90]

That same month the chief of naval operations, Adm. Elmo Zumwalt, sent a memorandum to the secretary of the navy recommending Cdr. Grace Murray Hopper, USNR (ret.) [U.S. Naval Reserve, retired] for appointment to captain. If the secretary approved the recommendation, it then had to wend its way via the secretary of defense to the president.[91]

Neither the widespread recognition of her work nor the accompanying push for her promotion meant time off for Hopper. Information Systems Division branch heads had to submit a monthly control listing of specific objectives for the month. In May 1972, under the heading "Milestone Action Due This Month," Hopper had written "Promulgate COBOL routines to vendors and conduct official validation of compilers. Develop library of validation and make initial distribution to ADPESO and Navy installations as required; commence maintenance phase, updates to routines, conducting new validations and distributing results as required." From the 18th of that month to 7 June Hopper was in Australia. She had been invited to give the keynote address at the Fifth Australian Computer Conference and also to lecture to the Brisbane Computer Society, the New South Wales Computer Society, the Canberra College of Advanced Education, the Adelaide Computer Society, and, on the way home, the Honolulu Chapter of the ACM. All of this was "at no cost to the government." From then on Hopper traveled overseas with increasing frequency, usually at the invitation of a foreign computing organization.[92]

Indeed, Hopper's work was spreading well beyond the DoD and even the U.S. government. On her return from Australia she received a letter from the Air Attaché to the Australian Embassy in Washington to whom she had evidently sent a copy of her Australian television broadcast. "I found it most amusing," wrote Wing Commander David Ingall; "it is obvious that your Australian audience appreciated your sense of humour." Moving on to the business of his letter, he reminded Hopper that while she was in Canberra "our Department of Defence made arrangements with you to obtain the latest version of the U.S. Navy COBOL and FORTRAN Evaluation Aids. . . . This letter," he continued, "conveys 2400 feet, $\frac{1}{2}$ inch magnetic tapes, one of which is the property of the US Navy. The second tape which belongs to our Defence Department is in exchange for your next version of the COBOL and FORTRAN routines as they become available. . . . The second half of the letter from our Defence Department requesting these routines," wrote the Wing Commander in closing, "discussed your visit to Australia; I won't embarrass you by repeating the flattery."[93]

On 1 August 1972 the Navy Programming Languages Section "attained the age of five years (1 August 1967–1 August 1972)," according to Hopper's weekly report to her boss, "alive and kicking, with a feeling of accomplishment, plenty of ideas and lots of work for the future."[94] The following year, on 2 August 1973, six years and one day after returning to active duty, Hopper was promoted to the rank of captain. Because she was overage for a regular promotion, it had taken a special act of Congress to put the promotion through. It was also the first time an officer of the naval reserve was promoted to captain while on the retired list. Hopper thought her promotion was mostly the result of her high public profile. In view of her heavy load of public speaking engagements she believed her bosses wanted her to have "enough ribbons to look impressive."[95]

The following year, navy computing was rocked by a devastating attack. In a scathing report drafted in 1974 and submitted to Congress in April 1975, the GAO charged that although the navy had poured over $2.8 billion into its data processing program since 1959, it had failed in its stated objective to develop standardized data systems in a timely and cost-effective manner. The focus of the GAO attack was on automated management information systems afloat and ashore, including those involved in research and development. These were precisely the systems with which Hopper dealt. By association, moreover, the report cast a shadow on the entire range of navy automation activities, all tactical systems, and all hardware and software. In its most damaging statement, the GAO blamed the navy's traditional "Right of Command" management philosophy for the failures. Centralized policy direction with decentralized execution allowed commanders to modify hardware and software regardless of navy policy, preventing the creation of a modern, standardized, navywide data processing system. "Command influence must not continue to deter standard systems," warned the report.[96]

Was this indictment justified? Could the very culture of independent command that had given the navy the lead in computing during World War II—and that had nurtured the first postwar generation of leaders in the computing field—have caused "inefficient and duplicative" computing thirty years later?[97] Or, as some in the navy angrily countered, was it both impossible and undesirable to create the kind of centralized control and uniform systems expected by the GAO?

Scrutiny of ADP budgets gave plenty of ammunition for attacks on computing programs throughout the federal government. The GAO is a service agency, often at odds with any administration, with broad powers to run investigations at the behest of any member of Congress. Even the NBS itself, among other government agencies, frequently faced GAO charges of poorly administered computer-acquisition programs. None of these criticisms was unusual. The entire Department of Defense's automatic data processing effort had been sharply criticized by a 1970 blue ribbon defense panel. The panel recognized that during the 1950s DoD had taken a lead in computing and had initiated and sponsored many early advances in the field but maintained that it had seriously lagged over the past ten years. The accusations were very similar to those the GSA leveled at the navy four years later—namely, that the DoD was distinguished by a "decentralized and fragmented" system characterized by the "proliferation of ADP systems and programs which are largely incompatible. . . ."[98]

The GAO report was thus part of a pattern of Congressional criticism of general inefficiencies in military and other governmental ADP dating back to the Brooks Bill. What made the 1974 attack on the navy different was the sweeping indictment of its very structure—its tolerance for independent command—presumably derived from the autonomy of ships at sea. The GAO portrayed the navy as more recalcitrant than the other services and less amenable to control.

In the summer of 1974 a draft of the report was circulated for comment to all concerned navy activities, eliciting a flood of indignant replies. By that time most management information systems ashore, including those for supply, security, communications, finance, and personnel, were automated or in the process of being automated. Many respondents privately admitted problems of lack of centralized planning and standardization in these administrative systems and agreed with the need for reform. They also pointed out that this characterized the development of other large-scale data systems—not only in the navy—and represented what seemed to be a general, if inadequate, state of practice in the field.[99]

Other respondents to the draft report pointed to the large number and variety of tasks they faced—on the surface of the sea, below it, and in the air. These, they argued, were unlike ADP tasks faced by any other organization. The navy increasingly relied on general-purpose digital computers as the basic data processing element for use in afloat and airborne tactical systems as well as for management information systems. General-purpose computers were used in command and control, sensor control and target detection and processing, weapons control, and navigation. The result of the spread of automation to tactical systems, as with the automation of administrative systems, had been the proliferation of different kinds and generations of computer hardware and associated software with minimal standardization.[100]

Unlike the indisputable case against the broad-based management information systems, however, the navy had a point when it defended some forms of diversity in ADP. Many one-of-a-kind systems had been created locally to handle specific needs. Such "uniques," as they were called, fulfilled vital functions unsuited to standardized systems and would not have emerged unless initiated by autonomous local commanders. The systems created for HFDF were of this kind. Respondents to the draft report also stressed the importance of creating systems sensitive to rapidly changing operational realities and independent of an inflexible, servicewide structure.[101]

The debate raged back and forth over what constituted justifiable uniqueness. The GAO report undoubtedly made some points that were hard to swallow. It noted, for example, that between 1966 and 1971 seven navy shipyards developed and used approximately 1,500 local "unique" programs as compared to about 280 standard programs. That certainly indicates the scope of the problem as characterized in the GAO report. These were not just a few specialized programs the navy was defending. In countering this accusation, however, the assistant secretary of the navy for financial management, responsible for the navy's ADP program, claimed that standard programs accounted for 80 percent of the data processing work performed on the navy's computers for supply activities at shipyards.[102]

The draft report cited many other egregious examples of lack of standard ADP practice in MIS. Since these examples were based on extensive quotation from the navy's own internal reviews, they were hard to refute. In general, therefore, the navy was forced to acknowledge the criticisms. At a July meeting convened to discuss the draft report Rear Adm. Frank S. Haak, who had just succeeded Admiral Spreen as head of OP-91, pointed out that although there were basically adequate instructions in the navy governing the management of ADP, they were not being complied with either internally, within OP-91, or externally within the whole navy. Gloomily admitting that "we were caught with our hands in the cookie jar," Admiral Haak noted that although the GAO report reflected only generalized findings, mostly regarding supply and logistics, the inevitable heat from Congress might very well impact funding for tactical computer systems as well.[103]

The possibility of an expansion of a specialized GAO criticism into a generalized attack on navy efficiency seemed all too likely. Most damaging of all, much of the report had been leaked to the press. Facing post-Vietnam appropriations fights, the navy was fearful of any negative publicity. "If our every internal effort at self assessment is liable to be picked up by the GAO and published in the newspaper," complained the head of the Policy Coordination Branch of the Information Systems Division, "there is little hope of aggressive internal criticism."[104]

In an effort at damage control, the assistant secretary of the navy detailed the navy's objections to the report. Among other things he noted that while there was no question that improvements could be made in navy ADP, the report spanned the fifteen years (1959–74) when computer systems applications were first established within both government and industry. During those pioneering days the navy had made significant strides in developing and operating effective automated information systems for a "wide range of command, management, operational and support functions ashore and afloat." It was hardly surprising, he wrote, that some errors might have been made at a time of rapid changes in technology, terminology, policy, and procedures, particularly given the pressure of urgent operational demands for increased ADP support generated by the war in Vietnam. On the whole, the assistant secretary of the navy noted with satisfaction, the navy's learning curve had kept pace with changes in the field.[105]

In defense of the navy's management philosophy characterized as the "Right of Command," the ASN waxed eloquent. He pointed out that the principle had been "continuously tested and repeatedly confirmed as an effective guideline for management of the navy's large-scale, complex and diverse operations." In 1966 the principle was reaffirmed not only as sound management policy, but specifically as valid within the context of the DoD computer programming system. Moreover, the principle promoted "the exercise of operational responsibilities at the lowest possible command echelon." The ADP program, he insisted, must accommodate the navy's traditional and still valid management philosophy.[106]

The CNO supported this argument in his written comments on the draft report. "In the Navy," he affirmed, "ADP systems are utilized to support the manager in accomplishing his missions and tasks. In many cases, these missions are, in fact, unique and must be supported by unique applications." An example of a computer processing workload almost exclusively dedicated to a unique assignment was the Naval Torpedo Testing Station in Keyport, Washington, the only navy activity with a primary mission to test live torpedoes. Among other things, the so-called uniques were also used to run numbers for the Polaris Missile Office Pacific and to run programs for Trident submarines and the Strategic Systems Project Office.[107]

As the main navy bastion of standardization, the NPLS often became involved in the issue of uniques as exceptions to the rule. Not infrequently, they pleaded the case for uniques. In February 1971, Dick Fredette had written a memo for Admiral Spreen to send to the ASN(FM) on behalf of a request from the Naval Weapons Lab at Dahlgren. Dahlgren wanted to execute a contract with a civilian company, Software Technology, Inc., to convert the automated engineering design compiler for their newly acquired CDC 6700 computer. The compiler would be used to expedite the generation of systems software for specialized computer systems such as fire control and ballistic missiles developed by Dahlgren. Other technical research installations such as the Naval Ship Research and Development Center, Carderock, Maryland, intended to make extensive use of the product generated by the contract.[108]

According to Fredette's brief, Software Technology, Inc. was the only organization with the experience to perform the conversion, and the GSA verified that government resources were not available to perform those services. Dahlgren, moreover, had the funds for the job. The final contract, for one hundred thousand dollars, specified that the federal government would be granted unrestricted use of the final product and that the vendor would provide a reasonable period of maintenance after delivery. Here was a case where even the GSA had to agree that because of the unique nature of the technical programs, a standard compiler would not work.[109]

Hopper, of course, faced decisions about uniques on a daily basis. Part of the success of her operation resulted from the excellent relations she and her crew maintained with every facility they visited. Each time they accomplished a conversion to Standard COBOL or helped to install a new standard program, they provided full support services. NPLS was always available for consultation, and a great deal of its time was spent in follow-up support. When, in response to the GAO attack, the navy outlined its ADP accomplishments, Hopper's contributions were notable among them.

Respondents to the GAO report pointed out that between 1960 and 1975 the navy was among the first to introduce real-time and online interactive systems, networking of large data systems over long distances, the use of COBOL and other higher-level languages, database management systems, computer aided design systems, modeling, simulation, and new, sophisticated decision-making systems. When the IBM-305 RAMAC (random access memory computer) with its limited memory and single terminal was the only such computer in commercial use, the navy already had multiple, remotely located terminals to interrogate and update online databases. At the time of the GAO draft report the navy was sponsoring several ADP software and hardware research and development efforts, including multiple large-scale batch processing and COBOL and FORTRAN for minicomputers.[110]

In 1972 a lieutenant commander in OP-916C, the Software Management Section, had been asked to comment on plans for a minicomputer for a destroyer. He was enthusiastic about the idea but very cautious about the software because of the lack of training in computers of most destroyer sailors. For that and other reasons he recommended the use of COBOL as "the ideal. It seems to meet the use requirements and has a well-defined interface with the outside world." Two years later, this recommendation would land the job in Hopper's lap.[111]

Automating shipboard nontactical systems would be no small task, though. A typical aircraft carrier or carrier tender package included approximately fifty-eight 3M (maintenance and material management) programs, sixty-two programs in support of supply requirements, and an assortment of programs supporting personnel, watchkeeping, and battle readiness. Developing these programs represented a considerable number of personnel-years of effort, which made it clear why standardization of programs for navywide application was an attractive economy measure. In December 1974, just as the GAO draft report was doing the rounds of navy ADP, Hopper was tasked with developing a program for shipboard ADP equipment support. Building compilers for shipboard minicomputers was a major part of her workload for the next two years. "The admiral has the notion that if he keeps me busy, I'll stay out of his hair," she told a reporter some months later, between puffs of her cigarette. "He's wrong. I keep starting new things that upset people."[112]

The GAO report, however, was much more upsetting to the navy than Hopper's criticisms were. The spur of the report led to a major reorganization of navy ADP that, among other things, reassigned Hopper from the Pentagon to the Washington Navy Yard. The GAO failed, however, to touch the autonomy of local commanders.

6

The Navy's Best Recruiter?
The NAVDAC Years: 1977–1986

I n January 1977 the navy responded to the criticisms in the GAO report by disestablishing the ineffectual Information Systems Division (OP-91). In place of the old organization it established the Naval Data Automation Command (NAVDAC), designed "to improve the overall management of the navy's ADP resources."[1] This major reorganization of nontactical ADP was carried out after comprehensive study and review, and with guidance from Congress and the Office of the Secretary of Defense. NAVDAC's goals included:

> Better planning and coordination navy-wide to anticipate, budget for, and satisfy ADP requirements before rather than after they become critical; standardization of systems and consolidation of facilities where it makes good sense; more aggressive and consistent exploitation of computers and teleprocessing; career development of ADP professional personnel; and the formulation of more responsive, up-to-date policy and procedures for the acquisition and management of ADP resources.[2]

NAVDAC was designed to handle the complex problems of meshing federal, DoD, and navy policies for automatic data processing equipment acquisition and systems development. It was responsible for collaborating with all navy ADP facilities and for oversight of all ADP contracts. It was hoped that NAVDAC would be more effective than OP-91 had been at controlling this specialized management area, which was driven by exceedingly fast-paced technology.[3]

NAVDAC was a second echelon command under the CNO. It consisted of a headquarters established in the Washington Navy Yard and two regional data automation centers (NARDACs)—one in Washington and one in San Diego—each the result of consolidation of multiple field activities. At least four more NARDACs, also to be created by the consolidation of other installations, were planned for the end of 1978. The ADP Selection Office of the navy and the DoD Computer Institute now reported to NAVDAC.

Mindful of the trouble caused by the GAO's criticism of too much local ADP autonomy as well as the difficulty of balancing competing requirements, NAVDAC's main focus was "to implement concepts which have the proper mix of command or operating management objectives with the technical and specialized management characteristics necessarily associated with computer systems." NAVDAC's contribution—by top-level evaluation and coordination—was intended to make possible the development and adoption of compatible plans navywide, the alignment of all projects with navy priorities, and the assurance of technical feasibility and navywide economic benefit. In other words, for the first time there was, in theory at least, a mechanism for the integration of ADP projects and plans with overall navy management objectives.[4]

At the end of the year Hopper, under NAVDAC's new commanding officer, Rear Adm. Peter K. Cullins, was among the core group of about twenty-five people from the disestablished OP-91 finally to make the move from the Pentagon to set up NAVDAC's new quarters in the Navy Yard. By May authorization had been received to begin hiring, but then everything had ground to a halt in October. The House Appropriations Committee had put a freeze on hiring pending a look at the propriety of the location of NAVDAC in Washington. It is not clear what the problem was, but six months later, the dispute apparently resolved, hiring was unfrozen and by September 1978 NAVDAC—almost two years after its establishment—was at about 70 percent of authorized strength.

Since her return to active duty Hopper had already been through one minor reorganization when her office was moved from the special assistant to the secretary of the navy to the ASN(FM). She had survived a major reorganization when the Office of Information Systems Planning and Development had been disestablished and the Information Systems Division (OP-91) had been set up instead under the CNO. Now OP-91 was gone too. Hopper remained with NAVDAC through its halting early days until her final, reluctant retirement from the navy in 1986.

At NAVDAC Hopper was one of five people designated Special Staff. She was named special advisor to the admiral commanding—a position he created specifically for her—and was given a special code: 00H, the H for Hopper. Her mission as defined in the NAVDAC organizational manual read in part: "Survey the state of the art in computer technology on a continuing basis. Review and evaluate the new knowledge from all sources, government and civilian, to determine the

applicability of such knowledge to major design and development problems. . . . Provide technical assessments of the possibility of applying
new concepts in existing systems." She was also responsible, in collaboration with Dick Fredette, for preparing an annual technical assessment of the navy's computer status. Finally, she was to serve as
NAVDAC representative to learned societies, industry associations, and
technical conferences. Within a year or two this last imperative became her major occupation. Traveling kept her so busy by then that
she was in her office only a couple of days a month.[5]

During these years Hopper continued to work most closely with
Dick Fredette, who had been made director of training and technology.
His job was to:

> Develop plans, policies, and procedures, and manage pro-
> grams for the career development and training of all civil-
> ians and military ADP personnel navy-wide. Assess and
> evaluate relevance, feasibility, and applicability of new
> technology. Promote transfer of new technology to opera-
> tional use in navy-wide ADP systems and applications.[6]

In 1977, Hopper was seventy-one years old but had not slowed
down her pace at all. The normal retirement age for a military officer
was sixty-two, yet she had been back on active duty for ten years and
still the Navy did not throw her out. She spent another nine years
continuing to tell her superiors what to do about computer technology.
Her outspokenness had by now become legendary, expected, and allowed for. Never awed by rank, she was forthright even when addressing the Joint Chiefs of Staff, as she recalled a few years later:

> And I went down and I told them I said: you're going to
> have to learn to listen to your juniors. They looked at me
> and I pointed out that they had piles of reports they had
> to read, major decisions to make, they had not had time to
> keep up with really rapidly changing technology. They were
> going to have to present their problems to their juniors
> who would come up with solutions; they could put on the
> political aspects and the strategic aspects, but they were
> going to have to learn from their juniors because they were
> the ones that knew today's technology.[7]

John F. Lehman, who became navy secretary in 1981, recalled
that Hopper once "gave me a stern lecture on computers. It was the
roughest wire-brushing I've had since I got this job." In the same interview Hopper's last navy boss, Kenton Hancock, director of NAVDAC,
admitted: "We never would presume to argue with her because we real-

ized that going in we can't win."[8] It seems there was a consensus among her coworkers and those who reported to her, as well as among her superiors, that Hopper was, as the *Washington Post* put it: "Always brilliant and tireless and sometimes contrary and cantankerous."[9]

In many ways Hopper was in an extremely fortunate position because of her age and her gender. She could cut through the nonsense of bureaucracy and politics and, for a while at least, no one wanted to risk looking bad by touching her. According to Dick Fredette, she did not know the word "intimidated." She not only held her own in meetings with her peers and superiors, but would end up dominating the conversation.[10] And yet, although always completely natural and forthright, Hopper was not one to stir up unnecessary trouble. She was one to get along, to placate, a peacekeeper, as Ruth Brendel had described her role at the Harvard Computation Lab so many years earlier. Eventually, of course, Hopper would have to retire, but no one could tell her that yet. Meanwhile there was, as always, a lot of nonsense, as she called it, and she was the person to cut through it. Reorganization and the creation of NAVDAC had not resolved all of the internal problems of navy ADP, nor did it remove the external constraints.

Theoretically, NAVDAC had the authority to override any subsidiary layers of responsibility for navy computing. In practice, however, as the GAO found later that year, control problems persisted. NAVDAC's commanding officer should have been able to reach down "into the bowels of an organization and remove" any errant computer, according to a GAO observer. In practice, though, Naval Material Command continued to exert management authority, thwarting all interference. Old equipment was still replaced with new without redesigning the system, contrary to DoD policy. Finally, the failure to report all equipment with ADP capability meant that the navy did not even know precisely what its ADP assets were.[11]

Right from the very beginning, too, NAVDAC had to contend with the customary external influence. In an early memorandum describing the reorganization and consolidation, NAVDAC somewhat plaintively stated that it would "proceed with overall objectives for Navy improvements as soon it is able to overcome constraints of organizing and staffing" imposed by congressional committees.[12] In a January 1977 description of NAVDAC's command organization, external authorities issuing ADP guidance to which the navy was subject were those first determined by the Brooks Act: the Office of Management and Budget, the General Services Administration, the National Bureau of Standards, the General Accounting Office, and the Office of the Secretary of Defense.[13]

But that did not mean that nothing had changed. Some progress had been made in consolidating and standardizing ADP resources since the General Accounting Office report of 1975, although not enough to suit Juanita Kreps, the secretary of commerce. In August 1977 she sent a letter to navy secretary W. Graham Claytor on the perennial issue of automatic data processing management. She explained that between 1968 and 1976 more than forty Federal Information Processing Standards (FIPS) and guidelines had been approved and issued. These standards were to be used by all federal agencies and departments unless the NBS granted a waiver. "Naturally," Secretary Kreps explained, "the benefits which may be expected from such standards depend upon their widespread acceptance and implementation. . . . We have been concerned of late," she continued, "that Federal agencies are not using the FIPS to the extent expected, and that the Brooks Act has, therefore, not been as effective as anticipated." As a result, another round of assessments was to take place to estimate FIPS compliance, and she wanted a navy representative to assist in the process.[14]

Then in September 1977 President Jimmy Carter set in motion a study for a sweeping reorganization of the whole Department of Defense. The data automation part of this initiative that affected the navy was the imperative to emphasize resource conservation through consolidation of ADP assets. The DoD, as part of its effort to improve relations with the other organs of government, was already heavily involved in supporting a federal ADP reorganization project and the federal and national ADP standards development program, as well as the assessment initiative recently set in motion by Secretary Kreps. The pressure was mounting to do even more.[15]

That same month the Department of Defense announced its new automatic data processing objectives. The four major areas for improvement were computer security, ADP technology forecasting, ADP career development and training, and improving congressional relations. Among the more specific objectives that fell under Hopper's purview were those to promote ADP standards, safeguard personal privacy and improve ADP security in compliance with the Privacy Act of 1974, and improve training and career management programs for ADP personnel. She had been interested in the issue of computer security for some time and had been working to develop what she described as a kind of internal "burglar alarm" for computers that would prevent attempts to gain illicit access to stored information. This was important not only for military security, but also had commercial implications when firms shared time on a common computer. This was the era when time sharing seemed to be the answer to the high cost of computers, but Hopper scornfully likened time sharing to "the laundry service in the [United] States—very efficient—but most people prefer to buy their own washing machine."[16]

Hopper also had to keep her eye on compliance with the call for expansion of data processing service centers, computer networks, and minicomputers, for each of which she was already a strong advocate. She was ahead of the curve in supporting the creation of an inventory of applications systems software to minimize the duplication of software development, acquisition, and use. The final objective in the DoD ADP program that fell within her area of responsibility was to "revise the data elements and codes standardization program." This work would never be complete. Like painting the Golden Gate bridge, as soon as one end was reached it was time to start at the other end again.[17]

What caused the seemingly endless imposition of political directives and the intense scrutiny of the military's management of ADP? Three factors seem to be involved. First, computer-based systems were costly in both time and money. Second, such systems had an enormous potential to improve the efficiency and effectiveness of military operations. And finally, the Brooks Bill of 1965 imposed a statutory requirement on the federal government to intensively manage its ADP resources.

It is also useful to bear in mind the size and scope of the task facing DoD to better understand why the effort to comply with standards was a never-ending struggle. By 1977, DoD had the largest ADP program in the federal government. Almost every phase of its activities involved some degree of computer support, including systems for business and administration; health care; command, control, and communications; intelligence; and tactical operations. The most recent addition to this list was computers embedded in weapons systems. In all, DoD had thirty-eight hundred general-purpose computer systems ranging from small, stand-alone computers to large, complex systems of interconnected computers linked to dozens of remote terminals. Including embedded computers, DoD operated 49 percent of the total computers used by the federal government. Fifty-four thousand people, military and civilian, were engaged in planning, operating, and maintaining these systems, roughly fourteen thousand in the army, twenty thousand in the air force, and thirteen thousand in the navy. The total cost to the taxpayer was almost two billion dollars a year, with an additional $0.7 billion estimated for embedded computers. The army share of the budget was $479 million, the air force share $784 million, and the navy share $480 million. There were sixteen central design and programming centers operated by the military departments and agencies across the country, and acquisition of ADP equipment was controlled separately by each service.[18]

One problem related to the size of the operation was the difficulty of finding sufficient numbers of properly trained personnel to handle all the specialized jobs now required of APD. Things had changed a lot since Hopper's days at the Harvard Computation Lab when she had had to know how to do everything from coding to tape punching to peering into the Mark I with a mirror to find what had caused it to stop. And yet, even with the passage of so much time and the proliferation of different specialties, terms were still vague and poorly understood. A 1976 Navy Department implementation plan for computer resources expressed serious concern over the lack of officers qualified in computers "due to a less than complete statement of requirements." It also noted "apparent deficiencies in assignment systems and officer coding," which made it difficult to identify qualified officers for prospective assignment. It was also unclear whether officers serving in computer and tactical data system areas were being selected for promotion at the same rate as officers in other subspecialty areas. The perception that this was not so might well have driven off otherwise qualified people.[19]

As far as civilian employees went, the problem may have been partially addressed the following year. A Civil Service Commission notice published in the *Federal Register* in April 1977 announced the establishment of prescribed minimum educational requirements for computer scientists employed in federal service. "Computer science is a new professional occupation," the announcement stated, "and the prescribed requirement will assure fair and equitable recruitment and placement." What was now institutionalized was the first professional position in the computer field—the first that required an academic degree. Thirty-three years after she wrote her first program, Hopper was working in a field that finally had begun to come of age.[20]

It was not until 1980, however, that Fredette's technology and training directorate produced a comprehensive plan to address some of the deficiencies in the navy's understanding of computing as it related to a naval career. The ADP billet structure was reviewed, validated, and arranged in priority order across all designations, grades, and activities. An ADP career pattern for computer technology subspecialists was also developed and promulgated, and relevant activities such as the Naval Postgraduate School and the Naval Academy were briefed on the changes. Training programs for ADP officers were revamped, as were those for enlisted data processors. In addition, the curriculum and training manuals for DP rates were reviewed and revised. Early the next year Fredette also designed and developed a brochure for use in college recruitment programs.[21]

In spite of rapid growth, unwieldy size, and imperfectly understood tasks, because all branches of the military knew it was Congress that approved their budgets, they did what they could to comply with federal computing requirements. They could all expect, at some point, to have to answer the question put succinctly by one member of the House of Representatives Appropriations Committee: "Let us get to the heart of the committee's concern—is it worth the money you are asking for?"[22] It was in response to federal standards that NAVDAC consolidated the four major computer installations in the Washington area into a single regional data automation center. The same impulse spurred the consolidation of twenty-four data processing installations nationwide into six regional data processing service centers (DPSCs). Similar efforts had been underway in the other services too. The Army Base Operations System project had consolidated over 160 systems into three standard systems. Under its Phase IV project, the air force had scheduled 234 local computer sites for consolidation into 140 sites. The Air Force Data Services Center in the Pentagon supported both the Air Staff and the Office of the Secretary of Defense.[23]

Hardware, and frequently also applications programs, had been standardized at activities and installations performing common functions. The Army Combat Services Support System, for example had ordered sixteen identical van-mounted systems for army divisions. Most impressive, perhaps, was the World Wide Military Command and Control System (WWMCCS), which included standard computer systems at thirty-five different sites. All sorts of technical support functions had also been standardized, ranging from establishing central design activities to developing specifications and selection of ADP equipment. In some cases where technical requirements were the same and relevant skills scarce, technical support had been consolidated into a single unit to serve the entire DoD. This was the case with the federal COBOL Compiler Testing Center. "The successful completion of the recent initiatives," maintained a defense department memorandum, "should guarantee that DoD's position of leadership in Federal ADP management continues for the foreseeable future." Obviously this would benefit each of the military services.[24]

Committed advocates of ADP were nevertheless mindful that there was a downside to excessive centralization. Consolidation and standardization tended to reduce responsiveness of ADP facilities and to lessen competition and technological innovation. The navy would not easily be weaned from its one-of-a-kind systems. Even with progressive improvements in technology they could still marshal good reasons against the sort of one-size-fits-all dream of some bureaucrats, especially those in the General Services Administration, which on the matter of standardization was the navy's usual nemesis. In response to a query from the office of the assistant secretary of defense who oversaw DoD computing, Rear Adm. C. A. Easterling, the director of the Command, Control and Information Systems Division, wrote bluntly: "Any suggestion that GSA rules should apply to tactical, embedded computers which are not commercially available, is viewed with concern. The continued integrity of necessary program management responsibility," he concluded, "would be seriously jeopardized by imposition of regulations appropriate for commercially available computers." [25]

The Chief of Naval Material went further. "The AN/UYK-7, AN/UYK-20 and AN/UYK-14 are not systems," he explained. "They are standard navy shipboard militarized computers, are not commercially available, and are under strict Navy configuration management." The point he was trying to make was that the standard navy shipboard and airborne computers were in no sense commercial, general-purpose equipment and did not, therefore, fall under GSA standardization requirements. In fact they were "well beyond the capabilities and responsibilities of GSA." [26]

Embedded computers and tactical systems aside, the navy's ADP continued to be heavily influenced and constrained by a complexity of external organizations. In many cases, changes in navy, as in defense, ADP policies and practices could not be made without at least considering their views, and very often their agreement had to be obtained. For that reason the DoD had as one of its stated ADP objectives for fiscal year 1978 to improve its relations with both executive and congressional offices. Here Hopper may well have been one of the navy's most valuable weapons. As the years progressed her profile became ever more recognizable. Each of her promotions henceforth took exceptional action on the part of either the legislature or the executive and was accomplished only because of the very strong support she had in both of those branches. She might well, in these later years, have been the most important promotional material in the navy's arsenal.

In many ways Hopper was a media dream by this time. She was a high-ranking female naval officer, of which there were few. She was approaching her eighties, feisty, and opinionated. She was a practiced public speaker and was always accessible to the press. Her one-liners made very good copy, and in uniform she took unbeatable photographs. It is no surprise that in December 1985 a newspaper headline read: "Is RADM Grace Hopper the Navy's Best Recruiter?" This question was sparked by a ceremony at the Navy Recruiting Command Headquarters, where Hopper was awarded the title of honorary recruiter. Part of the statement thanking her for her work said that "your recommendations to young men and women to join the navy are greatly appreciated. Recruiting is very difficult in the present environment and we need all the help we can get." The present environment included a good economy with plenty of good jobs available, a shrinking eligible population of young people between the ages of seventeen and twenty-five, and a growing need for enlisted men and women and officers for a navy expanding to a projected six hundred ships.[27]

There were some ADP problems, however, that could not be overcome, even by the best of public relations because they had been caused, in part, by an overly ambitious attempt to comply with the government's own directives. An important cautionary tale had recently played itself out when Congress decided to cancel one of the world's largest business computer systems efforts, the air force's Advanced Logistics System (ALS). This system was begun in 1967 just as Hopper was recalled to the navy to help with its much less ambitious standardization program. ALS was designed to be "a unifying force in helping the Air Force Logistics Command bring together several hundred separate data systems into a cohesive whole." This involved a complete change in hardware, software, and procedures, all at the same time, and for a while it had been the model against which other military systems were unfavorably compared. As it turned out, however, the project was just too big and had attempted too much at one time. After ten years and an estimated cost—at the time very high—of three hundred million dollars, the program had to be scrapped, much to the embarrassment of the air force. This was even more humbling to those in the know because it was to the air force that the Department of Defense had turned in 1965, at the beginning of this whole effort, as the service most fit to supervise the creation and implementation of information processing standards for all DoD computers.[28]

With an eye on the air force disaster, by 1978 NAVDAC had set in motion one of the largest single ADP software conversions ever attempted

in the navy. The Data Processing Service Center Project (DPSC Project),
which was to take two years, would initially convert all the software at
the six (and later two more) new major navy computer centers across
the nation. Over four thousand individual application programs woven
into 360 separate systems supporting navy business ashore and afloat
were to be transferred from existing computer hardware to new Sperry-
Univac U-1100 equipment. These systems, as the GAO had pointed out
in 1975, had been developed over many years and had been refined
and altered to use the old equipment to the greatest advantage. The
resulting diversity made the transfer to new computers and new operating systems all the more difficult, and the projected cost of the conversion was eighteen million dollars.[29]

By then microprocessor technology was already in the works, and
because of their small size and ruggedness it was believed that microprocessors would replace and improve hard-wired digital or analogue
devices in many military systems. An unclassified NATO study of microprocessors from October 1977 noted that they were not very well
understood yet, particularly with regard to systems software. It was
thought that such structures would probably be decentralized and asynchronous and would need operating systems very different from those
of conventional, centralized computer structures. It was foreseen that
new software production methods would have to be developed and that
the whole subject required a good deal more research. At the same
time advances were being made in the field of computer communications. The lieutenant commander who was the contact for information
about the NATO study could be reached at the ARPANET (predecessor
to DARPANET and the Internet) address: ONR-LONDON@ISIA. For
all the complaints about the slow pace of change, navy computing was
moving very fast in some ways.[30]

Hopper and Fredette were soon forced to grapple with the vexing
issue of databases. Converting a database management system and its
associated database from one computer to another was a costly and
time-consuming undertaking, yet replacement computers were seldom
selected for their compatibility with databases and their management
systems. Standards would not come to the rescue for some time, according to Fredette, "as they have been lagging disappointingly" in the
area of databases. "One particular standard, COBOL, had been a key
means for getting from one computer to another," Fredette maintained,
although it was not perfect. Still, it had "reduced the specter of conversion to a more manageable task."[31] Years later Hopper was still "trying
to change some admirals' minds about databases. I want our database

in special machines, not in those dinosaur mainframes. The future is in systems of computers that work together," she told an interviewer.[32]

When the first micros began to appear and Hopper got her hands on one, she naturally wanted to put COBOL on it. Of course she met with the usual opposition from people who said COBOL could not be adapted to a micro. According to Hopper, her succinct reply to these naysayers was "Tommy rot and nonsense." Not in the least deterred by opposition, she had immediately put her crew to work to create a mini-COBOL. Her available staff consisted of one DP2 (data processor second class) and two DP3s and a seaman. None of them were college graduates, but they knew COBOL from working with her. Accordingly, suppressing their own doubts, they set to work and within four months they had written the whole thing in independent modules, 80 percent of it in COBOL, with very clear instructions in English preceding each module. Because the navy does not sell things, Hopper gave the program to a small software house in Virginia. The owner modified and expanded the program and sold it to IBM. And the rest, as they say, is history. Hopper got what she wanted: the dissemination of a program for COBOL for microcomputers that would eventually find its way back to the navy. She and her staff did not make a penny, but according to Hopper at least one small, independent software company did, although, as always, the big money went to the giant IBM.[33]

By early 1979 the usefulness of minicomputers was spreading so fast that their increasing numbers in the navy inventory required the implementation of a stepped-up program to train operators in their use. At about that time a microcomputer was installed in the Subspecialty Development Branch of the Bureau of Personnel. According to a command history submitted by Fredette, "the system allows the subspecialty development officer to access at the press of a button such necessary information as billet availability, the incumbent's rotation date, and officers with the requisite qualifications available to fill the coded billets. . . . Through this system," Fredette's report ended, "BuPers is able to maintain better control over the subspecialty system."[34]

A microcomputer system was also being tested afloat. One system was installed in the carrier *Eisenhower* (CV-69) to assist in control functions for supply receipts. Programs written in standard COBOL were used to prepare input and verify data and provide local processing capability to ensure timely and accurate supply records. The system was supplied by NAVDAC "to demonstrate the capabilities of a commercial multi-terminal, microcomputer-based system in the shipboard environment of the future non-tactical computing systems." All the hard work Hopper had orchestrated to standardize COBOL in the commercial environment as well as in the navy was now paying off. COBOL was proving itself flexible enough to move to mini- and microcomputers and to be used effectively afloat.[35]

In a 1976 magazine article Hopper had already stated that the great big computers then in use—which cost over three million dollars each—were not needed anymore. Instead, she noted, people should use a whole chain of microcomputers, such as the micros and minis she had next door to her office, which cost only one hundred thousand dollars each. Some farsighted organizations such as the Bank of America, the Ford Motor Company, Citibank, and Ramada Inn were already using micro networks, but as always, fear of change inhibited a more widespread conversion.[36]

Hopper complained that she had been trying to push the use of multiple computers since she arrived at the Pentagon and was still fighting that battle. It was just common sense to her to build a computer out of microcomputers. In the old days, when people wanted to move around big heavy objects such as logs, they used oxen. And if the log was too heavy to move, they did not try to grow a bigger ox; they just hitched up two of them. "If you were running out of capacity in the computer," Hopper maintained, "don't try to build a bigger one, buy another one. Split your work." She saw no reason why payroll and inventory, for example, had to be on the same computer. The only reason many people believed that was how it had to be done was because, in the beginning, they could not afford more than one computer. Nobody could. But that had been a long time ago and the situation had changed entirely. The UNIVAC I had cost three million dollars, but in 1979 a Motorola with 64K of memory cost only four thousand dollars. Hopper's idea was to have a whole room full of computers hitched up in an assembly line, each doing one operation and sending the problem on down the line for the next operation. Long before it was popular, Hopper was thinking in asynchronous terms, but that was the way she had been trained. The assembly-line concept was what Howard Aiken had envisaged for the Mark I.[37]

This was, moreover, a common law of engineering. "Anything which gets beyond a certain stage of complexity must be broken up into components," Hopper insisted, "and become a system of components." She had always believed that would be inevitable for computers too, so it did not surprise her when people eventually came up with micros and minis. Hopper persevered in her push for the concept of networking minicomputers as an alternative to large-scale computers with complex operating systems, and eventually she achieved a measure of success. She was also instrumental in transferring applications from large-scale computers to the less expensive minicomputers, resulting in considerable savings to the navy.[38]

In spite of the rapidly advancing capability of computers, the political struggle to justify navy ADP continued throughout Hopper's last years in the navy. In fall 1980, a national security team of the Federal Data Processing Reorganization Study criticized the absence of integrated, long-range planning for ADP support by all navy components and commands. According to the team, this caused "difficulties with the Congress, OSD, GSA and OMB"—in other words, all the usual suspect organizations. Further, the team found that "Navy decisions on acquisitions of general purpose computing equipment have been made on an ad hoc basis, and not for the benefit of the navy as a whole." Perhaps NAVDAC had learned from the unfortunate experience of OP-91; certainly its response to this kind of external criticism was more sophisticated than in the past. Instead of overreacting and responding to perceived threats, NAVDAC merely noted that navy department managers had independently recognized the need for this sort of "bottom-up" planning and was adding it as an important input to the Navy Long Range Plan for Automated Information Systems.[39]

Just as complaints of lack of standardization continued, so too did the navy's promulgation of new standards. In fact NAVDAC's new head, Rear Adm. Paul E. Sutherland, went a step better and in spring 1982 announced the establishment of the Naval Data Automation Technical Standards (NDATS) program. This was to be an "organized program environment for the administration and management of data automation technical standards for navy-wide use/implementation." Apparently the meaning of this was clear to at least eight activities, which responded to NAVDAC's initiative with interest.[40]

In the fall of 1982 a World War II WAVE sent a note to Joy Bright Hancock, who had been WAVE director in the 1950s. Referring to the fortieth WAVES reunion in Seattle that she had attended she wrote: "One of the outstanding speakers was Capt. Grace Hopper, who kept everyone listening and laughing, with her wit and humor. After I returned home I learned she had been written about in the August 31 issue of *Forbes* Magazine. Then, in the September issue of *All Hands* they had a great feature story entitled 'Grace Hopper, a Living Legend.'"[41] During these last years in the navy as special advisor to the commander, NAVDAC, Hopper continued, and even expanded, her strenuous schedule of travel and talks. She gave well over two hundred talks a year, her lecture tours taking her all over the country and to Europe, Japan, Canada, and countless other places. In 1983, for example, she logged over one hundred thousand miles of air travel. While she loved to fly, Hopper used to say that she was always glad to get home on weekends to wash her hair and her shirts and to clean her apartment.[42]

Hopper's presentations were so well received because she had a way of speaking completely naturally, as though she was sitting next to you having a chat in her office. Her voice was rather low pitched and soft, even delicate in tone, which belied the vigor of her vocabulary and her sentiments. She had little accent, perhaps just a generic well-bred east coast intonation, and she had no affectations. If anyone asked her to stand up at a meeting and talk about her experiences with computers, she could go on for an hour without drawing breath. She never read from a prepared text; even for the most formal addresses she would have only a small note card with a few points on it, and she never even looked at that. Of course there was a lot of repetition among talks. She had a stable of stock stories and a selection of them came out in each of her speeches and interviews, although in varying order and with varying refinements.[43]

By this time young people, especially, had become enthralled by Hopper. She would talk to high school and college students and afterward they invited her to their graduation ceremonies to speak because they liked and admired her so much. "I would be sitting with her in the lobby of a hotel where she had just given a speech or something," Fredette recalled, "and some of the young college girls would come up and they'd just sort of stand around while we were talking and just sort of look at her in admiration. One of them, I remember, came up and said 'I just wanted to touch you.'"[44] But Hopper also related well to others of her own rank and distinction. Working closely with the air force on uniform DoD standards, she had come to know air force Brig. Gen. Wilma Voight. During these years the two of them became very friendly, chatting on the phone all the time and popping into each other's offices.[45]

During the last years, too, Hopper continued to battle institutionalized resistance to change. In 1983 she noted that the navy had just installed a database machine at Point Mugu, California. It had been sitting around out there for six months and, worse still, the concept was at least ten years old. In her office at the Navy Yard she had a similar computer destined for use in a neighboring building. At last the admiral for whom it had been ordered, whom she did not name, had finally recognized its value. Now he was going around "bragging about it, after he sat on it and argued against it for five years." Resistance to change was not just an occupational hazard of those who operated computers; it could be found at the very top of navy computing.[46]

It was also true that the increasing popularity of automatic data processing brought its own problems, including how best to manage the vast amount of data being generated. Hopper believed that, on the one hand, much information that should be retired to the historical files was being kept on line because of the prestige of being on line, while on the other hand too much data was being printed out and lay unread in heaps instead of staying in the computer until needed. Twenty years later the navy is still grappling with how best to manage its data. Now, however, with the ubiquity of email, the problem is that very little is being committed to paper, and those electronic records that survive may not be accessible to future hardware.[47]

Of course the navy was neither alone, nor even the worst offender, when it came to effective use of up-to-date computing power. Jan Prokop, a navy captain with a PhD in computer science, who had most recently served as director of the navy's ADPE Selection Office in Washington, D.C., on retirement from the navy had gone to the Social Security Administration during the Carter regime. There he hit what Hopper called a blank wall, including opposition from the Senate. The problem was not resources. Money had been poured into spacious new facilities with plenty of power to run a modern system. What was lacking was the will to embrace change. Social Security was still using a linear filing system by social security number, which Hopper called "insane in this day and age." Prokop had been unable to make anything move and had left, going instead to the Department of Energy. Hopper understood his frustration very well. Fifteen years earlier, when she had returned to active duty, she had tried to persuade the Social Security Administration to rewrite their programs in COBOL, one at a time. But they continued to use Autocode, which had been around since the 1950s, and now the equipment was obsolete and the people who knew the code were retiring. She foresaw a dangerous situation ahead. She also observed that the Internal Revenue Service, too, was still using Autocode, although the IRS had just signed a huge contract with UNIVAC to replace all its equipment and rewrite all its programs in COBOL.[48]

In part because she was so aware of the need to keep up with changing technologies, Hopper was glad to contribute her influence wherever she could to enhance the technical education of young people. She was also very good at bringing other people along on this mission.

One of the more tangible of her efforts was the creation of a computer center at Brewster Academy, a private school in Wolfeboro attended by her grandnephew and -nieces. Hopper had prevailed on some of her old friends in the computing industry to contribute equipment for the center, among them Ken Olsen, president and founder of Digital Equipment Corporation, who donated a top-of-the-line DECmate II system. Hopper had known Olsen for years, since his days working at MIT's computer lab.[49]

On 7 November 1983, a crisp, sunny day, Hopper was honored at the dedication of Brewster Academy's new Grace Murray Hopper Center for Computer Learning. Admiral Sutherland, her boss at NAVDAC, accompanied her to New Hampshire for the ceremony at the express request of the White House. Olsen flew in on one of his company helicopters to give the keynote address. Also present, in addition to members of Hopper's family, were officials from Wang Laboratories, NEC Laboratories, Computer Sciences Corporation, and many others, as well as members of the media and data processing trade press. Governor John Sununu sent his executive assistant to deliver an official declaration that 7 November 1983 had been designated "Grace Murray Hopper Day" throughout New Hampshire. Perhaps even more moving for Hopper was the presence of two old friends to help her celebrate, Bob Campbell and Dick Bloch from the Harvard Computation Lab days. To top off a perfect event, during the course of the proceedings Admiral Sutherland got news from Washington of Hopper's elevation to the rank of commodore, effective the next day, and was delighted to announce the news.[50]

John Lehman, Secretary of the Navy for seven years from 1981 to 1987, worked with Hopper "from time to time." When he first met her she was already seventy-four, but he helped to facilitate her promotion to commodore even though she was technically too old. "Before Hopper there were seventeen different computer systems in the Navy that didn't even talk to one another," he explained. "She was enormously helpful in putting together a road-map," the means to create a unified and standardized system. According to Lehman, Grace Hopper was not the least intimidated by what he called "the natural resistance to change and inertia of every big bureaucracy. . . . She had a tremendously forceful and creative personality as well as a sense of humor." She was "very, very bright," he recalled, and she "drove the Navy into the computer age with whips and scourges."[51]

On 15 December 1983, Secretary Lehman officiated at Hopper's promotion from captain to commodore in a special Oval Office ceremony hosted by President Ronald Reagan. In addition to her brother and sister, Hopper had also invited her nephews and their families. Her nephew Roger recalled noticing that the navy secretary was wearing a necktie with little submarines on it and the president wore cowboy boots with his brown suit. Reagan was tickled when Hopper insisted he have his picture taken with her teenaged grandniece, Jennifer, while Roger was "flabbergasted" at the way his aunt "basically ordered Reagan around." The president "was jumping when she spoke," he recalled with amusement. Of course, Hopper and the president were about the same age and seemed to have had a natural affinity for each other. As a lifelong Republican Hopper had been particularly pleased to have Reagan preside at her promotion even if, as Admiral Sutherland speculated later, the promotion was a "strictly political" move engineered by Secretary Lehman to placate navy women.[52]

During her last five years in the navy Hopper worked with computers at a higher and more theoretical level than she had before, and with less hands-on work. She preached about standards. She preached about office systems. She tried to create a vision of what computing could do in ordinary day-to-day living in an ordinary manner. Eventually, she thought, everyone would just have a little plastic card, sort of like a driver's license, that would hold all personal data. When stuck into a computer the card would be used to compute payroll, taxes, and a myriad other things as well. Hopper had a wonderful way of looking into the future and explaining the many possibilities with great clarity and enthusiasm. At this stage in her life she was less concerned with computers in missiles and more with plastic card technology. To get your social security check you will just plug in your card and collect, she would say.[53]

On 27 September 1985 Hopper was the guest of honor at the groundbreaking ceremony for the Grace Murray Hopper Service Center. The Naval Air Station, North Island, San Diego, had been selected as the prototype site for NARDAC's newest data processing center. NARDAC San Diego's mission was to provide ADP support for regional navy activities on land, at sea, and in the air, including managing remote facilities; providing data processing services; and designing, developing, and maintaining standard navy automated systems. This last task must have given Hopper particular pleasure. Admiral Sutherland, who had traveled out from Washington with her, gave a speech recognizing Hopper's many years of navy service, to which she gave a brief and gracious response. To complete the ceremony they all donned hard hats and posed for the cameras with shovels in hand. Once again,

Hopper was at the forefront of the computer revolution, this time as an honoree.[54]

On 8 November that same year, 1985, two years to the day since she had made commodore, Hopper's rank was changed to rear admiral (lower half) with the navy's change in title for that grade. The first woman to make rear admiral (lower half) had been, predictably, the Chief of the Navy Nurse Corps, who was promoted in 1972. Three other women were promoted to rear admiral in the 1970s and one more in 1981. Hopper was the sixth woman to attain that rank, not the first as some accounts erroneously state. She did not attend her promotion ceremony because she had taken a fall, was in a wheelchair, and was too proud to appear in that condition. Such accidents were to become the bane of her last years. Always practical, however, Hopper was especially delighted that as an admiral she was assigned a full-time aide. She also called her friends in Philadelphia to keep an eye on her great-grandfather Russell's grave because, she said, the thought of a female admiral might cause him to rise from the dead.[55]

Just as Hopper continued to work in her later years so, too, retirement to Wolfeboro did not mean slippers by the fire for her brother Roger. He served as director or trustee for more than thirty organizations and was a consultant and an expert witness in banking cases. His expertise was in retirement and pension plans, and he was the originator of the individual retirement account concept. Among other things, for many years he successfully guided the investments of Smith College and those of his alma mater, Phillips Academy, Andover, where he served as trustee.[56] Of course he was also in demand to help guide his sister with her finances. When she visited at Christmastime she would always consult with him about Remington stock and how IBM was doing.[57]

Like his sister, Grace, Roger was honored many times and feted for his philanthropy and his contributions to society. In March 1998, just a month before he died suddenly of a heart attack, he was named Citizen of the Year in Wolfeboro. That same day he had been defeated for a second term as town selectman. The local newspaper mentioned that his "age and/or health was rarely discussed in public, but some worried privately about his capacity to carry on for another three years." Murray was 86 at that time, but the paper noted that worry on his behalf was "scoffed at by the candidate." How like his sister![58]

A posthumous tribute to Roger Murray in the Andover *Alumni Bulletin* recognized his accomplishments in business and teaching and in his imaginative and successful management of retirement and pension plans for businesses, organizations, and institutions. A former colleague at Banker's Trust called him "one of the best-known and widely regarded investment thinkers in the country." Murray gave generously of the substantial fortune he had amassed, particularly in support of education. Like his sister, his passionate interest was in the young and in good teaching. At Yale, Roger had been the first undergraduate in twenty-five years to win the John Addison Porter prize, in competition with graduate students. He always credited his Andover education with making that possible. In 1977 he gave Andover a gift of $750,000 to establish the Roger F. Murray Teaching Foundation, writing at the time that he had "nurtured these 50 years a deep sense of gratitude to Phillips Academy for the great teaching and the personal interest of faculty in students like me." When he gave the Collegiate School in New York City a gift of one million dollars for support of teaching in 1982, Roger wrote: "Teachers, in my observation, either care or they don't; caring is the critical factor which makes a fine teacher great, an outstanding faculty excellent."[59]

Grace Hopper enjoyed her second full-time navy stint. She rented an apartment in Arlington, at River House on South Joyce Street, just behind the Pentagon, with a magnificent view of the capital. By this time she wore her thinning white hair in a hair net. That and her wrinkled face made her look ten years older than her age, an impression surely affected by years of heavy smoking and drinking. She was as thin as ever and had worn glasses for years. At this point in her life Hopper wore little makeup and no lipstick, but her nails were always well manicured with clear or light nail polish. In her younger days she had worn bright red polish. She was always, as everyone commented, very neat, tidy, and well groomed, and always wore gloves as her mother had taught her. When in uniform Hopper clutched a navy handbag as wrinkled as she. Fredette, of course, had many vivid memories of his former boss, all of them tinged with great respect and affection. He loved to tell, for example, how crestfallen he and his colleagues were when the boss would show up at parties at his house. It was not that they did not all esteem her highly, but this was supposed to be a chance to relax and unwind, and everyone knew that Hopper had no small talk. She would just corner some unfortunate soul and talk shop the whole evening. For her, business was never left behind. This was not just the product of advancing years and a long time living alone. Her World War II colleague and friend Ruth Brendel, who adored her, observed that even as a much younger woman "she was not one to just chat over nothing, she was pretty strictly business." Norma Gealt agreed, noting that she did not talk "household."[60]

In March 1986 with the departure of Rear Adm. Paul Sutherland, the Commander, NAVDAC billet and title were changed to Director, NAVDAC, and Sutherland was succeeded by Kenton B. Hancock, the first civilian to be appointed to that position. Five months later he had the difficult duty of overseeing Hopper's retirement, although it had fallen to Admiral Sutherland before he left to tell her that once again the navy felt it was time for her to go. She was not leaving because her work at the navy was done. It was not, nor, most likely, will it ever be. Standardization of navy computer languages is an ideal that probably cannot and should not be realized. From the early 1990s the navy struggled to impose the new universal computer language known as ADA, the standard of the Department of Defense, with little success.[61]

Named after Lord Byron's daughter Ada, Countess of Lovelace, sometimes called the first programmer, ADA was mandated for use across all applications, even though there were many areas where its use did not make sense. Finally, the ADA mandate was removed, which ironically ended resistance to it and enabled those who appreciated its capabilities to make use of its high-assurance, high-reliability properties. It used to be thought that a single language had to be used for an entire system, thus imposing a straitjacket of standardization that was often counterproductive. Finally, modern systems are being built using a multitude of languages, giving the kind of flexibility that Hopper would surely have appreciated.[62]

Since the retirement of Adm. Hyman G. Rickover in 1982, Hopper had been the navy's oldest serving officer. She wanted to retire on the navy's oldest commissioned ship, the 189-year-old frigate USS *Constitution*—Old Ironsides—in Boston Harbor, and as so often, she got her way. On 14 August 1986, wearing dress whites and gloves and carrying her ancient navy handbag, Hopper was piped on board *Constitution* with a boatswain's pipe. "I regret leaving active duty," Hopper told the 275 relatives, friends, and navy officers assembled on the deck to honor her, among them Bob Campbell and Dick Bloch. John Lehman attended, reminding everyone that this was Hopper's second retirement. She had been recalled after her first one when the navy found it could not do without her. At the end of his speech, he presented Hopper with the Defense Department's highest award, the Defense Distinguished Service Medal for exceptional meritorious service. Then the ship's crew, all in eighteenth-century uniform, scrambled up the rigging to give Hopper a rousing three cheers. A navy band played patriotic songs as an officer presented her with forty-three roses, one for each of her years of naval service. "What am I?" Hopper said to a journalist who had the temerity to ask. "Special Advisor to the Naval Data Automation Command, or something. I bug 'em." What was, perhaps, of more significance, at least to historians and to herself, Hopper was the last of the World War II WAVES to leave active duty.[63]

Letters of appreciation began to pour in as soon as word of Hopper's retirement got around. One was from President Reagan. "One person truly can make a difference," he wrote. "Setting an outstanding example throughout your naval service, you leave a living legacy in the careers and lives of all you meet."[64]

On 1 September, Hopper's name was returned to the inactive retired list.

7

Amazing Grace
Last Years and Legacy: 1986–1992

"When the Navy throws me out," Hopper had told an interviewer in 1979, "which they are bound to do eventually, because I'm going to be over age, . . . since UNIVAC made me famous, they cannot afford to have me wandering around the country in a starving condition. Therefore, they will hire me back at an extremely high salary. So I may be back at UNIVAC before too long," she concluded, "because the Navy is running out of money."[1]

The navy did not run out of money for Hopper for another seven years and then it was not UNIVAC, although they were agreeable, but Digital Equipment Corporation that took her off the streets. Without breaking stride, Hopper closed the door of her office in the Washington Navy Yard on 1 September 1986 and reported for work at Digital the next day. Digital was an easy choice for Hopper. In addition to her long friendship with Ken Olsen, Hopper had become very close to Rita Yavinsky, who was the business development manager for the Washington office of Digital, in the Government Systems Group.

Hopper and Yavinsky met for the first time at Logan Airport in Boston sometime in 1984 when they were both rushing for a plane to D.C. Hopper was in uniform, smoking, of course—in those days you could still do that—and Rita asked her if she had a spare match. Hopper just said "yes," and without another word handed her a navy Bic lighter. A couple of months later they both took the same flight again, and this time Yavinsky said hello to her and they talked as they got on the flight. A few months later still, they met at the airport again, this time on the way to Boston. Yavinsky told Hopper she was returning to D.C. that night and Hopper said she was too. On the return flight Yavinsky offered to give her a ride back to her apartment from the airport. Hopper accepted, and when they got there she invited her upstairs. When Yavinsky first saw Hopper's apartment she was overwhelmed. It was piled high with boxes bisected by what Yavinsky came to call Grace-width aisles. They went down one of the aisles where at the end Yavinsky could see a chair, a folding table, and a portable TV. Hopper lit up one of her Lucky Strikes and indicated a pile of boxes for her guest to sit on. She told Yavinsky that she was sitting on boxes of magnetic computer tapes and she pointed out other boxes that she said were full of steel tapes. These were the tapes of the original COBOL compiler. Another huge cardboard box held the punch cards from the same compiler. The two women talked for a while and became firm friends, seeing each other all the time after that.[2]

Once it was obvious that Hopper really would have to leave the navy, and for good this time, she was not yet ready to move back to Wolfeboro as she had always intended. Instead, she talked to Yavinsky about a job at Digital. Yavinsky concurred, naturally, but Hopper insisted on applying formally and going through the regular interview cycle. When she sent a letter to Yavinsky's boss at Digital, she proposed, much to his amusement, that she could be available on alternate Thursdays, at a very high salary and with an unlimited expense account, to be exhibited as a pioneer in their museum of computing.[3]

Instead, Hopper was hired as a full-time senior consultant, reporting to Rita. According to Digital's vice president for United States operations, Hopper's duties included representing the company at industry forums and serving on industry committees, speaking on government issues and the ADP environment, and participating with Digital's liaison programs with educational institutions. Explaining Hopper's expected contribution to Digital—and also the irresistible force she still represented—the vice president told the *New York Times*: "She has accomplished so much and experienced so much that younger people who associate with her will have the opportunity to learn at a rapid pace, whether they want to or not." An internal memo informed her new colleagues at Digital that the company also planned "to utilize Dr. Hopper's extensive knowledge on ADP issues and strategies in expanding our presence and stature within the computer industry." While acknowledging that she was past normal retirement age, Hopper noted that Digital had no mandatory rules on the subject.[4]

The Digital office where Yavinsky worked was on Pennsylvania Avenue, and while Hopper had been at the Navy Yard, not far away, they often met for lunch. When Hopper went to work for Digital it was even easier, of course, because Hopper was given an office right in Yavinsky's area. That was about the time that smoking was being banned from many offices around the country, Digital among them. When Hopper was told about the new rules she said, "You can either put an ashtray in my office or I won't be coming in." Her office was made a designated smoking area. Asked if Hopper had ever been concerned that the smoking might kill her, Yavinsky said, "She could care less."[5]

Digital was a good choice for Hopper, quite apart from the fact of her friendship with Olsen and Yavinsky. The company, which dominated the world minicomputer production, was at the time the leading supplier of networked computer systems and the leader in systems integration with its networks, communications, and software products. These were exactly the areas Hopper had been most interested in for a number of years.[6]

A glance at Hopper's calendar those first few months at Digital makes it clear that hiring her had been no mere window dressing; although pushing eighty, Hopper maintained a schedule someone half her age would find grueling. From 2 to 8 September Hopper was being briefed at Digital, had a physical, and hired an assistant. Tucked in between was an appearance at the Federal Computer Conference on the fourth. On 9 September Hopper testified before the Claude Pepper Committee's Subcommittee on Health and Long Term Care. On the evening of the tenth she was honored at a White House dinner, and on the eleventh she was interviewed in the morning by *USA Today* and in the afternoon she appeared on the National Public Radio program *All Things Considered*. The next day Hopper gave an interview for CBS *Nightwatch*.[7]

On Monday 15 September Hopper flew to Oak Ridge, Tennessee, for two days of meetings, still finding time for a telephone interview on the seventeenth. On the eighteenth she flew to an executive seminar at King's Point, New York, and on the nineteenth, after an all-day meeting at the Washington Navy Yard, she flew to Boston for two days of meetings. On 22 September Hopper met with an air force group at the Pentagon. She participated in a National Association of Engineering conference in Washington on the twenty-third, and the next day flew to Merrimac, New Hampshire, to visit Digital Engineering. While in New England, Hopper gave an interview to the *Worcester Telegram*. She returned home on 26 September to receive a distinguished achievement award from the American Aging Association. On 30 September Hopper flew to Boston, and from there was driven to Wolfeboro.[8]

The next day was a very important one for Hopper. She was honored at Brewster Academy, whose benefactress she was, and she was presented with a ship's print that she hung with great pride in her apartment in Arlington. On 2 October Hopper returned to Washington, resuming her normal round with a meeting of the Data Processing Management Association the next day. The following months were similar.

In October Hopper spoke at Maxwell Air Force Base in Montgomery, Alabama, and at the Federal Women's Program in the same state. She returned to Kings' Point for another seminar and spoke to GSA executives in Reston, Virginia. In November, Hopper gave a talk at Westminster College in Pennsylvania, traveled twice to Maxwell Air Force Base, and spoke in Houston, Atlanta, and Norfolk, Virginia. Again she was on the radio twice and gave interviews to the print media. Apart from a talk in Tulsa, Oklahoma, the high point of December was Hopper's appearance as Honorary Grand Marshall at the Orange Bowl Parade in Miami. She got four extra tickets for Rita Yavinsky and her three sons, and they all enjoyed the game immensely from a VIP box. Undeterred by the pouring rain, Hopper sat on a float in the parade wearing her rear admiral's uniform, hat, and white gloves, covered by a big navy coat.[9]

When Hopper had moved from Philadelphia to Washington in 1967, she continued her mania for collecting and hoarding. By the time she died, twenty-four years later, she had three apartments in River House in Arlington—a large corner one that she lived in and two smaller ones, one adjacent and another across the hall—all stuffed wall-to-wall with her possessions. Although she never wanted for money, she would not buy her apartments, even though Fredette often advised her to. She had loved her homes at Vassar and in Wolfeboro and perhaps she no longer felt a need to own property. She needed all the space, though, including six or seven walk-in closets, to house her many collections of books, American and British colonial stamps, china, dolls, and all sorts of memorabilia from her travels and from computing. According to her sister, Hopper loved to shop and adored jewelry, clothes, and especially shoes, of which she had a collection Imelda Marcos might have admired—in volume if not in style. She also had almost as many pairs of gloves as shoes. Hopper was always smart but conservative in appearance so it is no surprise that one of her favorite stores was Brooks Brothers; their tailored shirtwaists filled several of her closets. She needed that many because she refused to wear the same dress twice in any one year. Although she has become best known from her photographs in uniform, Hopper seldom wore one in summer, preferring cotton dresses instead.[10]

Hopper loved sets and series of things, perhaps reflecting her mathematical bent. She belonged to the Wedgwood club and had a lot of the company's chinaware, including the commemorative Christmas plates issued annually and whole sets of Christmas decorations. She also collected Hummel figurines, picking them up in duty-free shops for herself and for friends every time she traveled overseas. By the time she died, Hopper had also managed to amass over three thousand dolls. Yavinsky distributed as many as she could to the grandnieces. Then she and her sons loaded the rest into a truck and took them to the Children's Hospital. The apartments were also filled with pile on pile of books, most lying flat and stacked up in heaps. Yavinsky estimated that Hopper must have had at least ten thousand books when she died; they were even stuffed in the bathtubs. She read anything she could lay her hands on, picking books up wherever she was on her travels. For years she and her sister exchanged junky mysteries, but she also had piles of books on genealogy, biography, American naval history, English history, gardening, New England architecture, and lots of historical novels.[11]

Her interests were very broad. As long as she had her house in Wolfeboro she cultivated a flower garden; later she kept up vicariously, sending her nephew Roger books on gardening and on the Cape Cod style of architecture she loved. She also collected signs. "I don't think she ever went by a sign she didn't like," her nephew recalls, and it usually followed her home somehow or other. In the outhouse by her Wolfeboro farmhouse she had posted a telephone booth sign, and on the path leading up to it there was one reading something like "No Electioneering within Fifty Feet." "She swiped signs," Roger admitted with a grin.[12]

The apartment Hopper actually lived in, like the others, was always kept clean, although its huge living room was almost entirely filled with stacks of boxes two or three high. There were only the narrow aisles left clear, as Yavinsky had seen; one so that Hopper could sit and watch television and the other to get through to the kitchen. In her younger days Hopper had loved to drive but at this point she was no longer able to, nor did she any longer own a car. She still loved to fly, though, and would go off anywhere at the drop of a hat.[13]

As a rear admiral, Hopper had had a full-time aide and she found it hard to manage without one after she left the navy. From then on she had to rely once again on her longtime housekeeper, Pearl, to take care of all her needs and all her possessions. Hoarding, apparently, was a family trait; in later years Hopper's mother had had an eleven-room apartment, which was so full there was almost nowhere to sit down. Hopper had been a pack rat at the office too. When she went away on trips Dick Fredette would take the opportunity to clean out all her stuff. She did not even know what she had, he said, and never missed anything when she returned.[14]

Perhaps because she had gone so far in two fields dominated by men—computers and the navy—interviewers always asked Hopper what she felt about women's issues. Her nephew, Roger Murray, remembered her saying she was not a part of the women's movement. This might seem surprising from someone who had carved out a notable place for herself in a predominantly male world. From her Yale PhD in mathematics to her ascent to rear admiral in the navy, Hopper's trajectory had all the signs of a pioneering trailblazer. Her sharp humor, too, often expressed itself in gendered jokes. She was giving a speech once to a room full of men when she said: "Well, I see that there aren't many women here. But don't worry, I'll go slowly and hopefully you'll be able to keep up with me."[15] Still, she was right that she was not a part of any movement. She gave innumerable interviews during the 1960s, 1970s, and 1980s—informally to newspapers and magazines, and daylong formal sessions for oral history projects. In each of these she expressed reservations, and sometimes impatience, with what she saw as the counterproductive stridence of many women's groups. During those decades women's movements naturally evolved and changed. Sometimes women's issues had widespread popular support and sometimes, as in the 1980s, they were publicly embattled. Hopper was little affected by the public ebbs and flows. Over the course of thirty years her message to women was consistent: "They get there if they work hard."[16]

Hopper's sister Mary also maintained that Hopper "was never for this business of women's rights."[17] "In many cases today the women's movement is going to ridiculous extremes," Hopper is quoted as saying in 1976. "I would like to see them concentrate their efforts on lower level women seeing that they get equal pay for equal work. Older women around 40 and 50 who don't have management experience . . . putting them into management is just pushing a nervous breakdown."[18] She had said something similar in an interview a few months earlier in Florida. While denying that she herself had ever faced discrimination, she did admit that some women, particularly in the lower levels in manufacturing and industry, had not been treated fairly. Nevertheless, she continued to believe that women at higher levels would advance if they were good. Instead of trying to demolish the glass ceiling (an expression Hopper did not use) and trying to push older women into leadership positions for which they were ill-prepared, women should be fighting for young people, Hopper maintained, to secure for them the training and education they would need to assume leadership positions later on.[19]

Hopper firmly believed there were no innate differences in women's and men's abilities in math and science and saw the wide disparity in jobs as the result of lack of encouragement in school and at home.

"The first time a gal has a problem with her algebra, her father is apt to say, 'Well, girls can't understand that.'" Recent scholarship generally agrees with Hopper's premise of parity between the sexes in biological aptitude for science. It also confirms her identification of social, including familial, attitudes as one of several important negative influences on women's progress in science.[20]

In response to a journalist's question about whether she had suffered from gender prejudice in the navy, Hopper replied: "I'm asked that a lot and the answer is no."

Hopper explained that because the navy was the last service to admit women during World War II, when they finally did, "they went whole hog" in giving women equal status with men.[21] Of course the status of WAVES was not equal, nor could it be so long as they maintained a separate structure and name. But in her denial Hopper fit a pattern typical of the still-rare successful woman scientist. Only now, a decade after her death, are even much younger women beginning to publicly acknowledge the greater obstacles they faced because of their gender. Hopper was not unusual when she chose to overlook the fact that for decades there were congressional restrictions limiting her access to promotion.[22] In addition, her privileged experience in a small academic lab during World War II was by no means typical. Even more unusual were Hopper's recall from the retired reserve and the long extension of her second tour of active duty well past the normal retirement age. Loyalty to the navy clouded her usual clarity of vision when it concerned the treatment of women in the military.

The real changes for women in the navy did not begin until 1972 during Admiral Elmo Zumwalt's tenure as CNO when he set up committees to study equal rights for women. Earlier that year, Capt. Robin L. Quigley announced she would no longer use the misleading title of WAVES "Director" instead of her real title, Assistant Chief of Naval Personnel for Women, since she in fact directed nothing. She also issued a memorandum stating that continued use of the acronym WAVES implied that navy women were merely members of a ladies auxiliary and directed that it be discontinued. Navy women's separate personnel, communications, and advisory functions were gradually transferred or suspended. Admiral Zumwalt accepted Quigley's advice and allowed the disestablishment of the WAVES.[23]

The most authoritative history of navy women states categorically that "the majority of Navy women had experienced . . . [sexual harassment], and almost all had witnessed it."[24] But as Hopper herself admitted, "I was always too busy to notice. I was always trying to get something accomplished and I didn't take the time to even notice." To a careful observer this suggests—probably quite accurately—that she seldom wasted time fretting over what she viewed as secondary or even peripheral issues. Of course, this made Hopper a perfect advocate for the navy. Here she was, a woman who had for years been prevented from advancing to a rank commensurate with her position and responsibilities who nevertheless denied that there had been any such restrictions and praised the navy as an ideal place to work. She thought of herself not as a woman in the navy but as a person in the navy who was also a woman. As a woman, she stood up for herself. When a question was raised about the base for her retirement pay, since according to regulation she had been too old to be promoted, she did not hesitate for a moment to insist strenuously that she get full rear admiral's benefits. She did.[25]

When asked whether it had been hard to break into the field of computing in 1944, Hopper responded that it was not a field then, it was just a piece of equipment.[26] As the new field developed, though, during and right after the war, women were able to move into it fairly easily because there were no established precedents and there was no question of displacing men: the demand for mathematicians exceeded the available supply. Even then, though, there was nothing like parity in numbers. In May 1948, the recently formed Association for Computing Machinery had 459 members, only 26 of whom, or nearly 18 percent, were women. Nevertheless, a number of women contributed impressively to early computing, women such as Betty Holberton, Mina Rees, Nora Moser, Jean Smith (a Sperry engineer), Peg Harper of UNIVAC, and women who had worked with Holberton on the ENIAC, particularly Kathleen McNulty and Jean Bartik. Their names, however, have largely been forgotten.[27]

Hopper became the symbol, and perhaps the token, of the achievements of all the other women computer pioneers. Because of her ability, her age, her outspokenness, her navy uniform, her colorful personality, Hopper attracted all the media attention. Above all, her extensive speaking engagements set Hopper apart from the other women and generated the press coverage that made her an icon. Over the years, thanks to this publicity, Hopper became more than just a role model—she achieved, according to one view, "something akin to canonization in her own lifetime."[28] In magazine articles she was frequently referred to as "Amazing Grace" and even her younger colleagues took to calling her that. Yet in spite of all the headlines and Hopper's own earnest affirmation, the perception that computing was a field equally accessible to female talent did not outlast the first heady post-war days. Hopper never acknowledged the change.

A long article on Hopper in the San Diego *Evening Tribune* began: "Cmdr. Hopper is more worried abut the computer mystique than she is the feminine mystique." That probably sums up her frame of reference as well as anything. "Cmdr. Hopper knows how to handle a computer in no uncertain terms," the article continued, "and is dismayed by the mythology that has been built around its powers. 'It's just another tool,' Hopper said in an interview, 'like a wrench or a potato masher.'" She noted that housewives handled computers every day, but they were called thermostats, refrigerators, and toasters. Hopper blamed the computer manufacturers for promoting the mystery and complexity of computers in their advertising.[29] In reality, Hopper had told another interviewer, "It's as simple as an abacus."[30]

According to the *Evening Tribune* article, Hopper again said she put little store in the women's lib movement. She told the interviewer she believed that any woman could achieve her goal if she wanted it badly enough. She also believed that the computer field was wide open for women. "They seem to do better," she said.[31] At about the same time Hopper used similar homey language to make her point with another interviewer. "[Women's] experience in running a home is training enough to get started [in computer programming]," she said, optimistically. "Women have to be good in sequential operations to get a hot meal on the table, timing each item so that it's ready right at dinner time." And she added that a recipe was the equivalent of a technical flowchart. "In fact, a recipe for fudge is one of the best flowcharts I can think of," she said.[32]

Hopper's rosy view was contradicted by the facts, as she must have known. In spring 1971, she had been invited to cochair a workshop at a research conference called "Women in Engineering," where representatives from industry, government, and educational institutions would consider "a neglected and alarming facet of the growing gap that is developing between society and technology." "Women," the letter of invitation stated, "who represent the majority of consumers and who, as mothers, voters, and school teachers, have great power to shape the attitudes of our society, are practically absent from the pursuit of any professional activity in technology." The letter, written by the dean of the College of Engineering at the University of Illinois, cited just one example: Fewer than 1 percent of all engineers in the United States were women, versus 30 percent in the Soviet Union. Technology was viewed by most American women as an alien activity. The negative consequences of this attitude affected national policy on issues as diverse as pollution and educational innovation.[33]

To be sure, by the 1980s the tide seemed to be turning once again in favor of women in computing, but only at the lower levels of government service. A NAVDAC headquarters survey released in June 1980 found that 76 of the 163 civil service employees were women, representing 46 percent of the total. Twenty-five percent of the women were minorities, compared to only 9 percent of the men. Closer examination reveals, however, that women were concentrated at the lower grades, GS-5 to GS-9, doing data-entry sorts of jobs; as the grade increased the representation of women, and of minorities, decreased. In the computer specialist occupation, grades GS-12 to GS-17, women were concentrated in levels 12 and 13. There were equal numbers of men and women at the level of GS-11 but the numbers of women tapered off quickly after that. There were no minorities at grade GS-14 and above and only one woman GS-15, whereas there were seven men. Since the computer specialist occupation was the most important occupation at NAVDAC, the navy department identified it as an area needing "affirmative action and federal equal opportunity recruitment."[34]

Today, fifty years after it took off, computing is largely dominated by young men. Computing followed a typical postwar pattern, with a decline in women's status and participation in the field in the 1960s and 1970s, but then it failed to rebound like some other areas such as law and medicine in which women have been increasingly represented. It has been suggested that by the close of the 1980s, when Hopper retired, computing was well established as a "strangely single-gendered world."[35]

It is easy to see how the academic rigor and the sturdy independence of her upbringing, as well as living and working through the Depression and the Second World War, influenced Hopper's views. When asked whether it was possible for a woman to combine career and family, she noted that her sister had done it and so had her sister-in-law during the war. Her own career, and that of her sister, could hardly be a clearer endorsement of the enlightened way she was raised, although her success may have made her impatient with those facing more rigorous opposition with less preparation. "It's competitive," she would say. "I wouldn't want to get a job because I was a woman. I want to get a job because I do it better." Her advice to women was to "estimate your guy and give him what he needs to advance his purpose . . . being belligerent doesn't get you anywhere." The whole issue, to Hopper, was one of marketing. "You have to be pretty smooth to do a good marketing

job," she said. "Avoid the confrontations." When asked about problems
of unequal pay, Hopper denied she had ever experienced it. "You get
the bull if you do the job," was her only answer.[36]

There is little doubt that socially Hopper was far from a pioneer.
When asked what she thought about the first woman at Burning Tree—
an exclusive all-male country club in Bethesda, Maryland—she replied
that she "wished they'd [women] stay out of there. I don't know why
they can't let the guys have a nice, quiet place where they can go play
golf together." Work was vital, play was not, and she encouraged women
to enter all fields of work, but she was indifferent about recreational
spheres. Hopper had grown up in an era when the dominant status of
men was unchallenged. She saw herself not as challenging men, but as
asserting herself: an imperative she firmly believed was open to everyone of drive and ability. She believed that women had an important role
to play and that feminine wiles could be used in a constructive way.[37]

However she used her feminine wiles, Hopper had very good relationships with both women and men. For her, loyalty and leadership
were inextricably entwined. She used to say that she had learned about
old-fashioned leadership at midshipmen's school. "It's a two way street,"
she remembered being taught. "It's loyalty up and loyalty down. Respect for your superior—keep him informed of what you're up to, make
suggestions. Superior, take care of your crew, listen to them, pat 'em on
the back when they do a good job." She always took her leadership
position seriously—for example, seeing to it that the youngsters in her
group could get to their feet and give a report without saying "you know"
all the time. This she accomplished by keeping an empty coffee can on
her desk. Every time anyone said "you know" while reporting to her, he
or she had to put a quarter in the can. This tied up their capital but it
cured them all sooner or later. Hopper understood that things are managed but people must be led. Whenever she had to make a presentation
to an undersecretary or assistant secretary or admiral, she would take
her whole group with her. She would introduce each of the members
and have them give their part of the report. She watched the youngsters grow two inches, she said, when an admiral told them "well done."
Hopper also insisted that they each learn to write a report in plain
English. Judging from the lucidity of the reports written by George
Baird and others of her crew, and of the important liaison jobs with
government and industry groups with which they were entrusted,
Hopper's methods worked.[38]

Hopper did not tolerate fools or lazy people and she had an ex-
treme dislike for intellectual conventions and attitudes, but she did

have a great affinity for people of high intelligence. She very much admired Howard Aiken and gave him credit for many of the early innovative concepts in computing. This was not just blind loyalty. As Aiken's biographer has noted, it has been difficult to assess Aiken's place in computing history because he was not responsible for a specific invention or innovation that is easily identified. However, his role in establishing the computer age was recognized by his contemporaries with the Harry Goode Memorial Award in 1964, proof enough that he was, as Hopper always knew, "a major factor in producing the computer world in which we live."[39] Similarly, she remained convinced of John Mauchly's importance to the development of computing, calling him "one of the grandest people I ever met . . . he wanted to give everybody a chance, very supportive of his people, an ideal boss, I guess."[40]

Hopper's deep sense of loyalty probably also dictated her politics, although no one remembered her being particularly interested in party maneuverings. Dick Fredette recalled that while she did not talk much about politics per se, she often discussed national policy issues with him. When Ronald Reagan was elected president, Fredette was very surprised that she supported him, even endorsing his domestic financial policies. But she had been raised a staunch Republican and, as Fredette noted, she "had a tendency to maintain her allegiances."[41]

Those who knew her best remembered Hopper as considerate and extremely generous. She never returned from a trip without gifts for her staff. She always flew first class, almost always on her favorite Delta Airlines—where most navy pilots ended up when they left the service. In fact she was reluctant to fly anywhere not serviced by Delta; they treated her so well, it was almost like having her own private airline. During flights Hopper collected the little bottles of liquor she was given to take home for Fredette's parties. By then she herself had stopped drinking; typically, once she had decided to stop, she never touched another drop. When she traveled Hopper always carried two suitcases, one for clothes and one full of handouts and nanoseconds for her talks. She also took a couple of cheap string bags with her, usually red or green. On her return the bags would be bulging with presents. She was particularly lavish with her secretary, Norma Gealt, to whom she often brought expensive Hummel figurines. She did the same for her sister. To everyone's amusement Hopper could be seen, any day, walking along in the Pentagon with those bulging string bags—one on each side for balance, she would say as she brushed off offers of help. Of course, she slowed down over the years, but only physically. Her mind still operated at high speed and always in one direction: straight ahead.[42]

Hopper never lost the zeal to push people in new directions. Dick Fredette said she was a joy to work for because she set lofty goals, always planning for one hundred years hence. At the age of seventy-two she addressed a meeting of software professionals and chastised them for not planning ahead before "invalidating our older programs." First, she warned the audience that she was going to "put a burden on the programming languages people." Then she attacked: "I'd like to insist that if they add something to a language, or change something in a language, they also provide us with the algorithm . . . so that we can automatically translate our programs, say from COBOL 68 to COBOL 74. If they don't do something like that pretty soon," she added, "I'm personally going to go around and shoot up members of the language defining committees because they are providing a large number of headaches."[43] "I always try to persuade people to do completely reasonable things," Hopper had told an interviewer some time earlier, "and I'm always told I'm on cloud 9."[44]

It was important in this fast-developing field, as it is now, to keep up to date with changes. Hopper was always keen to be at the forefront of her profession, never satisfied with the status quo, never satisfied with the present state of the art. It was her ability to sustain this eager probing and questioning with undiminished energy even through her seventies that set her apart from so many others. She once said of a book that she particularly enjoyed that it "so beautifully matches my own experience of having new and wild ideas." That is how she thought of herself, and how others saw her too.[45]

In 1973 Hopper had become the only woman, and the only American, to be made a Distinguished Fellow of the British Computer Society. Arrayed in full dress uniform she had been escorted to the London event by Lord Louis Mountbatten, a cousin of Queen Elizabeth. Her initial awe at being hosted by royalty dissipated when she recalled that Mountbatten was also an admiral. From then on she felt at ease. Addressing the guests after dinner, Hopper began, as she always did, by thanking them for the award. Then, as always, she said that for her there was only one higher award, "the privilege and the responsibility of serving proudly in the United States Navy." Hopper later admitted that she had wondered whether she should say such a thing in a foreign country and then had decided she would anyway. She knew she had made the right decision when Mountbatten, always a navy man, had said to her as she turned to sit down, "Oh, well done, Captain." She never forgot that; it moved her deeply.[46]

Also in 1973, Hopper had been elected to membership in the American National Academy of Engineering. Unsentimental, as always—Ruth Brendel called her "totally unsentimental"—Hopper liked to point out the dates of her awards. While not unappreciative of the honors, she nevertheless knew that she was the first woman to receive many of them and believed she was selected in large part because of her gender. "What they were doing," she recalled in 1983, "was looking for a woman to give it to, because the uproar about women and things was getting started. . . . And there I was," she concluded perceptively.[47] She was probably quite right in this matter of timing. One study of women scientists noted that even when women did receive prestigious awards, they often came too late in life to help their careers.[48]

Some of the praise for Hopper was so specific and personal, however, that it cannot be written off as the usual professional courtesy nor even as a politically motivated sop to women. In this category fall the folders full of letters of appreciation buried among boxes of naval records in the Washington National Records Center in Suitland, Maryland. These were letters of thanks for the hundreds of talks Hopper gave every year to academic institutions, business organizations, computer groups of all sorts, and military groups. Some, of course, are indeed the usual perfunctory bread-and-butter thank-you letters. What is moving, however, is not only the sheer volume of the letters, but the fact that the vast majority were written with obvious sincerity and warmth.

Just one such letter gives the flavor of many others. On 28 May 1971, Capt. H. M. Chandler, USNR, the commanding officer of the Naval Reserve Systems Analysis Division of the Naval Reserve Training Center in Philadelphia, wrote to thank Hopper for the "outstandingly good" presentation she gave at their drill the previous month. "Captain Froscher, commanding officer of the Naval Air Engineering Center, was thoroughly impressed and spoke very highly of your talk," he wrote, and "as Commander Jim Maginnis so well and succinctly put it—wow! . . . During the week following your visit," the captain continued, "I listened to 51 technical papers and presented the 52nd myself at the Fourth Symposium on Engineering Problems in Fusion Research at NRL, Washington, DC. Not one of them came close to matching your presentation to us." Captain Chandler ended, "You may be pleased to know that there were strong sentiments expressed in the unit that you should be serving in the grade of captain. We only wish we knew how this might be accomplished."[49]

Hopper's great gift was the ability to talk to each of her different audiences in language they understood. She could stand up in front of a group of seventy- and eighty-year-olds or a group of seven- and eight-year-olds and explain to them what computing was all about. According to Yavinsky, she "had a wonderful way of expressing her view of standards in computing. She had a wonderful way of expressing where she thought we were in the evolution of computers."[50] She thought computers were in the era of the DC-10, but were progressing very fast. She used to say that when she looked out from her house in Wolfeboro she could see streams rushing down the mountain. A little bit of water would be diverted from one stream and it would flow through a mill and would be used to grind wheat into flour. The little diversion would go back to the mainstream and descend a little further and there would be another little diversion where a farmer had put up a dam to make a pond for his cows and sheep, and the water would be used to make milk and wool. And that little diversion would go back to the mainstream. As it came down the mountain into Wolfeboro, everybody used the water for something different, but it was the same water. That is what Hopper thought would happen with computers. The time was coming when small businesses would be the ones to profit most from computers in a myriad different ways, and even individuals would own their own and they would all be connected like the streams of water.[51]

Hopper's touch was sure in all kinds of situations, even with royalty. This she had a chance to demonstrate again when she was invited to Stockholm to receive an honorary doctorate to be presented by the king of Sweden. As was required, Hopper wore evening dress: full navy evening dress. This consisted of a long straight black skirt with gold cummerbund, a white ruffled shirt with a small velvet tie, a white mess jacket, and a tiara with navy insignia. Award recipients were all instructed that when they received the diploma from the provost they should then turn to face the king; the men should bow and the women curtesy. "In the first place," Hopper enjoyed recalling, "I knew darn well you couldn't curtesy in that straight skirt, and in the second place, if I tried I'd fall over." Instead, without saying a thing, she just waited her turn. When it came, because she was in naval uniform and the king was a naval officer, she saluted him instead of curtesying. "He smiled all over," she said, "it was the only time he smiled and looked gay during the whole time there."[52]

Among the thirty-four honorary degrees Hopper received over the course of her life, one of the most gratifying must have been the one awarded in 1974 by the University of Pennsylvania, where she taught as an adjunct associate professor for many years. On that memorable occasion she shared the podium with her former boss, John Mauchly, as they were both made honorary doctors of laws. Two years earlier she had been awarded an honorary doctorate of engineering by the Newark College of Engineering. In her letter of reply to the invitation to attend the commencement exercises she wrote: "I shall be delighted to be present in full dress white uniform." She only asked for one or two favors. She was landing at Kennedy airport at 6 A.M., having flown straight from Australia, and Dick Fredette was going to meet her. She asked if he might accompany her to the ceremony. She also asked for directions and for the name of a nearby motel where she could "wash up, rest a bit and dress before appearing."[53]

Obviously, Hopper never took herself or her success too seriously. Not long before she retired from the navy for the second time, she met up again with Ruth Brendel, her colleague from Harvard days. It was probably in 1984 at the celebration held by IBM and other computing companies to commemorate forty years of computing since the inauguration of the Mark I. Hopper told her old friend that she had received something like thirty honorary degrees, and each one came with a brightly colored hood. Ever practical, and irreverent, Hopper confided that she was planning to cut them all up to make a quilt.[54]

In later years Hopper became the perfect publicist for the navy's computing because her genius lay in making accessible this highly specialized field. Even her technical reports were models of spare prose, clear structure, and logical purpose. They were filled with apt examples, making them readily understandable to the nonexpert. She passionately believed in the broad application of computers and made it her business to see that they should be increasingly easy to use. Since 1952 she had published more than fifty papers and articles on computer software and programming languages, helping to spread her influence even further. She also challenged her crew to question, to innovate, and to write. As a result she had been the inspiration for the navy computer magazine *CHIPS Ahoy,* which eleven years after her death is still going strong. The editors of *CHIPS* had promised "a wrinkled little lady in an admiral's suit to take care of the baby," and they did. Grace Hopper "has been a key part in the introduction of computers to human beings," Ken Olsen said in a speech in 1983. "She has been motivated by the desire to make work fun and exciting, to introduce innovation into all factors of our life . . . and above all, to make computers part of ordinary life for ordinary people."[55] Hopper retained her faith in technology to the end. In her later years she advocated the use of technology, and particularly information technology, to help combat pollution and protect the environment, and for weather and earthquake prediction. She often said that computers were humanizing, not the opposite, because, for example, bank accounts, insurance statements, and the like could now be tailor-made for each individual. In a paper she wrote in 1971, Hopper summed up these concerns. She believed that a world concerned with population, food supplies, and ecology would need to manipulate huge numbers of facts and would have to understand complex interrelationships in order to better manage the future. "The Computer can assist," Hopper pointed out, "but only insofar as they are recognized as man's most sophisticated tool, and as they are reformed to meet each man's specific needs rather than to flood the world with an unrequired avalanche of raw data."[56]

By this time Hopper had developed a grand, cosmic view of life. Looking ahead, she believed that the human race would one day have to leave Earth or be incinerated by the sun. She strongly supported space exploration and travel to prepare for that day, and she knew that computers were needed to solve many of the logistics problems of space travel such as the shape of vehicles, their metal composition, and life-support systems. Computers were needed to plot the course for space-ships, and small computers had to be developed to use onboard. She predicted that, even as everyone was being evacuated, there would be those who would not board the last spaceship to leave Earth because they would refuse to accept that the Earth would be burned up. Still, she had the satisfaction, she said, of knowing that she would have helped the human race to survive, because it was computers, among other things, that made space travel possible.[57]

This does not mean that Hopper was a blind advocate of computing. She had always understood its limitations and spent almost as much time warning people about what computers could not do as she had persuading them of what they could do. "Computers never have a new idea," she told an interviewer in 1972. "They have no imagination. They do only what they are told to do."[58] Or, as she put it more succinctly in other interviews: "garbage in, garbage out." "We spend a great deal of time training people for the technological side of things," she told a graduating class at the College of William and Mary in 1985. "How often have we remembered that we must train those people with a broad judgment to look at that information and make good use of it? They must know history; they must know economics; they must know philosophy, if they are going to make proper use of that information as we move into the future."[59] Computers may not replace human judgment but, according to Hopper, neither do they make mistakes. When Hopper had trouble with an account that confused her record with that of someone called Hooper, she sent a certified letter of complaint to the president of the company. "And don't try to put the blame on the computer," she admonished him. She received a very civil reply by return mail saying "Thank you for realizing I didn't make your error." It was signed, "Your favorite computer."[60]

She was certainly aware that she had seen, participated in, and influenced the development of modern computing. In the 1970s she began carrying around the latest technological marvel, a 3/8-inch square computer chip, which she kept in her purse to show to people. She explained that it had eight thousand components and was, in itself, a complete computer. Her historical sense made her concerned for the preservation of the record of these developments. She thought about giving her own records to the Naval Historical Center in the Washington Navy Yard but believed that the center was focused on collecting material on missiles and weapons rather than on computers. She therefore gave some of her papers to the Smithsonian Institution, even though she knew it was really more interested in earlier, mechanical computing devices than in electronic computing. Her hope was that the recently established Charles Babbage Institute at the University of Minnesota would become the repository for all the important documents relating to computing, including her own extensive collection. A great deal had been lost already: for example, the records of the Mark III, which had disappeared in the shuffle between navy and air force control. What she feared was that everything would remain scattered and eventually disappear. In spite of the excellent job done by the Charles Babbage Institute, much has in fact been lost.[61]

Hopper had seen many significant changes in her lifetime beyond those in computing. When she was growing up, the tallest building in New York City was only seven stories high. As a child looking across at the city from her grandfather's boat, Hopper remembers it looked flat. Riverside Drive along the Hudson River was still an unpaved dirt road. Families would sit outside next to the road on the weekends and watch the horses and carriages go by. Every electric light fixture in the city had a backup gas system because the electricity was still so unreliable. The trolley cars on Broadway had overhead wires, and of course the subway did not exist, nor did the tunnels under the Hudson. Hopper remembered their construction very well. She also remembered that when she moved to Philadelphia there were two phone companies, each one servicing half the city. You had to know which half you were calling in order to get the correct phone number.[62]

Hopper had kept up her strenuous travel schedule for the first two-and-a-half years with Digital until increasingly debilitated by a series of falls. She suffered from osteoporosis and her bones became more and more brittle. In 1990 she broke her arm for the second time in a fall at Dulles Airport from which she took a long time to recover. She left her apartment less and less, relying increasingly on Yavinsky for groceries and Dick Fredette to balance her checkbook. With the help of an assistant from Digital she did, however, continue to write articles occasionally. Her last, "Prioritizing Information," came out in *Byte* magazine only seven months before her death. In the article she took on the computer industry, chastising it for being seduced by any new technology instead of considering how to use it most effectively. "I'm afraid we'll continue to go out and buy pieces of hardware with flashing lights and lovely 'user friendly' software," she wrote, "and totally neglect the underlying subjects" such as how to ensure the best flow of information.[63]

On 16 September 1991, President George H. W. Bush awarded Hopper the nation's highest technology award, the National Medal of Technology. She was not well enough to attend the White House Rose Garden ceremony in which she and thirteen other recipients were honored for their "monumental accomplishments." "Today's award winners," noted President Bush, "range in age from the Pegasus Team of precocious 40-something scientists . . . who built the world's first private space rocket to Admiral Grace Hopper, born in 1906, who pioneered the revolution that put personal computers on the desks of millions of Americans—and dragged even this President into the computer age." Hopper was the first woman to win the award individually. Typically, she told her sister Mary, who had received the medal on her behalf, just to send it to her in the mail.[64]

Apparently unmoved by the antismoking campaign, Hopper continued to smoke more than a pack a day of her unfiltered Lucky Strikes until near her death. It was not the smoking that killed her directly, though. Her last fall in 1990 had seemed to sap some of her boundless energy and enthusiasm and she had become increasingly reclusive. When she was finally confined to her bed in mid-1991, she was cared for by Rita Yavinsky and Pearl until she finally needed twenty-four-hour care.[65]

Hopper was a die-hard Washington Redskins fan and knew the whole team by name. She would always abruptly end any telephone conversation when a Redskins game started on television. She used to tell Yavinsky that there was only one thing in Washington everybody knew about and that was the Redskins, so it was a safe topic. You could talk about the Redskins whether you were a Republican or a Democrat.

The Redskins were to play in the Super Bowl in 1992, and Hopper was thrilled. She told her nephew Roger that although she could not get up any more she would just have to watch them on television from her bed. But Hopper did not get to see them play. She died in her sleep on the first of January, "apparently of natural causes," according to the *New York Times*.[66] She had been ready to go, Yavinsky said, and was on her daybed under her two favorite ship prints and her admiral's seal when she slipped away. Five days later *Computerworld* magazine, calling Hopper the "mother of cobol," said that according to a Digital spokesman she died of "old age after a long period of ill health."[67]

Her obituary in the *New York Times* had a number of errors, but perhaps none so misleading as her comparison with the "combative personality" and "unorthodox approach" of Adm. Hyman Rickover.[68] Hopper, who often aptly described herself as a boat rocker, would have taken pleasure in the adjective "unorthodox." However, her approach, although straightforward and uncompromising, was never described as "combative" by those who knew her. Contrary occasionally, usually outspoken, but not aggressive. Of course, there were parallels; Rickover was known as the "father" of the nuclear navy, while Hopper was often called the mother of COBOL. She also resembled Rickover in another way: she, too, had to be forced out of the navy she loved. Early press reports in August 1986 reported Hopper's retirement as involuntary. The *Navy Times*, however, quoted a spokesman for navy secretary John Lehman as saying that Hopper was not being forced out. "It was her choice. She sent in a letter requesting voluntary retirement." Hopper herself denied that, telling the *Navy Times* that she had not planned on retirement. "I would have loved to stay in the navy and I wasn't ready to leave," she said. "But it's all about numbers and I guess they needed mine." Anyone who has read John Lehman's account of the painful scene when he asked Rickover for his resignation must sympathize with him for having to ease out two of the oldest and longest-serving naval officers of the twentieth century. Unlike Rickover, though, Hopper comported herself well. She came off as an officer and a lady, a credit to the service she loved.[69]

Hopper had originally intended to be buried at sea, but later in life she was captivated by genealogy and became the family historian. During her travels, particularly in Europe, she would always make time to plunge into the archives, noting with satisfaction on her return that she had "dug up another relative." This impressed on her the need for a gravestone so she could be found, so she decided on burial in Arlington National Cemetery.[70] The service was in the old

Ft. Myer chapel on 7 January, and Rita Yavinsky had insisted that Hopper have a pair of white gloves with her in the casket. Ever the lady, Hopper had never gone anywhere without her gloves. From the chapel a horse-drawn caisson slowly carried the flag-draped coffin to a grassy spot overlooking the Washington Memorial in the distance. Family, friends, and navy men and women followed, gathering around the gravesite for a brief ceremony, "Much like the way Grace liked her introductions," as one navy commander noted. Admiral Sutherland, who was there, thought there should have been more admirals in attendance, although nobody else seemed to notice any omissions. A navy chaplain wished her fair winds and following seas, a navy band played, there was a rifle salute, and then, finally, a cannon salute. Following the military honors, Hopper's youngest grandnephew, John Murray, was presented with the flag that had been draped over the casket. This was at the request of Hopper's brother Roger, to underline Hopper's belief in youth and the future.[71]

Adm. Frank B. Kelso II, the chief of naval operations, said of Hopper after her death that she was "a visionary in every sense of the word, and her contributions to the navy cannot be replicated. Our navy and our nation have lost an innovator, a teacher, a patriot, and a friend. At the same time that we grieve her death we remain grateful for the depth of her vision, her commitment to excellence and her boundless energy."[72]

Even after her death Hopper continued to receive awards and recognition. It was seventeen degrees below zero on 6 January 1996, and a bitter wind blew off the Kennebec River in Portland, Maine, but Hopper's nephew, Roger Murray, recalls that he did not care how cold it was. It could have been twenty degrees colder and he would have been perfectly warm because he was so proud to be there. Early that morning the Bath Iron Works Corporation launched *Hopper*, the eleventh *Arleigh Burke*–class destroyer, DDG-70. The ship was launched in the traditional manner, down the ways, although Bath Iron Works was turning more and more to floating new vessels out of flooded dry docks.[73]

True to its namesake, the ship surged purposefully ahead in spite of the temperature and the stiff wind, a tug pulling it out into the river to begin the trip to Portland for final fitting. A golden lion on the ship's emblem referred to Hopper's Scottish heritage, while its motto, *Aude et Effice*, Dare and Do, perfectly reflected her personal courage. In addition to Hopper's sister, Mary, her brother, Roger, and many family members and friends, the ceremony was attended by John H. Dalton, the secretary of the navy, as well as most of Maine's most prominent dignitaries, including the governor, Angus King; Senator Olympia Snowe; and Congressmen John Baldacci and James Longley. The speeches had to be cut short because of the intense cold.

Hopper took on its crew for the first time six months later, almost fifty-three years from the day its namesake began active duty at the Harvard Computation Laboratory, setting in motion the long career for which she was honored. In August, *Hopper* set sail for San Francisco, its home port, where it was commissioned on 6 September 1997. The ship carried a crew of 340, 45 of them women. It was 465.9 feet long and could reach a speed of 31 knots. It was very fitting that Grace Hopper, whose navy career had been entirely ashore and whose function was quintessentially support, should have a powerful warship named for her. Both she and the guided-missile destroyer were lean, purposeful, and high-tech. The Aegis destroyers, armed with stealth technology, are protected against most modern forms of attack. They can be shut down completely—for example, they can be made airtight in case of a chemical attack and then washed off after the attack. "Without . . . [Grace Hopper], computers would still be as big as ships," said *Hopper*'s new commanding officer at the commissioning, with pardonable zeal. There was a reception the evening before the ceremony and then a luncheon on deck after the commissioning, at which Senator Barbara Boxer spoke. Family and friends were given a tour of the vessel that Roger Murray still refers to as "my aunt's destroyer." At the end of the commissioning ceremony a piper played *Amazing Grace* on the bagpipes.[74]

One of the posthumous tributes that would have given Hopper the greatest pleasure was a three-day conference in September 1997 in San Jose, California. Organized to honor her, the conference was called the Grace Hopper Celebration of Women in Computing. With funding contributed by the National Science Foundation and other organizations, the conference had eight technical sessions, workshops, panels, and plenaries. Among the topics were some of Hopper's favorites, such as "Theory to Practice: Languages" and "Fundamentals: Systems." Others, including "Robotics" and "JAVA," showed how far the field had traveled since her death five years earlier.[75]

Hopper's navy work might best be summed up in a posthumous award presented by navy secretary Dalton on 13 May 1998. This was the Acquisition Pioneer Award, given to Hopper for her "visionary and innovative leadership in the development of computing technology for Naval warfare and mission support from 1944 to 1986."[76] Hopper never forgot that the navy got her into computing. Whenever she gave major addresses she did not want people bored with long lists of her accomplishments and honors, invariably asking to be introduced merely as "the third programmer on the first large-scale digital computer, the Mark I." Hopper was undoubtedly a key person in the early days of programming languages. In fact, she represented in her own person their entire history from MATH-MATIC in the 1950s to the development of COBOL for minicomputers in the 1980s.[77]

Roger Murray once said of his sister, and in her presence too, "You should not be deceived, by the uniform which she wears, into thinking that she is fundamentally a military type. . . . You have to remember that 'once a teacher always a teacher.'" His sister had dedicated her life to teaching, he maintained.[78]

Hopper began as a teacher, and from mentoring Ruth Brendel at Harvard to adjunct teaching at the University of Pennsylvania and George Washington University, she never really left the field. Even her move into computing was not as much of a change as it might at first appear. Like teaching, data processing was a support activity. In 1973 a Department of Defense memorandum on automatic data processing objectives stated: "Automatic data processing systems exist solely to provide responsive support to the operating and support forces. Supporting automatic data processing systems will be designed, developed, implemented, and operated with this paramount fact in mind."[79]

Hopper knew she was providing the tools of support. In a 1979 interview she was typically frank:

> To me, I guess basically when you come down to it, I have never done anything that's intellectually great. Everything I have done has been based on common sense. If I was going to copy subroutines out of a notebook I might as well let the computer do it. . . . It's basically common sense in everything I did—no mathematical genius, no theory.[80]

And yet she could never have changed the practice of computing as she did without some very particular gifts. Always unconventional in her thinking, Hopper scorned the customary and traditional, was impatient with the status quo, and approached problem solving with instinctive innovation. Putting aside the excessive rhetoric and the overblown claims that were made on her behalf, Hopper did make real contributions to programming languages and information processing. The most critical were her development of the compiler, her creation of FLOW-MATIC, and her understanding of the significance of Howard Aiken's design for the Mark I: the idea of the separation of data from procedures. Even more important, perhaps, was her persistent and persuasive advocacy of higher-level languages, which helped to shape the early advances in programming. But the contribution of which Hopper remained most proud was not any of these; she believed they would eventually have been made by someone else if not by her. She thought her greatest accomplishment was all the young people she had taught over the years. The brand-new programmers she trained went on to become heads of programming departments and vice presidents, and they in turn trained others. This was her legacy; these were her offspring.[81]

Looking back from the lofty vantage point of a rear admiral, Hopper wrote down her personal recollections of Howard Aiken and the Mark I. "For me the Mark I will always be my favorite computer," she wrote, "because I know exactly how to tell her what to do." Howard Aiken "didn't only teach us about computers," she continued. "He taught us to be part of the navy . . . and that, too, is a lesson which has stayed with me ever since, and which I value highly." She ended, "No matter how long I live, no matter how many more different jobs I may have, I have already been given the highest reward I'll ever receive, the privilege and the responsibility of serving very proudly in the United States Navy and of programming and operating the Mark I."[82]

Notes

Abbreviations Used in the Notes

ACNP(W)   Records of the Assistant Chief of Naval Personnel for Women, microfilm, Lehman College Library, CUNY, Bronx, NY

CBI BCF   Biography and Clippings File, Charles Babbage Institute, University of Minnesota, Minneapolis

CBI Bloch   Richard Bloch Interview by William Aspray, 22 February 1984, OH66, Charles Babbage Institute, University of Minnesota, Minneapolis

CBI Campbell   Robert V. D. Campbell Interview by William Aspray, 22 February 1984, OH67, Charles Babbage Institute, University of Minnesota, Minneapolis

CBI Fox Papers   Margaret Fox Papers, CBI 45, Charles Babbage Institute, University of Minnesota, Minneapolis

CBI Hopper   Grace Hopper Interview by Christopher Evans, 1976, OH81, Charles Babbage Institute, University of Minnesota, Minneapolis

CBI Stein Papers   Marvin Stein Papers, CBI 10, Charles Babbage Institute, University of Minnesota, Minneapolis

Fredette Interviews   Richard L. Fredette Interviews by author, 9 January 2001 and 7 June 2001

Gealt Interview   Norma Gealt Interview by author, 11 June 2001

Hagley   Sperry Univac Records accession 1825, The Hagley Museum and Library, Greenville, DE

Hagley Hopper Interview   Grace M. Hopper Oral History Interview by Philip Holmer, 20 July 1979, Sperry Univac Records accession 1825, The Hagley Museum and Library, Greenville, DE

HUA   Harvard University Archives, Cambridge, MA

JVHW Interview   John V. H. Westcote Interview by author, 23 November 2002

MMW Interview   Mary Murray Westcote interviews by author, 1, 23 October 1999; 2, 11 December 1999

MMW Papers   Mary Murray Westcote Papers, courtesy MMW

NA2   National Archives II, College Park, MD

NAMAR   National Archives Mid-Atlantic Region, Philadelphia, PA

NDL Hopper   Grace Hopper File, Navy Department Library, Naval Historical Center, Washington Navy Yard, Washington, DC

NHC/OA   Operational Archives, Naval Historical Center, Washington Navy Yard, Washington, DC

NMAH Hopper Collection   Grace Hopper Collection, 1944–1965, National Museum of American History Archives Center, Smithsonian Institution, Washington, DC

NMAH Hopper Interview 1968   Grace Hopper Interview by Uta Merzbach, July 1968, folders 5, 6, 7, box 11, series 1, Computer Oral History Collection acc. 196, National Museum of American History, Smithsonian Institution, Washington, DC

NMAH Hopper Interview 1972   Grace Hopper Interview by Henry Tropp, 5 July 1972, folder 9, box 11, series 1, Computer Oral History Collection accession 196, National Museum of American History, Smithsonian Institution, Washington, DC

NPRC/OMPF   Grace Murray Hopper, Officer Fitness Report [OFR], Official
Military Personnel File, National Personnel Records Center, National
Archives and Records Administration, St. Louis, MO
NRL   Naval Research Laboratory Archives, Anacostia, Washington, DC.
NYU   Vincent Foster Hopper Biographical Files, New York University Archives,
NYU Libraries, New York, NY
RBN Interview   Ruth Brendel Noller Interview by author, 23 December 1996
RFMIII Interview   Roger F. Murray III Interview by author, 1 July 2001
RG   Record Group
SL Hopper Interview   Capt. Grace Hopper Interview by Linda Calvert, 3
September 1982 to 28 February 1983, OH46, Women in Federal Government
Oral History Project, Schlesinger Library, Radcliffe Institute, Cambridge,
MA.
SL Reynard Papers   Elizabeth Reynard Papers, A-128, Schlesinger Library,
Radcliffe Institute, Cambridge, MA
VCL Hopper   Grace Hopper, Biographical Files, Special Collections, Vassar
College Libraries, Poughkeepsie, NY
WMW Letters   Walter Murray Westcote Letters to author, August 2003
WNRC   Accession numbers 75-0056, 82-0007, 82-0011, 78-0033, 75-0045, 75-
0056, 78-0034. All in Record Group 38 (CNO), Washington National Records
Center, Suitland, MD
WTWIII Letters   William T. Westcote III Letters to author, December 2002 to
May 2003
Yavinsky Interview   Rita Yavinsky Interview by author, 7 July 2001
Yavinsky Papers   Rita Yavinsky Papers, courtesy Rita Yavinsky

Chapter 1. Remember Your Great-Grandfather the Admiral

1. Whitelaw, *Grace Hopper*, 11–12; Billings, *Hopper*, 20. Parts of this book appeared previously in Williams, *Improbable Warriors*.
2. CBI Hopper Interview, 11; for quote see, "Computer Sciences Man of the Year," 7.
3. For "maverick" remark see SL Hopper Interview, 18; MMW Interview, 2: 7.
4. WTWIII Letters.
5. WTWIII Letters; MMW Interview, 1: 24–26; WMW Letters.
6. "Computer Sciences Man of the Year," 7.
7. Tim Clark, "The Commodore and the *Constitution*," *Yankee*, July 1985, n.d., VCL.
8. Alexander Wilson Russell, Rear Admiral, USN, biography in Hopper File, NDL; Nofi, *Marine Corps Book of Lists*, 141–44; SL Hopper Interview, 22. Hopper's ancestry, dating to the American Revolution, is on file at the Daughters of the American Revolution in Washington, DC, as is Hopper's own application to the DAR dated March 1951 #401-440.
9. Family tree compiled by Pieter Van Horne, courtesy of William Westcote; Whitelaw, *Grace Hopper*, 12; "Navy Computer Grandmother Keeps Moving," *The* [Baltimore] *Sun*, September 26, 1975, B8.
10. Whitelaw, *Grace Hopper*, 13–14; "Navy Computer Grandmother Keeps Moving," *The* [Baltimore] *Sun*, 26 September 1975, B8; MMW Interview, 1: 61; JVHW Interview, 1–2; SL Hopper Interview, 3; WMW Letters.
11. MMW Interview 2: 2–3; JVHW Interview, 1–2.
12. MMW Interview, 1: 10; JVHW Interview, 1.
13. RMIII, 12; MMW Interview, 1: 13.
14. SL Hopper Interview, 18, 154; JVHW Interview, 2.
15. *The Agora*, Centennial Year Book, 1816–1916, The Graham School, New York City, 38, MMW Papers; I am grateful to the Collegiate School for information on its history.
16. *The Agora*, 38, MMW Papers.
17. *The Agora*, 55, MMW Papers.
18. RMIII. Interview, 30–31; JVHW Interview, 15–16; WMW Letters.
19. SL Hopper Interview, 157.
20. MMW Interview, 1: 26, 56; JVHW Interview, 4–5.
21. RMIII Interview, 12; JVHW Interview, 5.
22. MMW Interview, 1: 19.
23. SL Hopper Interview, 17; Chafe, *American Woman*, 103–4; Hopper's sister Mary graduated in 1930 and her brother Roger graduated from Yale in 1932.
24. Sussman, "Pentagon Computer Pioneer—They Won't Let Her Retire," n.p.
25. SL Hopper Interview, 5,113.
26. NMAH Hopper 1968, 5; "1928 in 1938," Vassar Class Bulletin 11: 16, VCL; Rhodes, *The Making of the Atomic Bomb*, 126–27.
27. Brooks, *Government of Science*, 21–23; Rees, "The Mathematical Sciences and World War II," 607, the quote is by William Prager; Penick et al, *Politics of American Science*, 5; Brown, *A Radar History of World War II*, 79, 315. Courant's bother-in-law was the famous German radar engineer, Wilhelm Runge.
28. MMW Interview, 1: 54, 59.
29. SL Hopper Interview, 4–5, 7. For similar observations see Chafe, *American Woman*, 89–111; and Rees, "Support of Higher Education," 374.
30. "Grace Murray Hopper and Devils, Too," Letters, *Vassar Quarterly*, vol. 93, no. 1 (Winter 1996): 2, VCL; MMW Interview, 1: 41.

31. MMW Interview, 1: 20–21.
32. "Memorial Minute for Vincent Foster Hopper," NYU Graduate Faculty Minutes, 1 March 1976, NYU.
33. MMW Interview, 1: 19–21; SL Hopper Interview, 151.
34. SL Hopper Interview, 151; Yavinsky Interview, 33.
35. NMAH Hopper Interview 1968, 17.
36. NMAH Hopper Interview 1972, 2.
37. NMAH Hopper Interview 1968, 17–29, 37.
38. NMAH Hopper Interview 1968, 31–32; RMIII, 1–6.
39. Tropp, "Grace Hopper," 8; NMAH Hopper Interview 1968, 4; Hopper Biographical File, VCL; Etzkowitz, Kemelgor, and Uzzi, *Athena Unbound*, 44–45; Murray, *Women Becoming Mathematicians*, 5.
40. Chafe, *American Woman*, 89–111; Rees, "Support of Higher Education," 374; SL Hopper Interview, 114.
41. For marriage and career paths of women mathematicians see Murray, *Women Becoming Mathematicians*, 35–39, 155–60.
42. NMAH Hopper Interview 1968, 38.
43. SL Hopper Interview, 18, 153; Phillips Academy, Andover, *The Andover Bulletin*, 90, MMW Papers.
44. NMAH Hopper Interview 1968, 41–42.
45. NMAH Hopper Interview 1968, 32–33; "Memorial Minute for Vincent Foster Hopper," NYU Graduate Faculty Minutes, 1 March 1976, NYU.
46. MMW Interview, 1: 21; Cushman, "Admiral Hopper's Farewell," *New York Times*, 14 August 1986.
47. MMW Interview, 1: 21–22; JVHW Interview, 10, 30.
48. Gildersleeve, *The "Waves" of the Navy*, 267; Letters/Memorandum to District/ Air Command Directors (1943–1948), roll 4, series I, ACNP(W), NHC/OA.
49. Holm, *Women in the Military*, 26–27; R. Adm. Jacob's quote is from Senate hearings on S 2527, 19 May 1942, Hearings on WAVE Legislation and Public Laws, 1942–48, roll 19, series III, ACNP(W), NHC/OA. See also Hancock, *Lady in the Navy*, 55–56.
50. Grace M. Hopper, "Howard H. Aiken and the Mark I: Some Personal Recollections," 1, typescript, Yavinsky Papers; MMW Interview, 2: 47.
51. SL Hopper Interview, 10.
52. NMAH Hopper Interview 1972, 17.
53. "Plainfielder's Niece is Operator of Robot Einstein," *Plainfield Courier-News*, Plainfield, NJ, 8 August 1944, 1; Vincent Foster Hopper, Faculty Biography, March 1953, NYU; *Granite State News*, Wolfeboro, NH, 24 December 1943, Wolfeboro Public Library; NMAH Hopper Interview 1972, 55.
54. David Taylor Model Basin memo, 27 April 1943, folder AMP, box 36, RG298 (ONR), NA2.
55. U.S. Office of Education, Information Bulletin, February 1942, file 127, box 8, A-128, SL Reynard Papers.
56. U.S. Office of Education, Information Bulletin, February 1942, Faculty National Service Committee Report of Progress, 13 March 1942, School of Engineering to Dean Gildersleeve, 28 January and 19 February 1942, file 127, box 8, A-128, SL Reynard Papers.
57. Williams, *Improbable Warriors*, 13–14.
58. NMAH Hopper Interview 1968, 35.
59. "Ordnance Unit 4-3 Boasts of Expert," *4ND Naval Reserve News* (June 1953): 26, MMW Papers.
60. Hopper, "Aiken and the Mark I," 2, typescript, n.d., Yavinsky Papers; NMAH Hopper 1968, 37.

61. NMAH Hopper Interview 1968, 35–36.
62. Ibid.
63. Ibid., 35, 38.
64. Text of the commission is RBN Interview, 64. No emphasis in original. NMAH Hopper Interview 1968, 40; NMAH Hopper Interview 1972, 14.
65. NMAH Hopper Interview 1972, 13.
66. SL Hopper Interview, 46.

Chapter 2. You're in the Navy Now

1. Navy Liaison Office to Chief, BuShips, 3 July 1944, folder NC1/Harvard, box 374, Gen. Corr. 1940–45, RG19, NA2. Mitchell, *Grace Murray Hopper,* 1–11, 24–37, 50–51, 63–64; Billings, *Hopper,* 30, 36–38, 47–53, 111, 115.
2. NMAH Hopper Interview 1968, 1, 43.
3. Capt. Solberg to Director, Rad. Lab., 14 June 1944, folder NC1/Harvard, box 374, Gen. Corr. 1940–45, RG19, NA2.
4. Quoted in Cohen, *Makin' Numbers,* 185.
5. NMAH Hopper Interview 1968, 43–44.
6. CBI Hopper Interview, 1.
7. NMAH Hopper Interview 1968, xx–xxi; Samuel S. Snyder, "Influence of U.S. Cryptologic Organizations on the Digital Computer Industry," box 4, SRH-03, RG457, NA2; Boslaugh, *When Computers Went to Sea,* xxiii, 76–77. CSAW, generally known simply as the Communications Annex, was based in a former girls' school in northwest Washington. Barlett, "Sugar Camp Reunion," 1.
8. Folder "Bell Telephone Labs," box A-C, 289.2005, Aiken Correspondence, HUA; Hartree, *Calculating Instruments and Machines,* 80; Cohen, "Howard Aiken and the Beginnings of Computer Science," 303; Spencer, *Great Men and Women of Computing,* preface.
9. Hodges, *Alan Turing,* 298–99; Cohen, "Howard Aiken and the Beginnings of Computer Science," 306; Burke, *Information and Secrecy,* 264–65, 281.
10. CBI Hopper Interview, 2.
11. "Robot Brain at Harvard Hot News Copy," *Boston News Week,* n.d., clipping from IBM Archives, Somers, NY; for "algebraic superbrain:" see: "Algebra Machine Spurs Research Calling for Long Calculations," *New York Times,* 7 August 1944.
12. Welch, "Computer Scientist Howard Hathaway Aiken," 47.
13. "Highbrow Harvard Bows to a Robot Brain," *Sunday Mirror Magazine,* 5 August 1945.
14. Welch, "Computer Scientist Howard Hathaway Aiken," 43–44; CBI Campbell Interview, 12.
15. Bloch interview by author, 12 September 1997; CBI Bloch Interview, 5; Cohen, new foreword, *A Manual of Operations for the Automatic Sequence Controlled Calculator,* xiii, for Aiken quote.
16. Pugh, *Memories That Shaped an Industry,* 6; "General Purpose Digital Computers," n.d., folder "Bell Telephone Labs," box A-C, UAV 289.2005, Aiken Correspondence, HUA.
17. Aiken to Dr. Arnold Lowan, 1 November 1944, folder "(dead) BuOrd," box A-C, UAV 289.2005, Aiken Correspondence, HUA.
18. Hopper, "Aiken and the Mark I," 6, Yavinsky Papers.
19. "IBM Automatic Sequence Controlled Calculator," 6, IBM Archives; "Plainfielder's Niece is Operator of Robot Einstein," *Plainfield Courier-News,* Plainfield, NJ, 8 August 1944, 1.
20. "IBM Automatic Sequence Controlled Calculator," 6, IBM Archives; "Plainfielder's Niece is Operator of Robot Einstein," *Plainfield Courier-News,* 1;

Grant, "35-Ton Super-Brain," *New York Herald Tribune;* "Algebra Machine Spurs Research," *New York Times,* 1.

21. "IBM Automatic Sequence Controlled Calculator," 5, IBM Archives; Hartree, *Calculating Instruments and Machines,* 74–79; Aiken and Hopper, "The Automatic Sequence Controlled Calculator - I," 1–4.

22. George Stibitz, "History of 7.5," n.d. but forwarded with letter of 22 March 1946, folder "Division 7," box 10, RG227, NA2.

23. NMAH Hopper Interview 1972, 32 for quote; CBI Hopper Interview, 3.

24. NMAH Hopper Interview 1972, 44–45.

25. RBN Interview, 3–4, 20.

26. RBN Interview, 22, 64.

27. RBN Interview, 3, 5; Cohen, *Howard Aiken,* 245, for 1964 Goode Award quote and for Cohen's view of Aiken as a teacher.

28. RBN Interview, 7–8.

29. RBN Interview, 7, 43.

30. RBN Interview, 7, 41–42.

31. CBI Campbell Interview, 61; Petty Officer Delo A. Calvin, letter to author, 10 March 1998, 2; RBN Interview, 18.

32. Calvin letter to author, 1–2; NMAH Hopper Interview 1968, 52.

33. "Harvard Gets Huge Calculator," Boston *Daily Globe,* 7 August 1944, n. p., folder 9, box 6, NMAH Hopper Collection; Grant, "35-Ton Super-Brain," *New York Herald Tribune,* 7 August 1944; Campbell-Kelly, *Computer,* 75–76.

34. Conant, foreword to *A Manual of Operation for the Automatic Sequence Controlled Calculator, Annals of the Computation Laboratory of Harvard University,* vol. 1 ; CBI Campbell Interview, 15–19, 21; CBI Bloch Interview, 17–18; Pugh, *Memories,* 6.

35. NMAH Hopper Interview 1972, 72–75; Shapley to Aiken, 22 September 1944, box Correspondence P-S, UAV 298.2005, Computation Laboratory, HUA.

36. *Harvard Alumni Bulletin* 47, no. 1 (September 1944), folder 21, box 6, NMAH Hopper Collection.

37. Contract NObs-14966, folder "BuShips Computing Project," box 6, UAV 885.95.2, World War II Government Contract Records, HUA; Hershberg, *James B. Conant,* 128; Spencer, *Great Men and Women of Computing,* 55; Stewart, *Organizing,* for administrative history of OSRD.

38. Bush, foreword, in Stewart, *Organizing,* ix–x; Burke, *Information,* 224, 291, 276, 297.

39. Mina Rees to Cdr. H. H. Aiken, 2 January 1945, folder "(dead) BuOrd," box A-C, UAV 289.2005, Aiken Correspondence, HUA; Letter to Capt. T. A Solberg, BuShips, from Warren Weaver, NDRC, 26, June 1944, folder June 1944–July 1944, box 72, series II, Sperry Acc.1825, Hagley.

40. Burke, *Information,* 290–303; Cortada, *Before the Computer,* 203.

41. Stewart, *Organizing,* 57. For an account of organizing science for war in major Allied and Axis countries see Hartcup, *The Effect of Science on the Second World War.*

42. Light, "When Computers Were Women," 455–83; Warren Weaver to Cdr. J. T. Flynn, 30 November 1943, folder AMP, box 36, RG298 (ONR), NA2. For "girl hours" see, for example, Memo, Visit to Harvard, 18 September 1944, folder September–October 1944, box 72, series II, Sperry acc. 1825, Hagley.

43. "Anonymous Research Contracts and Approximate Number of Employees at 8/31/44," folder "Personnel," box 2, UAV 885.95.2, WWII Government Contract Records, HUA.

44. Baxter, *Scientists against Time,* 21–22; Hartcup, *The Effect of Science,* 9–10.

45. Rees, "Mathematics and the Government," 1–4, Rees Collection, CUNY.

46. Rees, "The Mathematical Sciences and World War II," 608–9; Rees, "Mathematics and the Government," 4, Rees Collection, CUNY.

47. Rodgers, *Think*, 143; Cohen, "Howard Aiken and the Beginnings of Computer Science," 30; Capt. W. G Schindler, Officer-in-Charge, Naval Ordnance Laboratory, to Dr. John Mauchly, 20 June 1944, folder 01891-02549, box 70, series II, Sperry acc. 1825, Hagley.

48. Cortada, *Before the Computer*, 203; Goldstine, *The Computer*, 130–31.

49. Richard M. Bloch, "Programming the Mark I," 3, unpublished typescript courtesy of Dick Bloch; CBI Hopper Interview, 6.

50. SL Hopper Interview, 13–14, 26; NMAH Hopper Interview 1972, 21–22; Spencer, *Great Men and Women of Computing*, 107–9; Shapley to Aiken, 9 February 1945, box Correspondence P-S, UAV 298-2005, Computation Laboratory, HUA.

51. CBI Hopper Interview, 20–23; NMAH Hopper Interview 1972, 39; MMW Interview, 57; Campbell interview by author, 12 September 1997; and Bloch interview by author, 12 September 1997 for "tough hombre" remark.

52. NMAH Hopper Interview 1972, 41.

53. Campbell interview by author, 12 September 1997; Cohen, "Howard Aiken and the Beginning of Computer Science," 306.

54. RBN Interview, 9, 41.

55. NMAH Hopper Interview 1972, 50; RBN Interview, 7, 57.

56. Campbell interview by author, 12 September 1997; NMAH Hopper Interview 1968, 50–51.

57. NMAH Hopper Interview 1972, 42.

58. Ibid., 46–47.

59. NMAH Hopper Interview 1972, 36–37; Bloch, "Programming the Mark I," 59.

60. NMAH Hopper Interview 1972, 49.

61. Bloch, "Programming the Mark I," 3; CBI Campbell Interview, 62; Hopper, "Aiken and the Mark I," 15, Yavinsky Papers.

62. NMAH Hopper Interview 1968, 45; NMAH Hopper Interview 1972, 25.

63. Diary of Mina Rees, EXCO AMP, 6 March 1944, folder AMP Mtgs. 1943–46, box 1, RG227, NA2; Diary of Mina Rees, EXCO AMP, 25 February 1945, folder AMP Mtgs. 1943–46, box 1, RG227, NA2.

64. NMAH Hopper Interview 1968, 52–55; Cohen, *Makin' Numbers*, 60, 126.

65. Report No.7, July 1944, BuShips Computation Project Reports 1944–1945, NRL; *Annals of the Computation Laboratory*, vol. 26, (1951), 5; CBI Hopper Interview, 2, for quote.

66. Report No.11, December 1944, BuShips Computation Project, NRL; Bob Campbell to author, 16 August 1998; Cohen, *Makin' Numbers*, 101; Solberg to Weaver, 6 July 1944, folder June 1944–July 1944, box 72, Sperry acc. 1825, Hagley. Cohen, *Howard Aiken*, 165, believed that no one at the lab knew the purpose of von Neumann's calculations until Hiroshima.

67. CBI Campbell Interview, 23; Cohen, "Howard Aiken and the Beginnings of Computer Science," 318.

68. Chief BuShips from NRL, 3 January 1945, folder "(Dead) BuOrd," box A-C, UAV 289.2005, Aiken Correspondence, HUA.

69. Navy Liaison Officer to Chief, BuShips, 21 July 1944, folder NC1/Harvard, box 374, Gen. Corr. 1940–45, RG19 (BuShips), NA2; CBI Campbell Interview, 22.

70. Chief BuShips from NRL, 3 January 1945, folder "(Dead) BuOrd," box A-C, UAV 289.2005, Aiken Correspondence, HUA; Navy Liaison Officer to Chief, BuShips, 21 July 1944, folder NC1/Harvard, box 374, Gen. Corr. 1940–45, RG19, NA2; CBI Campbell Interview, 22; Reports no.10, October 1944, no.8, August 1944, no.5, June 1944, BuShips Computation Project, NRL; Cohen,

Makin' Numbers, 3; Chief, BuShips to Navy Liaison Officer, 25 May 1944, folder NC1/Harvard, box 374, Gen. Corr. 1940–45, RG19, NA2.

71. Computation Project, Report of Activity to 16 August 1944, folder NC1/Harvard, box 374, RG19, NA2.

72. Interim Progress Reports to AMP, 21 August 1944, 23 October 1944, 24 January 1945, folder "Project No. 10–Harvard Univ.," box 13, RG 227, NA2; quote is from Interim Report to AMP, 24 June 1944, folder "Project No. 10–Harvard Univ.," box 13, RG 227, NA2.

73. Warren Weaver to Mina Rees, 9 March 1945, folder "Project No.2," box 4, RG 227, NA2; Mina Rees to Oswald Veblen, 9 June 1945, folder "War Science," box 19, RG 227, NA2.

74. NMAH Hopper Interview 1968, 46; Hopper, "Aiken and the Mark I," 16, Yavinsky Papers.

75. NMAH Hopper Interview 1968, 46.

76. Campbell and Bloch interview by author, 12 September 1997; NMAH Hopper Interview 1972, 1–2.

77. SL Hopper Interview, 139–40; NMAH Hopper Interview 1968, 47–48.

78. NMAH Hopper Interview 1968, 48.

79. Ibid., 47.

80. Hopper, "Aiken and the Mark I," 12, Yavinsky Papers.

81. RBN Interview, 6, 43; NMAH Hopper Interview 1968, 51–52.

82. L. S. Dederick to W. Weaver, 20 March 1945, folder "Aberdeen Proving Ground," box 5, RG 227, NA2.

83. CBI Hopper Interview, 11.

84. Ibid., 6, 11.

85. Ibid., 7, 11–12.

86. Hopper, "Aiken and the Mark I," 17, Yavinsky Papers; RBN Interview, 37.

87. Hagley Hopper Interview, 2; CBI Hopper Interview, 14; Hopper, "Aiken and the Mark I," 19, Yavinsky Papers.

88. EMCC of Remington Rand, product literature, 1951, box 7, CBI#8, CBI Fox for quotes; Hartree, *Calculating*, 81; CBI Hopper Interview, 7–9; Campbell interview by author, 1 February 1998.

89. SL Hopper Interview, 24; Stevens, "New, Faster Mechanical Brain," 11.

90. *New York Times*, 3 January 1992. See also *New York Times*, 22 April 2000.

91. Hopper, "Aiken and the Mark I," 6, Yavinsky Papers.

92. Hopper, "Aiken and the Mark I," 9, Yavinsky Papers.

93. Aiken to Dr. Arnold Lowan, 1 November 1944, folder "(dead) BuOrd, 13-11," box A-C, UAV.289.2005, Aiken Correspondence, HUA.

94. NMAH Hopper 1972, 18–19; RBN Interview, 54.

95. NMAH Hopper Interview 1972, 26; Tim Clark, "The Commodore and the Constitution," *Yankee*, July 1985, Grace Hopper, Biographical File, Special Collections, VCL; RBN Interview, 42, 51.

96. JVHW Interview, 5; WTW Letters.

97. RBN Interview, 30.

98. NMAH Hopper Interview 1972, 27; CBI Hopper Interview, 20 for quote.

99. CBI Hopper Interview, 3.

100. EMCC of Remington Rand, product literature, 1951, box 7, CBI#8, CBI Fox; "30-ton 'Brain'," 58; SL Hopper Interview, 15, 32.

101. Hopper interview, OH81 4, CBI.

102. CBI Hopper Interview, 4, for ENIAC quote; Hagley Hopper Interview, 13.

103. Bashe et al., *IBM's Early Computers*, 32.

104. Hopper, "Aiken and the Mark I," 13, Yavinsky Papers; EMCC of Remington Rand product literature, 1951, box 7, CBI#8, CBI Fox.

105. R&D Div. to BuOrd, 24 October 1945, folder R&D October 1945, box 11, RG298, NA2 for quote; Chief, ORI to Chief, BuPers, 5 November 1945, folder Staff—November 1945, box 112, Gen. Corr. 1941–46, RG298, NA2.

106. ORI to CO, Boston Branch, ORI, 5 December 1945, folder Staff December 1945, box 112, Gen. Corr. 1941–46, RG298, NA2.

107. "Recommendation for Centralized Computation Laboratory," 14 November 1944, folder Mathematical Laboratory, box 46, Gen. Corr. 1941–46, RG298, NA2.

108. Navy Liaison Officer to Chief, BuShips, 14 November 1944, folder Mathematical Laboratory, box 46, Gen. Corr. 1941–46, RG298, NA2.

109. Memo: "Calculating Machine—Probable uses at NRL," 31 July 1945, folder Mathematical Laboratory, box 46, Gen. Corr. 1941–46, RG298, NA2; Memo: "Mechanics and Electricity Division's Use of Computing Machine," 1 August 1945, folder Mathematical Laboratory, box 46, Gen. Corr. 1941–46, RG298, NA2.

110. "Progress Report No. 12, Harvard Computation Laboratory," September 1950–October 1950," 1, box 1, series I, Technitrol Suit Records, Accession 1901, Hagley.

111. "The President's Report," Harvard University, 1946, 10–11, folder 9, box 4, NMAH Hopper Collection; "Highbrow Harvard Bows to Robot Brain," *Sunday Mirror Magazine*, 5 August 1945.

112. Hopper interview 1972, 36–37.

113. SL Hopper Interview, 13.

114. Stevens, "New, Faster Mechanical Brain," 11.

115. The two books are: I. Bernard Cohen, *Howard Aiken: Portrait of a Computer Pioneer*, 1999, and I. Bernard Cohen and Gregory W. Welch, eds., *Makin' Numbers: Howard Aiken and the Computer*, 1999.

116. Cohen, "Howard Aiken and the Beginnings of Computer Science," 320–22; "Aiken, Howard," in Ralston, ed., *Encyclopedia of Computing*, 41. See also *Annals of the Computation Laboratory*, vols.16, 26.

117. Welch, "Computer Scientist Howard Hathaway Aiken," 4, 76, 101–2, 109, 115; Campbell interview by author, 12 September 1997; Cohen, "Babbage and Aiken," 183; "Harvard Receives $25 Million," 1, 6.

118. Hopper, "Aiken and the Mark I," 21, Yavinsky Papers.

119. RBN Interview, 4.

120. Hagley Hopper Interview, 1; WMW Letters.

121. SL Hopper Interview, 43–46; Billings, *Hopper*, 60.

122. SL Hopper Interview, 142.

123. SL Hopper Interview, 15; "Harvard Computation Laboratory," 856; NMAH Hopper Interview 1972, 21–22; Spencer, *Great Men and Women of Computing*, 107–9.

124. Sara White, "MIT Scientist Rebels at War Research Talk," *Boston Traveler*, n.d., folder 24, box 6, NMAH Hopper Collection.

125. Rodgers, *Think*, 173–74, for Watson; NMAH Hopper Interview 1972, 73.

126. NMAH Hopper Interview 1972, 51–53.

127. Hopper, "Aiken and the Mark I," 20, Yavinsky Papers.

128. Wexelblat, ed., *History of Programming Languages*, 21.

129. Hopper, "Aiken and the Mark I," 21–22, Yavinsky Papers.

130. Hopper, "Aiken and the Mark I," 20, Yavinsky Papers; NMAH Hopper Interview 1972, 86–87, for quote.

Chapter 3. Women Enter the World of Technology

1. McCartney, *ENIAC,* 154–55.
2. Schimelpfenig, "Navy's Computer Expert."
3. "Announcements," 593; SL Hopper Interview, 28, and 41 for quote.
4. NMAH Hopper Interview 1972, 14.
5. SL Hopper Interview, 30–31, 47; "Aiken" in Ralston, ed., *Encyclopedia of Computer Science and Engineering,* 685–86; Hagley Hopper Interview, 1; McCartney, *ENIAC,* 152.
6. SL Hopper Interview, 162.
7. SL Hopper Interview, 162; for "kick" quote see Trudy Willis, "Women, Computers Called a Good Team," *The Roanoke Times,* 27 January 1972, folder Dr. Hopper thank you letters, box 20, acc. 75-0056, RG38, WNRC.
8. NMAH Hopper Interview 1972, 80–81.
9. Stibitz Report on Computing Machines, 25 May 1946, 16, box 10, CBI #4, CBI Fox.
10. "The UNIVAC SYSTEM," product literature (emphasis in original), box 7, CBI #8, CBI Fox.
11. EMCC contract with National Bureau of Standards, 25 June 1948, box 10, CBI #4, CBI Fox; "Relations with Eckert-Mauchly Computer Corporation," box 8, CBI #8, CBI Fox. For an explanation of how early computer designers failed to allow for the difficulty of programming their devices, I am indebted to Beyer, *Grace Hopper and the History of Computer Programming.*
12. H. A. Bruno and Associates, "Background Material in Connection with the Dedication of the UNIVAC," n.d., box 7, CBI #8, CBI Fox.
13. EMCC of Remington Rand product literature, 1951, box 7, CBI #8, CBI Fox.
14. Ibid.
15. H. A. Bruno and Associates, "Background Material in Connection with the Dedication of the UNIVAC," n.d., box 7, CBI #8, CBI Fox; "Performance of the Census Univac System," paper presented December 10–12, 1951, box 11, CBI #4, CBI Fox.
16. H. A. Bruno and Associates, "Background Material in Connection with the Dedication of the UNIVAC," n.d., box 7, CBI #8, CBI Fox.
17. SL Hopper Interview, 42; Billings, *Hopper,* 65, for "logic" quote.
18. SL Hopper Interview, 32.
19. Levitas, "Thinking Machine Tamer," 27.
20. CBI Hopper, 22.
21. SL Hopper Interview, 40, 49, 178.
22. CBI Hopper, 22.
23. "Grace Hopper Mixes Insight, Foresight," 4.
24. Rossiter, *Women Scientists in America, 1940–1972,* 259, 299; Woodfield, *Women, Work, and Computing,* 3–4.
25. McCartney, *ENIAC,* 95–97, 151–52; SL Hopper Interview, 168.
26. Hagley Hopper Interview, 1–2.
27. Ibid. Holberton went with the UNIVAC machine to work for the navy at the David Taylor Model Basin. She has only recently received some long-overdue recognition for her accomplishments. See McCartney, *ENIAC,* 95–97, 151–52, and Petzinger's two 1996 *Wall Street Journal* articles.
28. SL Hopper Interview, 3.
29. Grace Hopper, "The Education of a Computer," reprinted from *Proceedings, Symposium on Industrial Applications of Automatic Computing Equipment,* Midwest Research Institute, Kansas City, MO, 8–9 January 1953, CBI BCF.
30. Hopper, "Automatic Programming," undated typescript, 10, CBI Stein Papers.

31. Ibid., 10–12, CBI Stein Papers.
32. Wexelblat, ed., *History of Programming Languages,* 11.
33. Hopper, "Automatic Programming," undated typescript, 12, CBI Sein Papers; Wexelblat, ed., *History of Programming Languages,* 9.
34. Wexelblat, ed., *History of Programming Languages,* 12.
35. Ibid., 10.
36. Grace Hopper, "The Education of a Computer," 141, reprinted from *Proceedings,* Symposium on Industrial Applications of Automatic Computing Equipment, Midwest Research Institute, Kansas City, MO, 8–9 January 1953, CBI BCF.
37. Ibid.
38. Grace Hopper, "The Education of a Computer," 142, CBI BCF.
39. CBI Hopper interview, 14–15.
40. Grace Hopper, "The Education of a Computer," 144, CBI BCF.
41. WMW Letters; SL Hopper Interview, 38.
42. SL Hopper Interview, 13.
43. Wexelblat, ed., History of Programming Languages, 261.
44. Billings, *Hopper,* 74; McCartney, *ENIAC,* 168–71; NMAH Hopper Interview 1972, 54–55; Wexelblat, ed., *History of Programming Languages,* 18.
45. Leatherman, "Getting Faster," 7–8.
46. CBI Hopper interview, 12–13.
47. Ibid.
48. The A-2 Compiler System, Operations Manual, 15 November 1953, folder 1, box 6, NMAH Hopper Collection. Emphasis in original.
49. Hagley Hopper Interview, 9. See SL Hopper Interview, 36, for another version of this story.
50. Emil Schell to Hopper, 14 December 1953, folder 1, box 6, NMAH Hopper Collection; Second Workshop on Automatic Programming, the Pentagon, 1 December 1953, folder 1, box 6, NMAH Hopper Collection.
51. Wexelblat, ed., *History of Programming Languages,* 262.
52. Ibid., 15.
53. "Grace Hopper Mixes Insight, Foresight," 4.
54. Levitas, "Thinking Machine Tamer," 26.
55. Hagley Hopper Interview, 6.
56. Hopper, "Automatic Programming," undated typescript, 19–20, CBI Stein Papers.
57. Hopper, "Compiling Routines," reprint from *Computers and Automation,* May 1953, folder 11, box 5, NMAH Hopper collection.
58. Hagley Hopper Interview, 9.
59. Billings, *Hopper,* 97.
60. Wexelblat, ed., *History of Programming Languages,* 17.
61. Hopper, "Automatic Programming," undated typescript, 48, CBI Stein Papers.
62. Wexelblat, ed., *History of Programming Languages,* 17.
63. Hopper, "Automatic Programming," undated typescript, 21, CBI Stein Papers.
64. Wexelblat, ed., *History of Programming Languages,* 18.
65. Hagley Hopper Interview,11.
66. Hopper, "Automatic Programming," undated typescript, 30, CBI Stein Papers.
67. Wexelblat, ed., *History of Programming Languages,* 19.
68. Hagley Hopper Interview, 11–12, 20.
69. SL Hopper Interview, 117.
70. Hagley Hopper Interview, 12, 22.

71. Aline, "Through Texas Eyes."
72. Hagley Hopper Interview, 11. See McCartney, *ENIAC*, for the role of marketing in the early computer industry .
73. Wexelblat, ed., *History of Programming Languages*, 6.
74. Hagley Hopper Interview, 14.
75. Ibid., 8.
76. Ibid., 19–20.
77. Ibid.
78. Wexelblat, ed., *History of Programming Languages*, 202.
79. Jean E. Sammet quoted in Wexelblat, ed., *History of Programming Languages*, 263.
80. Hagley Hopper Interview, 23.
81. Ibid., 20–21.
82. Wexelblat, ed., *History of Programming Languages*, 263.
83. Cdr. Grace M. Hopper, "Standardization of High Level Programming Languages," folder Programming Langs. Standardization, box 19, acc. 75-0056, RG38, WNRC.
84. SL Hopper Interview, 48, 189; Spencer, *Great Men and Women*, 87–96.
85. "Computer Programming Pioneer," *New York Times*, 18 August 1961.
86. MMW Interview, 50; Vassar College, Class of 1928, Thirty-Eight Year Report, 1966, 45, VCL.
87. Hagley Hopper Interview, 21; SL Hopper Interview 10; Rossiter, *Women Scientists in America, 1940–1972*, 271–72.
88. SL Hopper Interview, 147–48; Hagley Hopper Interview, 18.
89. Hopper's Position Description at Remington Rand, enclosure 4, Hopper OFR, 14 July 1964, NPRC/OMPF.
90. Ibid.
91. Vassar College, Class of 1928, Thirty-Eight Year Report, 1966, 45, VCL.
92. "Grace Hopper Mixes Insight, Foresight," 4.
93. Hopper quoted in Betts, "Grace Hopper, Mother of Cobol," 14.
94. Levitas, "Thinking Machine Tamer," 26.
95. See interview with J. Presper Eckert in Betts, "Grace Hopper, Mother of Cobol," 14.
96. MMW Interview, I: 17; *The Brewster Review*, Spring–Summer 1984, 11, MMW Papers; WMW Letters. I am grateful to Frederic A. Stott for information on Roger Murray.
97. NMAH Hopper Interview, 1968, 5.

Chapter 4. A WAVE Ordnance Officer?

1. Rees, "The Computing Program of the Office of Naval Research, 1946–1953," 833.
2. Stern, *From Eniac to Univac*, 99. The Whirlwind Project was initially the inspiration of navy captain Luis de Florez.; *Fourth Naval District Navy Department News*, 2 August 1953, Hopper, NPRC/OMPF.
3. Mitchell, *Grace Murray Hopper*, 44; SL Hopper Interview, 13.
4. Boslaugh, *When Computers Went to Sea*, xxiii, 2, 92–98. NTDS first went to sea in 1962; For NSA's link to commercial computer developers see Samuel S. Snyder, "Influence of Cryptologic Organizations on the Digital Computer Industry," 10–16, SRH 003, box 4, RG457, NA2.
5. Herman Goldstine wrote of the Harvard Computation Lab that it was "the training ground for a large number of first-rate men active in the field today." Goldstine, *The Computer from Pascal to von Neumann*, 119. See also

Smith, *Electronic Digital Computers,* viii; Boslaugh, *When Computers Went to Sea,* 70, 81–81; Stern, *From Eniac to Univac,* 116–117; Rees, "The Computing Program of the Office of Naval Research, 1946–1953," 102–20.

6. NMAH Hopper Interview 1972, 69.
7. NMAH Hopper Interview 1968, 40.
8. NMAH Hopper Interview 1972, 78–79.
9. Stern, *From Eniac to Univac,* 94, 99, 138–39; for Hopper on Ed Berkeley see NMAH Hopper Interview 1968, 2–4; Cohen, *Howard Aiken.* For Gene Smith see NMAH Hopper Interview 1968, 15; Rees, "The Computing Program of the Office of Naval Research," 834–35.
10. Boslaugh, *When Computers Went to Sea,* 102, 106–7.
11. NMAH Hopper Interview 1972, 57.
12. "Ordnance Unit 4-3 Boasts of Expert," *Fourth Naval District Reserve News,* June 1953, 26, NPRC/OMPF.
13. NMAH Hopper Interview 1972, 31, 57–59.
14. Hopper Officer Fitness Report [hereafter Hopper OFR], 15 March 1950, NPRC/OMPF.
15. See for example, Hopper OFR for 26 June 1950, 1 July 1951, 4 May 1952, 14 October 1956, etc., NPRC/OMPF; "Ordnance Unit 4-3 Boasts of Expert," *Fourth Naval District Reserve News,* June 1953, 26, NPRC/OMPF.
16. Hopper OFR, 4 May 1952, and Hopper OFR for 1 July 1952, to 30 June 1953, NPRC/OMPF.
17. Hopper OFR, 30 June 1951, to 30 June 1952, NPRC/OMPF; Holm, *Women in the Military,* 260–67; Godson, *Serving Proudly,* 223–26.
18. Hopper OFR for period 1 July 1952, to 30 June 1953, NPRC/OMPF.
19. Capt. H. R. Wright to Remington Rand, Inc., 19 May 1953, Hopper, NPRC/OMPF.
20. *Fourth Naval District Navy Department News,* 2 August 1953, Hopper, NPRC/OMPF.
21. "Ordnance Unit 4-3 Boasts of Expert," *Fourth Naval District Reserve News,* June 1953, 26, NPRC/OMPF; MMW Interview, 23.
22. Hopper OFR, 19 April 1953, 4 October 1953, 5 August 1954, NPRC/OMPF.
23. Ibid., 12 September 1954, NPRC/OMPF; Billings, *Hopper,* 73.
24. Hopper OFR, 14 October 1956, NPRC/OMPF.
25. Ibid., 9 October 1957, NPRC/OMPF; Transcript of Naval Service, 1 July 1985, Grace Hopper Officer Biography, box 313, NHC/OA.
26. Hopper OFR, 19 March 1959, NPRC/OMPF. See also OFR for 30 June 1961, NPRC/OMPF.
27. Gustafson, "Parallel Computing Forty Years Ago," 49–50, 57.
28. See Williams, *Secret Weapon.*
29. Gustafson, "Parallel Computing Forty Years Ago," 50–51, 59. See also an account of postwar HFDF operations in James Bamford, *The Puzzle Palace,* 161.
30. Gustafson, "Parallel Computing Forty Years Ago," 51.
31. Ibid., 52–59.
32. Ibid.
33. "Commandant Fourth Naval District Consolidated Study of Management Advisory Services at Mechanicsburg Complex," October 1962, folder 5450, box 13, gen. corr. RG181, NAMAR.
34. Col. Miller quoted in Hopper, "Automatic Programming," undated typescript, 31–33, CBI Stein Papers.
35. Commanding Officer, U.S. Navy Ordnance Supply Office, Mechanicsburg, PA, to Chief, Bureau of Supplies and Accounts, 6 March 1962, folder 5450, box 13, gen. corr. RG181, NAMAR.

36. Godson, *Serving Proudly,* 271; SL Hopper Interview, 40.

37. Hopper OFR, 30 June 1961, NPRC/OMPF; Holm, *Women in the Military,* 119–20. Public Law 90-130, signed on 8 November 1967, removed the percentage restrictions on women's ranks.

38. Hopper OFR, 14 July 1964, NPRC/OMPF; Hopper OFR, 22 July 1965, NPRC/OMPF; Hopper OFR, 5 July 1966, NPRC/OMPF; Grace Hopper Officer Biography, box 313, NHC/OA.

39. Rear Adm. C. K. Duncan to Hopper, 24 April 1963, NPRC/OMPF.

40. Capt. D. J. Carrison to Hopper, 10 June 1963, NPRC/OMPF.

41. Ibid. The bureau hired Booz, Allen and Hamilton to consult on the reorganization.

42. Capt. W. R. McQuilkin to Hopper, 16 August 1963, NPRC/OMPF.

43. Ibid.

44. Commandant, Fourth Naval District to Hopper, 17 February 1964, NPRC/OMPF; Hopper to Commandant, Fourth Naval District, 27 February 1964, NPRC/OMPF.

45. Hopper OFR, 2 August 1963, NPRC/OMPF.

46. Ibid., 14 July 1964, OMPR/NPRC. See a similar comment in Hopper OFR, 22 July 1965, NPRC/OMPF, and again in Hopper OFR, 5 July 1966, NPRC/OMPF.

47. "Univac Systems Expert Visits," *The Mainsheet,* U.S. Naval Training Center, Bainbridge, MD, vol. 22, no. 49 (8 December 1966), 6, NPRC/OMPF.

48. Hopper OFR, 20 December 1966, NPRC/OMPF.

49. Ibid.

50. For a complete list of Hopper's awards see Grace Hopper Officer Biography, box 313, NHC/OA.

51. Quoted in typescript memo "Management Evaluation of ADP Systems," 9 February 1977, no folder, box 9, acc. 82-0007, RG38, WNRC.

52. Billings, *Hopper,* 87.

53. Hopper OFR, 26 February 1967, NPRC/OMPF.

54. Billings, *Hopper,* 87.

Chapter 5. I'm in the Reserve, Retired, and on Active Duty

1. Bob Corbett, "Computer? Just Another Potato Masher," *Evening Tribune,* San Diego, folder Dr. Hopper thank you letters, box 20, acc. 75-0056, RG38, WNRC.

2. Dick Fredette to author, 16 April 2003.

3. Memo for CNO from Norman J. Ream, 18 October 1967, folder GAO Reports NAVSUP, box 1, acc. 82-0011, RG38, WNRC.

4. Fredette Interview, 9 January 2001.

5. In FY52, 540,000 line items were carried at NSC Oakland, and 11,400 personnel handled 3,200,000 demands. In 1967 the same terminal carried 900,000 line items and only 4,000 personnel were required to handle more than 5,500,000 demands. "Specific CNO Comments on GAO Draft Report Codes 77814 and 73802," n.d., 7, folder GAO Draft Report, box 1, acc. 82-0011, RG38, WNRC; Commanding Officer, Naval Supply Systems Command to Chief, NavMat, 3, n.d., but July 1974, folder GAO Reports NAVSUP, box 1, acc. 82-0011, RG38, WNRC.

6. CBI Hopper Interview, 12–13; Godson, *Serving Proudly,* 207.

7. One of the first graduate courses in computing machinery was offered by Howard Aiken at Harvard in 1947–1948, but it was to be nearly a decade before computer courses became widely available; Rees, "The Computing

Program of the Office of Naval Research, 1946–1953," 835. The University of Colorado, for example, offered its first course in digital computing in 1957–1958; K. Gustafson, "Parallel Computing Forty Years Ago," 48.

8. "Automatic Digital Computing: A Thumbnail History," no author, 7, folder Higher Level Programming Languages, 1969, box 23, acc. 75-0056, RG38, WNRC.

9. Capt. William M. Oller, "Navy's Management of Information Systems," 36, *Armed Forces Comptroller,* October 1968, acc. 75,0056, RG38, WNRC.

10. Memo from Assist. Sec. of Defense, Subj. Data Elements and Data Codes Standardization Program, 9 December 1964, folder Navy ADP Standards, box 23, acc. 75-0056, RG38, WNRC.

11. R. W. Bemer, "A View of the History of COBOL," typescript, 10, folder Higher Level Programming Languages, 1969, box 23, acc. 75-0056, RG38, WNRC; Memo for File, OP-913C, 20 January 1972, folder 1972, Unnumbered Memos, box 1, acc.78-0033, RG38, WNRC. The terms of the Brooks Bill remained largely unchanged for a decade, in some cases hampering ADP development.

12. "Information Processing Standards for Computers, Status Report," 1 July 1977, no folder, box 9, acc. 82-0007, RG38, WNRC.

13. Memo for the Admin. Officer, Navy Dept., 21 March 1968, folder IPSC committee, box 21, acc. 75-0056, RG38, WNRC.

14. Memo for CNO, 18 October 1967, folder GAO Reports NAVSUP, box 1, acc. 82-0011, RG38, WNRC.

15. IPSC Status Report, 1 July 1977, 2, no folder, box 9, acc. 82-0007, RG38, WNRC.

16. Memo for undersecretary of the navy, 1 June 1971, folder 5230 (ADP), box 130, Double Zero Files 1971, NHC/OA.

17. Commanding Officer, Fleet Computer Programming Center, Pacific to Commanding Officer, Rome Air Development Center, 23 February 1972, folder Jovial, box 20, acc. 75-0056, RG38, WNRC.

18. Ibid.; Hopper quoted in: "Computers in the Navy," *New Scientist,* 12 June 1969, 594.

19. Ruth, "What Can the Navy Learn from the Air Force's Logistics System?" 101.

20. "Computer Sciences Man of the Year," 6–7.

21. Navy COBOL Audit Routines, 22 October 1970, folder Programming Langs. Standardization, box 19, acc. 75-0065, RG38, WNRC.

22. Fredette Interview, 9 January 2001.

23. SL Hopper Interview, 166–68.

24. Trudy Willis, "Women, Computers Called a Good Team," *The Roanoke Times,* 27 January 1972, folder Dr. Hopper thank you letters, box 20, acc. 75-0056, RG38, WNRC.

25. SL Hopper Interview, 166–68. Quote is on 167.

26. Ibid., 171–72.

27. Ibid., 164–65.

28. "Some of the Skills of Program Diplomacy," *Computer Weekly,* 12 June 1969, 14.

29. SL Hopper Interview, 117.

30. Cdr. Grace M. Hopper, "Standardization of High Level Programming Languages," undated typescript, folder Programming Langs. Standardization, box 19, acc. 75-0056, RG38, WNRC.

31. Ibid.

32. Ibid.

33. Wexelblat, ed., *History of Programming Languages,* 19–20.

34. Cdr. Grace M. Hopper, "Standardization of High Level Programming Languages," folder Programming Langs. Standardization, box 19, acc. 75-0056, RG38, WNRC.

35. "Some of the Skills of Program Diplomacy," *Computer Weekly*, 12 June 1969, 14.
36. NBS Draft Handbook for Data Standardization, 7 July 1970, no folder, box 21, acc. 75-0056, RG38, WNRC; SL Hopper Interview, 170.
37. "Computer Sciences Man of the Year," 7.
38. NMAH Hopper Interview 1968, 7.
39. For several examples see Williams, *Improbable Warriors*.
40. OPNAV Notice 5430, 10 June 1974, no folder, box 1, acc. 82-007, RG38, WNRC.
41. OP-91 for distribution, 1 October 1970, folder Policy File, box 19, acc. 75-0056, RG38, WNRC.
42. Information Systems Div., Mission and Function Statement, 10 December 1970, 3, folder Policy File, box 19, acc. 75-0056, RG38, WNRC.
43. Ibid.
44. Memo for CNO, 20 November 1970, folder Dr. Hopper thank you letters, box 20, acc. 75-0056, RG38, WNRC.
45. News Release, 1970 Joint Fall Conference American Federation of Information Processing Societies, n.d., folder Programming Langs. Standardization, box 19, acc. 75-0056, RG38, WNRC.
46. American Federation of Information Processing Societies, pamphlet announcing the 1970 Harry Goode Memorial Award to Grace Murray Hopper, folder Programming Langs. Standardization, box 19, acc. 75-0056, RG38, WNRC.
47. Kin Thompson to Adm. Spreen, 13 October 1970, folder Programming Langs. Standardization, box 19, acc. 75-0056, RG38, WNRC; Brooks to Hopper, 24 November 1970, folder Dr. Hopper thank you letters, box 20, acc. 75-0056, RG38, WNRC.
48. McAdams to Hopper, 8 December 1970; Hopper to McAdams, 16 December 1970, folder Programming Langs. Standardization, box 19, acc. 75-0056, RG38, WNRC.
49. NPLS to K. B. Thompson, 5 February 1971, folder Programming Langs. Standardization, box 19, acc. 75-0056, RG38, WNRC.
50. OP-915 to OP-916, 2 August 1971, folder Policy File, box 19, acc. 75-0056, RG38, WRNC.
51. Cdr. Grace M. Hopper, "Standardization of High Level Programming Languages," n.d., folder Programming Langs. Standardization, box 19, acc. 75-0056, RG38, WNRC.
52. Ibid.
53. MMW Interview, 31.
54. NPLS to K. B. Thompson, 23 December 1971, folder Programming Langs. Standardization, box 19, acc. 75-0056, RG38, WNRC.
55. OP-91 to OP-09B21, 11 August 1971, folder, Originator File—Mr. Fredette, box 19, acc. 75-0056, RG38, WNRC; RFMIII Interview, 9.
56. DP1 George Baird to CNO, 15 October 1970, folder military (general), box 20, acc. 75-0056, RG38, WNRC.
57. NPLS to K. B. Thompson, 18 February 1972, folder Programming Langs. Standardization, box 19, acc. 75-0056, RG38, WNRC; OP-916 to OP-91B, 8 November 1971, folder Memo File, box 19, acc. 75-0056, RG38, WNRC.
58. Fredette Interviews, 9 January 2001 and 7 June 2001; Gealt Interview, 11 June 2001.
59. William Westcote Interview by author, 3.
60. "Captain Grace Murray Hopper, U.S. Naval Reserve," July 1981, Grace Hopper Officer Biography, Box 313, NHC/OA.
61. "Computer Sciences Man of the Year," 7.
62. Ibid.

63. David R. Eaton, Memo for the Record, 20 April 1971, folder Programming Langs. Standardization, box 19, acc. 75-0056, RG38, WNRC.
64. GSA Special Notice No. 5 to Ordering Offices, 10 August 1971, folder Originator File, box 19, acc. 75-0056, RG38, WNRC.
65. Dodson to Spreen, 18 October 1971, folder Originator File—Mr. Fredette, box 19, acc. 75-0056, RG38, WNRC.
66. Hopper brief attached to Spreen to Dodson, 16 November 1971, folder Originator File—Mr. Fredette, box 19, acc. 75-0056, RG38, WNRC.
67. Hopper brief attached to Spreen to Dodson, 16 November 1971, folder Originator File—Mr. Fredette, box 19, acc. 75-0056, RG38, WNRC.
68. Ibid.
69. Hopper brief attached to Spreen to Dodson, 16 November 1971, folder Originator File—Mr. Fredette, box 19, acc. 75-0056, RG38,WNRC.
70. BuPers Notice 530, 8 March 1971, folder 5230 (ADP), box 130, Double Zero Files 1971, NHC/OA.
71. NPLS to K. B. Thompson, 18 June 1971, folder Programming Langs. Standardization, box 19, acc. 75-0056, RG38, WNRC; David R. Eaton., Memo for the Record, 16 June 1971, folder Programming Langs. Standardization, box 19, acc. 75-0056, RG38, WNRC; David R. Eaton, Memo for the Record, 17 June 1971, folder Programming Langs. Standardization, box 19, acc. 75-0056, RG38, WNRC; OP-916 to OP-915, 2 August 1971, folder Policy File, box 19, acc. 75-0056, RG38, WNRC.
72. Billings, *Hopper,* 91; Grace Hopper Officer Biography, Box 313, NHC/OA; Sussman, "Pentagon Computer Pioneer"; NMAH Hopper 1972 Interview, 59; RFMIII Interview, 40.
73. RFMIII Interview, 13.
74. Navy Programming Languages Div. to Capt. J. W. Riehl, 2 October 1970, folder, Programming Langs. Standardization, box 19, acc. 75-0056, RG38, WNRC.
75. MMW Interview, 3; Billings, *Hopper,* 97–98.
76. NMAH Hopper Interview 1972, 59–60.
77. NPLS to K. B. Thompson, 5 February 1971, folder Programming Langs. Standardization, box 19, acc. 75-0056, RG38, WNRC; Grace M. Hopper, Memo for the Record, 9 June 1971, folder Programming Langs. Standardization, box 19, acc. 75-0056, RG38, WNRC.
78. Memo to the Chief, U.S. Army STAG, 12 March 1971, folder Originator File—Mr. Fredette, box 19, acc. 75-0056, RG38, WNRC.
79. Chief, BuMed to CNO, 8 June 1971, folder Programming Langs. Standardization, box 19, acc. 75-0056, RG38, WNRC.
80. Ibid.
81. Brief for OP-91, 17 June 1971, folder Originator File—Mr. Fredette, box 19, acc. 75-0056, RG38, WNRC.
82. OP-916 to OP-91B, 2 September 1971, folder Originator File, box 19, acc. 75-0056, RG38, WNRC; Navy COBOL Audit Routines, 22 October 1970, folder Programming Langs. Standardization, box 19, acc. 75-0056, RG38, WNRC.
83. Fredette Interview, 9 January 2001.
84. Memo for ASN (FM), 20 October 1971, folder Originator File, box 19, acc. 75-0056, RG38, WNRC.
85. Ibid.
86. NPLS to K. B. Thompson, 18 February 1972, folder Programming Langs. Standardization, box 19, acc. 75-0056, RG38, WNRC; NPLS to K. B. Thompson, 25 February 1972, folder Programming Langs. Standardization, box 19, acc. 75-0056, RG38, WNRC.
87. NMAH Hopper Interview 1972, 70–71.

88. OP-91 to OP-916, 11 April 1972, folder Policy File, box 19, acc. 75-0056, RG38, WNRC.

89. Ibid.

90. OP-91B to OP-916, 5 April 1972, folder Memo File March/April 1972, box 19, acc. 75-0056, RG38, WNRC; NPLS to K. B. Thompson, 30 June 1972, folder Programming Langs. Standardization, box 19, acc. 75-0056, RG38, WNRC.

91. OP-91B to OP-916, 20 April 1972, folder Memo File March/April 1972, box 19, acc. 75-0056, RG38, WNRC.

92. Branch Heads Monthly Control Listing For Specific Objectives, 916D, 5/72, folder Memo File March/April 1972, box 19, acc. 75-0056, RG38, WNRC; NPLS to K. B. Thompson, 7 April 1972, folder Programming Langs. Standardization, box 19, acc. 75-0056, RG38, WNRC.

93. David Ingall to "Dear Grace," 16 August 1972, folder Programming Langs. Standardization, box 19, acc. 75-0056, RG38, WNRC.

94. NPLS to K. B. Thompson, 4 August 1972, folder Programming Langs. Standardization, box 19, acc. 75-0056, RG38, WNRC.

95. Sussman, "Pentagon Computer Pioneer"; SL Hopper Interview, 170.

96. *Report to Congress,* "Ways to Improve Management of ADP Resources, 16 April 1975," Department of the Navy, by the Comptroller General of the United States, 16 April 1975 [hereafter *Report to Congress,* 16 April 1975], i–iv, 1–33, folder, GAO Draft Report, box 1, acc. 82-0011, RG38, WNRC. In general, computers that were part of a weapon system or that were built to military specifications were addressed separately from those that were not. See CNO to CNM (Chief of Naval Material), 14 January 1972, folder IBM Case, box 6, acc. 78-0033, RG38, WNRC.

97. Rear Adm. Peter K. Cullins, "Why a NAVDAC?" *Access, the Navy Data Automation Review* 1, no.1 (September–October 1978), 1, folder NAVDAC Command History 1978, Command File Post-1974, NHC/OA.

98. Rees, "The Computing Program of the Office of Naval Research," 836, n.4; "Automatic Data Processing," Report of the Blue Ribbon Defense Panel, 100–51, folder, Blue Ribbon, box 1, acc. 82-0011, RG38, WNRC.

99. Memo from OP-911 (Head, Policy Coordination Branch) to OP-91 Branch Heads, subj. "Navy ADP Problems," 30 August 1974, no folder, box 1, acc. 82-0007, RG38, WNRC. This memo is attached to fifteen pages of navy-identified ADP problems.

100. "Automatic Data Processing," chapter 2, 49, n.d., folder DON ADPM letters, box 1, acc. 78-0033, RG38, WNRC; NAVMAT Instruction 4130 from Chief of Naval Material, n.d., but internal evidence confirms fall 1970, subj. Standard Automatic Data Processing Hardware and Software, folder AN/UYK-7, box 4, acc. 78-0033, RG38, WNRC.

101. See among many other examples OP-914 (ADP Acquisition and Review Branch) to OP-915 (Navy Integrated Command Management and Information Systems Branch). Both OP-914 and OP-915 reported to OP-91, Information Systems Division, 8 May 1975, folder GAO Report April–May 1975, box 1, acc. 82-0011, RG38, WNRC; "Specific CNO Comments on GAO Draft Report Codes 77814 and 73802," unsigned, undated; memo from OP-911 (Policy Coordination Branch) to OP-915 (Navy Integrated Command Management and Information Systems Branch), 3 July 1974, folder GAO Draft Report, box 1, acc. 82-0011, RG38, WNRC; Special Assistant for Data Automation, to Assist. SecNav (FM), subj. Comments on the Recent GAO Report on Ways to Improve Management of ADP Resources in the Dept. of the Navy," 22 April 1975, folder GAO Draft Report, box 1, acc. 82-0011, RG38, WNRC.

102. *Report to Congress,* 16 April 1975, 16, 24, folder GAO Draft Report, box 1, acc. 82-0011, RG38, WNRC; G. D. Penisten, Asst. SecNav (FM), to Dir., Logistics and Communications Div., GAO, 16 October 1974, folder GAO Draft Report, box 1, acc. 82-0011, RG38, WNRC.
103. Commanding Officer, Naval Supply Systems Command to Chief of Naval Material, 5–6, n.d., but July 1974, folder GAO Reports NAVSUP, box 1, acc. 82-0011, RG38, WNRC; Rear Adm. Haak noted that he believed that the last GAO investigation of navy computing had been in 1969 and that he did not know what had sparked the present investigation. "Memo for the Record: A Meeting to Discuss the Subject Report," 9 July 1974, folder GAO Draft Report, box 1, acc. 82-0011, RG38, WNRC.
104. Memo from OP-911 (Policy Coordination Branch) to OP-915 (Navy Integrated Command Management and Information Systems Branch), 3 July 1974, folder GAO Draft Report, box 1, acc. 82-0011, RG38, WNRC.
105. G. D. Penisten, Asst. SecNav (FM), to Dir., Logistics and Communications Div., GAO, 16 October 1974, folder GAO Draft Report, box 1, acc. 82-0011, RG38, WNRC.
106. Ibid.
107. "Specific CNO Comments on GAO Draft Report Codes 77814 and 73802," n.d., folder GAO Draft Report, p. 2, box 1, acc. 82-0011, RG38, WNRC. Adm. James L. Holloway III took over as CNO from Adm. Elmo R. Zumwalt, Jr., in July 1974, just days after the draft report was delivered to the navy. A new SECNAV, J. William Middendorf II, had taken over from John W. Warner in April. This changing of the guard made it more difficult for the navy to mount a coordinated response; Commanding Officer, NAVSUP, to Commanding Officer, NAVMAT, n.d., Enclosure 5, UADPS-SP chronology, 1–3, folder GAO Reports NAVSUP, box 1, acc. 82-0011, RG38, WNRC.
108. Spreen to ASN (FM), 25 February 1971, folder Originator File—Mr. Fredette, box 19, acc. 75-0056, RG38, WNRC.
109. Spreen to ASN (FM), 25 February 1971, folder Originator File—Mr. Fredette, box 19, acc. 75-0056, RG38, WNRC; Memo for the CNO, 8 March 1971, folder Originator File—Mr. Fredette, box 19, acc. 75-0056, RG38, WNRC.
110. "Recommendations and Comments," Appendix I, *Report to Congress,* 16 April 1975, p.41, folder GAO Draft Report, box 1, acc. 82-0011, RG38, WNRC; "Specific CNO Comments on GAO Draft Report Codes 77814 and 73802," n.d., folder GAO Draft Report, p. 4, box 1, acc. 82-0011, RG38, WNRC; "Evolution of the Navy ADP Utilization," Enclosure 1 in G. D. Penisten, Asst. SecNav (FM), to Dir., Logistics and Communications Div., GAO, 16 October 1974, folder GAO Draft Report, box 1, acc. 82-0011, RG38, WNRC.
111. OP-916C to OP-91, 18 May 1972, folder Memo File, box 19, acc. 75-0056, RG38, WNRC.
112. Commanding Officer, NAVCOSSACT, to CNO (OP-91), 15 December 1970, folder AN/UYK-7, box 4, acc. 78-0033, RG38, WNRC; OP-911 Current Projects as of 16 December 1974, no folder, box 1, acc. 82-0007, RG38, WNRC; "Navy Computer Grandmother Keeps Moving," *The* [Baltimore] *Sun,* 26 September 1975, B8, for Hopper quote.

Chapter 6. The Navy's Best Recruiter?

1. Rear Adm. Peter K. Cullins, "Why a NAVDAC?" *Access: The Navy Data Automation Review,* 1, no. 1 (September–October 1978), 2, folder NAVDAC Command History 1978, Command File Post-1974, NHC/OA.

2.   *Access: The Navy Data Automation Review* 1, no.1 (September–October 1978),4, folder NAVDAC Command History 1978, Command File Post-1974, NHC/OA.

3.   "Data Automation Accomplishments," November 1977, no folder, box 9, acc. 82-0007, RG38, WNRC.

4.   Ibid.

5.   SL Hopper Interview, 49; "NewsBriefs," *Vassar Quarterly,* 1978/80, 75–76 (Summer 1980), 36, VCL.

6.   *Access: The Navy Data Automation Review* 1, no.1, (September–October 1978), 7, folder NAVDAC Command History 1978, Command File Post-1974, NHC/OA.

7.   Hagley Hopper Interview, 16.

8.   Associated Press, "Navy's Oldest Officer Logs Off," *New Haven Register,* 15 August 1986.

9.   Richard Pearson, "Adm. Hopper Dies," *The Washington Post,* 4 January 1992.

10.   Fredette to Author, 12 April 2003.

11.   Memo for the Record, subj. GAO Visit, 14 November 1977, folder GAO Reports, box 1, acc. 82-0011, RG38, WNRC.

12.   "Data Automation Accomplishments," November 1977, no folder, box 9, acc. 82-0007, RG38, WNRC.

13.   NAVDAC Command History 1976 and 1977, folder Washington NAVDAC Command History 1976/77–1978, Washington Naval Data Automation Command Histories, Post 1974 Command File Shore Establishment, NHC/OA.

14.   Kreps to Claytor, 2 August 1977, no folder, box 9, acc. 82-0007, RG38, WNRC.

15.   Memo for the Record: Informal Discussions with OSD, 31 October 1977, no folder, box 9, acc. 82-0007, RG38, WNRC.

16.   "Computer Sciences Man of the Year," 7.

17.   "Objectives for the Defense ADP Program," FY 1978, no folder, box 9, acc. 82-0007, RG38, WNRC.

18.   Memo for the Special Asst. to the Sec. and Deputy Sec. of Defense, 11 November 1977, no folder, box 9, acc. 82-0007, RG38, WNRC; Management Evaluation of ADP Systems, 9 February 1977, no folder, box 9, acc. 82-0007, RG38, WNRC. Numbers vary slightly in these two reports.

19.   Quoted in Management Evaluation of ADP Systems, 9 February 1977, 4, no folder, box 9, acc. 82-0007, RG38, WNRC.

20.   "Civil Service Commission Prescribed Minimum Educational Requirements; Establishment," *Federal Register,* vol. 42, no. 73, (15 April 1977), no folder, box 9, acc. 82-0007, RG38, WNRC.

21.   NAVDAC Command History, 18 February 1981, folder Wash. NAVDAC Command History, 1981–1986, box 1193, Command File Post 1974 Shore Establishment, NHC/OA.

22.   Quoted in Management Evaluation of ADP Systems, 9 February 1977, 4, no folder, box 9, acc. 82-0007, RG38, WNRC.

23.   Memo for the Special Asst. to the Sec. and Deputy Sec. of Defense, 11 November 1977, no folder, box 9, acc. 82-0007, RG38, WNRC.

24.   Ibid.

25.   Memo for the director for Data Automation, OASD (C) (MS), 14 September 1977, no folder, box 9, acc. 82-0007, RG38, WNRC.

26.   Chief, Naval Material to CNO, 12 September 1977, no folder, box 9, acc. 82-0007, RG38, WNRC.

27.   Misc. newspaper clipping, 12 December 1985, Grace Hopper, Ready Reference File, NHC/OA.

28.   Ruth, "What Can the Navy Learn from the Air Force's Logistics System?" 100–101.

29. Cdr. C. E. Harlow, "Software Conversion Via the Data Processing Service Center Project," *Access,* September–October 1978, 7–8, folder C.H. NAVDAC 1978, Command File Post-1974, NHC/OA.

30. Commanding Officer, ONR London to CNO, 6 October 1977, no folder, box 9, acc. 82-0007, RG38, WNRC.

31. Richard C. Fredette, "The Backend DBMS," *Access: The Navy Data Automation Review,* 1, no.1 (September–October 1978),17–19, folder NAVDAC Command History 1978, Command File Post-1974, NHC/OA.

32. Tim Clark, "The Commodore and the *Constitution,*" *Yankee,* July 1985, Grace Hopper, Biographical File, Special Collections, VCL.

33. Hagley Hopper Interview, 17.

34. Command History, 4 January 1979, folder NAVDAC Command History 1979, Command File Post-1974, NHC/OA.

35. Ibid.

36. Mason, "Grand Lady of Software," 86.

37. Hagley Hopper Interview, 13.

38. CBI Hopper Interview, 21; Memo for CNO, 24 December 1975, NPRC/OMPF.

39. NAVDAC Command History, December 1980, folder, NAVDAC Command History 1980, Command File Post 1974, NHC/OA.

40. NAVDAC Command History 1982, April–September 1982, folder Washington NAVDAC Command History 1980, box 1193, Post 1974 Command File Shore Establishment, NHC/OA.

41. Alsmeyer to Hancock, 16 October 1982, Marie Bennett Alsmeyer, Personal Papers, folder E-H, box 3, series 3, NHC/OA.

42. *Business Software,* 1, no. 4 (July/August 1983), Grace Hopper Biographical File, NHC/OA.

43. Fredette to author, 12 April 2003; JVHW Interview.

44. Fredette Interview, 9 January 2001, 5.

45. Yavinsky Interview, 50.

46. SL Hopper Interview, 136.

47. Ibid.; Hattendorf, "The Uses of Maritime," 33–35.

48. Prokop, ed., *Computers in the Navy,* 23; SL Hopper Interview,135.

49. *The Brewster Review,* Spring–Summer 1984, 9–12, courtesy Brewster Academy, Wolfeboro, NH.

50. Ibid.

51. Author's telephone interview with John F. Lehman, 26 June 1998.

52. RFMIII Interview, 11, 30; Mitchell, *Grace Murray Hopper,* 64, for Sutherland quote.

53. Yavinsky Interview, 47.

54. Program for the Grace Murray Hopper Service Center Groundbreaking Ceremony, 27 September 1985, Grace Hopper, Biographical Files, Special Collections, VCL.

55. Holm, *Women in the Military,* 202–4; Godson, *Serving Proudly,* 271–72, 277; RFMIII Interview, 10; MMW Interview, 14; another version of the story about the admiral's aide is that Hopper resisted having one until she was ordered to. See Mitchell, *Grace Murray Hopper,* 64–65.

56. RFMIII interview, 42–45; Phillips Academy, Andover, *Alumni Bulletin,*90, MMW Papers; WMW Letters.

57. RFMIII Interview, 54.

58. "Keniston Elected Wolfeboro's New Selectman," *The Granite State News,* 1; WMW Letters.

59. The Phillips Andover Academy *Alumni Bulletin,* 90; MMW Papers.

60. Fredette to author, 12 April 2003; RBN Interview, 21; Gealt Interview, 11 June 2001.

61. Cushman, "Admiral Hopper's Farewell, *New York Times,* 14 August 1986.
62. I am grateful to Currie Colket, The Mitre Corporation and chair, ACM SIGAda, for this information on ADA.
63. Associated Press, "Female Admiral, Age 79, Ends 43-Year Navy Career," *The [Baltimore] Sun,* 15 August 1986; MMW Interview, 29; Cushman, "Admiral Hopper's Farewell, *New York Times,* 14 August 1986, for quote.
64. Reagan to Hopper, 15 September 1986, Yavinsky Papers.

Chapter 7. Amazing Grace

1. Hagley Hopper Interview, 15.
2. Yavinsky Interview, 2–5.
3. SL Hopper Interview, 18.
4. "Digital Hires Dr. Hopper,"*New York Times,* 3 September 1986; memo, Weiss to "Distribution," 7 October 1986, Yavinsky Papers.
5. Yavinsky Interview, 8.
6. "Digital Hires Dr. Hopper," D.E.C. Press Release, 2 September 1986, Yavinsky Papers.
7. Hopper calendar, September 1986, Yavinsky Papers.
8. Ibid.
9. Hopper calendar, September–December 1986, Yavinsky Papers; Yavinsky Interview, 22–23.
10. Fredette Interview, 9 January 2001; MMW Interview, 23; WMW Letters.
11. MMW Interview, 10; Yavinsky Interview, 35; WMW Letters.
12. RFMIII Interview, 37–39.
13. Fredette to author, 12 April 2003.
14. RFMIII Interview, 18; MMW Interview, 9, 30.
15. RFMIII Interview, 14.
16. MMW Interview, 8.
17. Ibid.
18. Schimelpfenig, "Navy's Computer Expert," 12 January 1976.
19. Sussman, "Pentagon Computer Pioneer," 28 August 1975.
20. SL Hopper Interview, 119; Etzkowitz, Kemelgor, and Uzzi, *Athena Unbound,* 32–48.
21. Schimelpfenig, "Navy's Computer Expert," 12 January 1976.
22. Etzkowitz, Kemelgor, and Uzzi, Athena Unbound, 24–25; Murray, *Women Becoming Mathematicians,* 40–41.
23. Holm, *Women in the Military,* 282–83; Godson, *Serving Proudly,* 224–25.
24. Godson, *Serving Proudly,* 246.
25. Schimelpfenig, "Navy's Computer Expert," 12 January 1976; Yavinsky Interview, 45.
26. Sussman, "Pentagon Computer Pioneer," n.p.
27. ACM Members, 21 May 1948, folder 06461-24905, box 71, series II, Sperry acc., 1825, Hagley.
28. Mahoney, "Boys' Toys and Women's Work," 169.
29. Bob Corbett, "Computer? Just Another Potato Masher," *Evening Tribune,* San Diego, n.d. but 1971 or 1972, folder Dr. Hopper thank you letters, box 20, acc. 75-0056, RG38, WNRC.
30. Elma Broadfoot, "Computer Age Has Far to Go," *The Wichita Beacon,* 30 April 1971, folder Dr. Hopper thank you letters, box 20, acc. 75-0056, RG38, WNRC.
31. Bob Corbett, "Computer? Just Another Potato Masher," *Evening Tribune,* San Diego, n.d., folder Dr. Hopper thank you letters, box 20, acc. 75-0056, RG38, WNRC.

32. Trudy Willis, "Women, Computers Called a Good Team, *The Roanoke Times*, 27 January 1972, folder Dr. Hopper thank you letters, box 20, acc. 75-0056, RG38, WNRC.
33. George Bugliarello to Hopper, 13 April 1971, folder Dr. Hopper thank you letters, box 20, acc. 75-0056, RG38, WNRC.
34. Memo, NAVDAC EEO Statistics, 10 September 1980, folder NAVDAC Command History, Command File Post 1974, NHC/OA.
35. Woodfield, *Women, Work and Computing*, 2.
36. SL Hopper Interview, 117. For very similar expressions from other senior women scientists at the end of the twentieth century see: Etzkowitz, Kemelgor, and Uzzi, *Athena Unbound*, chapters 5 and 6.
37. SL Hopper Interview, 177; Fredette Interview, 9 January 2001.
38. *The Brewster Review*, Spring–Summer 1984, 11, courtesy Brewster Academy, Wolfeboro, NH.
39. Cohen, *Howard Aiken*, 245–46.
40. SL Hopper Interview, 23, 130–31. Quote is on 42.
41. Fredette to author, 16 April 2003; RFMIII Interview, 11.
42. Fredette to author, 12 April 2003; Mitchell, *Grace Murray Hopper*, 67–68; Gealt Interview, 11 June 2001.
43. Wexelblat, ed., *History of Programming Languages*, 20.
44. Elma Broadfoot, "Computer Age Has Far to Go," *The Wichita Beacon*, 30 April 1971, folder Dr. Hopper thank you letters, box 20, acc. 75-0056, RG38, WNRC.
45. SL Hopper Interview, 150.
46. Ibid., 182.
47. RBN Interview, 43; SL Hopper Interview, 176.
48. Etzkowitz, Kemelgor, and Uzzi, *Athena Unbound*, 23.
49. Capt. H. M. Chandler to Cdr. Grace Hopper, 28 May 1971, folder Dr. Hopper thank you letters, box 20, acc. 75-0056, RG38, WNRC.
50. Yavinsky Interview, 46.
51. Ibid., 48–49.
52. SL Hopper Interview, 181.
53. "Receive Honorary Degrees from Penn," *Sperry Univac Sphere*, vol. 4, no. 3, March 1974, 4, MMW Papers; Hopper to Pres. William Hazell, 17 April 1972, folder Dr. Hopper thank you letters, box 20, acc. 75-0056, RG38, WNRC.
54. RBN Interview, 21.
55. Diane Hamblen, "Editorial," *CHIPS*, April 1992, 3; T*he Brewster Review*, Spring–Summer 1984, 9, courtesy Brewster Academy, Wolfeboro, NH, for Olsen quote.
56. Grace Hopper, "Progress: Challenge to Computers," typescript, folder Dr. Hopper thank you letters, box 20, acc. 75-0056, RG38, WNRC.
57. NMAH Hopper Interview 1972, 63–64; Bob Corbett, "Computer? Just Another Potato Masher," *Evening Tribune*, San Diego, n.d., folder Dr. Hopper thank you letters, box 20, acc. 75-0056, RG38, WNRC.
58. NMAH Hopper Interview 1972, 66.
59. *The Navy Times*, 1 July 1985, Grace Hopper, Capt., Officer Biography, box 313, NHC/OA.
60. Bob Corbett, "Computer? Just Another Potato Masher," *Evening Tribune*, San Diego, n.d., folder Dr. Hopper thank you letters, box 20, acc. 75-0056, RG38, WNRC.
61. Sussman, "Pentagon Computer Pioneer," n.p.; SL Hopper Interview, 183–87.
62. NMAH Hopper Interview 1972, 61; Billings, *Hopper*, 94.
63. Quoted in Mitchell, *Grace Murray Hopper*, 76–77.

64. The White House, Office of the Press Secretary, "Remarks by the President during Presentation of National Medal of Science and National Medal of Technology," 16 September 1991, MMW Papers; MMW Interview, 29.

65. RFMIII Interview, 32; Yavinsky Interview, 28–30.

66. RFMIII Interview, 33; Yavinsky Interview, 18–20; Markoff, "Rear Adm. Grace M. Hopper Dies."

67. Betts, "Grace Hopper, Mother of Cobol, Dies," 14.

68. Markoff, "Rear Adm. Grace M. Hopper Dies."

69. Lehman, *Command of the Seas*, 1–36; Sharon B. Young, "Hopper Won't Retire, She'll Just Fade into Another Computer Job," *Navy Times*, 11 August 1986, 1, MMW Papers.

70. RFMIII Interview, 8.

71. Quote is from Navy Women's 50th Anniversary Convention. Grace Hopper, Ready Reference File, NHC/OA; Mitchell, *Grace Murray Hopper*, 78, for Adm. Sutherland's observation.

72. "Navy Computer Pioneer, Innovator, Hopper dies," *Sea Services Weekly,* vol. 14, no. 2, 17 January 1992, Grace Hopper Ready Reference File, NHC/OA.

73. RFMIII Interview, 25; MMW Interview, 45.

74. Class Notes, 1928, *Vassar Quarterly*, 94, no. 2 (Spring 1998), 39, VCL; RFMIII Interview, 47–51.

75. "1997 Grace Hopper Celebration of Women in Computing—Agenda," Yavinsky Papers.

76. Dalton quote read into transcript, MMW Interview, 4.

77. MMW Interview, 4; Wexelblat, ed., *History of Programming Languages,* 7. Lists of Hopper's awards and publications can be found in Mitchell, *Grace Murray Hopper*, 89–92, and Billings, *Hopper*, 120–24.

78. *The Brewster Review*, Spring–Summer 1984, 11, courtesy Brewster Academy, Wolfeboro, NH.

79. *NOMIS News*, March 1973, 3, folder Navy Ordnance Management Info. Sys., box 3, acc. 75-0045, RG38, WNRC.

80. Hagley Hopper Interview, 13.

81. CBI Hopper Interview, 22.

82. Hopper, "Aiken and the Mark I," 23, Yavinsky Papers. Part of the Mark I is at the Smithsonian in Washington and another part can be seen in the lobby of Harvard's science center.

Bibliography

Author's Interviews and Correspondence

Bloch, Richard M. Harvard Computation Laboratory

Campbell, Robert V. D. Harvard Computation Laboratory

Fredette, Richard C. Navy civilian colleague of Grace Hopper

Gealt, Norma. Grace Hopper's secretary

Lehman, Hon. John F. Secretary of the Navy, 1981–1987

Murray, Roger F. III. Nephew of Grace Hopper

Noller, Ruth Brendel. World War II WAVE, Harvard Computation
    Laboratory

Westcote, John V. H. Nephew of Grace Hopper

Westcote, Mary Murray. Sister of Grace Hopper

Westcote, Walter M. Nephew of Grace Hopper

Westcote, William T. Nephew of Grace Hopper

Yavinsky, Rita. Digital Equipment Corporation colleague and
    friend of Grace Hopper

Unpublished Sources

Brewster Academy Archives, Wolfeboro, NH
    Grace Murray Hopper Collection

Charles Babbage Institute, University of Minnesota, Minneapolis
    Hopper, Grace Murray. Biographical Files
    Oral Histories: 66 (Richard Bloch), 67 (Robert Campbell), 81
        (Grace Hopper)
    Margaret Fox Papers
    Marvin Stein Papers

City University of New York, Graduate School and University
Center Archives
    Mina Rees Collection

Grace Murray Hopper Museum, NavComTel, Naval Air Station, San Diego, CA
>   Grace Hopper memorabilia and papers

Hagley Museum and Library Archives, Greenville, DE
>   Sperry Univac Records, Accession 1825
>   Technitrol Suit Records, Accession 1901
>   Grace M. Hopper, 20 July 1979, Oral History Interviews

Harvard University Archives, Cambridge, MA
>   Records of the Computation Laboratory, 1944– (Aiken Correspondence)
>   Welch, Gregory Webb. "Computer Scientist Howard Hathaway Aiken: Reactionary or Visionary?" (Thesis, A.B., Harvard University, 1986)
>   World War II Government Contract Records

IBM Archives, Somers, NY
>   *Biography of Howard Hathaway Aiken.* n.d.
>   *IBM Automatic Sequence Controlled Calculator.* IBM Corporation, 1945

Lehman College Library, City University of New York, Bronx, NY
>   Records of the Assistant Chief of Naval Personnel for Women

Mary Murray Westcote Papers
>   Grace M. Hopper Collection

National Archives II, College Park, MD
>   Record Group 19, Bureau of Ships; Record Group 24, Bureau of Personnel; Record Group 38, CNO; Record Group 227, OSRD; Record Group 298, Office of Naval Research; Record Group 457, Special Research Histories

National Archives, Regional Archives, Mid-Atlantic Region (Philadelphia)
>   Record Group 181, Fourth Naval District

NARA, National Personnel Records Center, St, Louis, MO
>   Grace Hopper Official Military Personnel File

NARA, Washington National Records Center, Suitland, MD
>   Record Group 38, CNO

Naval Historical Center, Navy Department Library, Washington Navy Yard
>   Grace Hopper File

Naval Historical Center, Operational Archives, Washington
Navy Yard
    Command File, post-1974
    Double Zero Files, 1971
    Grace Hopper Officer Biography
    Grace Hopper Ready Reference File
    Marie Bennett Alsmeyer, Personal Papers
    Records of the Assistant Chief of Naval Personnel (Women),
    Shelf File Boxes

Naval Research Laboratory, Anacostia, DC
    Bureau of Ships Computation Project Reports, 1944–1945

New York University Archives, New York, NY
    Vincent Foster Hopper Papers

Schlesinger Library, Radcliffe Institute for Advanced Study
    Women in Federal Government Oral History Project, OH46
    (Grace Hopper)
    Elizabeth Reynard Papers

Smith College Archives, Northampton, MA
    War Service, WAVES Collection

Smithsonian Institution, National Museum of American History,
Archives Center
    Grace Murray Hopper Collection, 1944–1965
    Grace Hopper Oral Interviews

Vassar College Archives, Poughkeepsie, NY
    Hopper Collection

Wolfeboro Historical Center, Wolfeboro, NH
    Hopper Collection

Wolfeboro Public Library, Wolfeboro, NH
    Granite State News

Published Sources

Books

"Aiken, Howard." In *Encyclopedia of Computer Science and Engineering*, ed. Anthony Ralston. New York: Van Nostrand Reinhold, 1983.

Annals of the Computation Laboratory of Harvard University, 35 vols. Cambridge, MA: Harvard University Press, 1945–1962.

Bashe, Charles J., Lyle R. Johnson, John H. Palmer, and Emerson W. Pugh. *IBM's Early Computers*. Cambridge, MA: MIT Press, 1986.

Baxter, James Phinney. *Scientists Against Time*. Boston: Little, Brown, 1946.

Billings, Charlene W. *Grace Hopper: Navy Admiral and Computer Pioneer.* Hillside, NJ: Enslow, 1989.

Boslaugh, David L. *When Computers Went to Sea: The Digitization of the U.S. Navy.* Los Alamitos, CA: IEEE Computer Society Press, 1999.

Brooks, Harvey. *The Government of Science*. Cambridge, MA: MIT Press, 1968.

Brown, Louis. *A Radar History of World War II: Technical and Military Imperatives*. Bristol and Philadelphia: Institute of Physics Publishing, 1999.

Burke, Colin. *Information and Secrecy: Vannevar Bush, Ultra, and the Other Memex*. Metuchen, NJ, and London: Scarecrow, 1994.

Campbell-Kelly, Martin, and William Aspray, *Computer: A History of the Information Machine*. New York: BasicBooks, 1996.

Ceruzzi, Paul E. *A History of Modern Computing*. Cambridge, MA: MIT Press, 1998.

Chafe, William Henry. *The American Woman: Her Changing Social, Economic, and Political Roles, 1920–1970*. New York: Oxford University Press, 1972.

———. *The Paradox of Change*. Revised ed. of *The American Woman* (1972). New York: Oxford University Press, 1991.

Cohen, I. Bernard. *Howard Aiken: Portrait of a Computer Pioneer.* Cambridge, MA: MIT Press, 1999.

———. New Foreword to *A Manual of Operation for the Automatic Sequence Controlled Calculator.* Cambridge: MIT Press, 1985.

Cohen, I. Bernard, and Gregory W. Welch, eds. *Makin' Numbers: Howard Aiken and the Computer.* Cambridge, MA: MIT Press, 1999.

Cortada, James W. *Before the Computer: IBM, NCR, Burroughs, and Remington Rand and the Industry They Created, 1865–1956.* Princeton, NJ: Princeton University Press, 1993.

Etzkowitz, Henry, Carol Kemelgor, and Brian Uzzi. *Athena Unbound: The Advancement of Women in Science and Technology.* Cambridge, MA: Cambridge University Press, 2000.

Gildersleeve, Virginia C. *The "Waves" of the Navy: How They Began.* New York: Macmillan, 1956.

Godson, Susan H. *Serving Proudly: A History of Women in the U.S. Navy.* Annapolis, MD: Naval Institute Press, 2001.

Goldstine, Herman H. *The Computer: From Pascal to von Neumann.* Ormond Beach, FL: Camelot, 1996.

Hancock, Joy Bright. *Lady in the Navy.* Annapolis, MD: Naval Institute Press, 1972.

Hartcup, Guy. *The Effect of Science on the Second World War.* New York: Palgrave, 2000.

Hartree, Douglas R. *Calculating Instruments and Machines.* Urbana, IL: University of Illinois Press, 1949.

Hershberg, James G. *James B. Conant: Harvard to Hiroshima and the Making of the Nuclear Age.* New York: Alfred A. Knopf, 1993.

Hodges, Andrew. *Alan Turing: The Enigma.* New York: Simon and Schuster, 1983.

Holm, Maj. Gen. Jeanne, USAF (ret). *Women in the Military: An Unfinished Revolution,* rev. ed. Novato, CA: Presidio Press, 1992.

Hughes, Thomas Parke. *Elmer Sperry: Inventor and Engineer.* Baltimore and London: The Johns Hopkins University Press, 1971.

Lehman, John F. Jr. *Command of the Seas.* Annapolis, MD: Naval Institute Press, 2001.

McCartney, Scott. *ENIAC: The Triumphs and Tragedies of the World's First Computer.* New York: Walker, 1999.

Mahoney, Michael S. "Boys' Toys and Women's Work: Feminism Engages Software." In *Feminism in Twentieth Century Science, Technology and Medicine,* eds. Angela N. H. Creager, Elizabeth Lunbeck, and Londa Schiebinger. Chicago: University of Chicago Press, 2001.

Murray, Margaret A. M. *Women Becoming Mathematicians: Creating a Professional Identity in Post-World War II America.* Cambridge, MA: MIT Press, 2000.

Nofi, Albert A. *Marine Corps Book of Lists.* Conshohocken, PA: Combined Publishing, 1999.

Penick, James L. Jr., Carroll W. Pursell, Jr., Morgan B. Sherwood, and Donald C. Swain, eds. *The Politics of American Science, 1939 to the Present.* Cambridge, MA: MIT Press, revised edition 1972.

Prokop, Jan. ed. *Computers in the Navy.* Annapolis, MD: Naval Institute Press, 1976.

Pugh, Emerson W. *Memories That Shaped an Industry: Decisions Leading to IBM System 1360.* Cambridge, MA: MIT Press, 1984.

Randell, Brian. *The Origin of Digital Computers: Selected Papers.* New York: Springer-Verlag, 1973.

Rhodes, Richard. *The Making of the Atomic Bomb.* New York: Touchstone, 1986.

Rodgers, William. *Think: A Biography of the Watsons and IBM.* New York: Stein and Day, 1969.

Rossiter, Margaret W. *Women Scientists in America: Before Affirmative Action, 1940–1972.* Baltimore, MD: Johns Hopkins University Press, 1995.

Smith, C. V. L. *Electronic Digital Computers.* New York: McGraw-Hill, 1959.

Spencer, Donald P. *Great Men and Women of Computing.* Ormond Beach, FL: Camelot, 1996.

Stern, Nancy. *From Eniac to Univac: An Appraisal of the Eckert-Mauchly Computers.* Bedford, MA: Digital Press, 1981.

Stewart, Irvin. *Organizing Scientific Research for War: The Administrative History of the Office of Scientific Research and Development.* Boston: Little, Brown, 1948.

Wexelblat, Richard L. ed., *History of Programming Languages.* New York: Academic Press, 1981.

Whitelaw, Nancy. *Grace Hopper: Programming Pioneer.* New York: W. H. Freeman, 1995.

Williams, Kathleen Broome. *Improbable Warriors: Women Scientists and the U.S. Navy in World War II.* Annapolis, MD: Naval Institute Press, 2001.

———. *Secret Weapon: U.S. High-Frequency Direction Finding in the Battle of the Atlantic.* Annapolis, MD: Naval Institute Press, 1996.

Woodfield, Ruth. *Women, Work and Computing.* Cambridge, UK: Cambridge University Press, 2000.

Yost, Edna. *Women of Modern Science.* New York: Dodd, Mead, 1959.

Periodicals

Aiken, H. H., and Grace M. Hopper. "The Automatic Sequence Controlled Calculator, I–III." *Electrical Engineering* 65 (August–September 1946): 384–91, 449–54, 522–28.

Aiken, H. H. "Proposed Automatic Calculating Machine." Ed. and preface by A. C. Oettinger and T. C. Bartee. *IEEE Spectrum* (August 1964): 62–69.

"Algebra Machine Spurs Research." *New York Times,* August 7, 1944.

Aline. "Through Texas Eyes." *Christian Science Monitor,* April 13, 1959.

"Announcements." *Science* 104 (December 20, 1946): 593.

Associated Press. "Navy's Oldest Officer Logs Off after 43 Years on Computers." *New Haven Register,* August 15, 1986.

Barlett, R. Elaine. "Sugar Camp Reunion." *Cryptolog* 17 (Spring 1996): 1.

Betts, Mitch. "Grace Hopper, Mother of Cobol," *Computerworld* (January 6, 1992): 13–14.

Cohen, I. Bernard. "Babbage and Aiken: With Notes on Henry Babbage's Gift to Harvard, and to Other Institutions, of a Portion of His Father's Difference Engine." *Annals of the History of Computing* 10 (1988): 175–77.

———. "Howard Aiken and the Beginnings of Computer Science." *CWI Quarterly* 3 (1990): 303–4.

"Computer Programming Pioneer Promoted By Remington Rand." *New York Times,* August 18, 1961.

"Computer Sciences Man of the Year." Dataweek 7 (June 18,1969): 7.

"Computers in the Navy," *New Scientist* (June 12, 1969): 594.

Cushman, John H. "Admiral Hopper's Farewell." *New York Times,* August 14, 1986.

"Digital Hires Dr. Hopper." *New York Times,* September 3, 1986.

"Grace Hopper Mixes Insight, Foresight; Has Important Role in 'Man's World.'" *UNIVAC News* 7 (March 1967): 4.

Grant, Lester. "35-Ton Super-Brain Can Solve Hardest Mathematical Problem." *New York Herald Tribune,* August 7, 1944.

Gustafson, K. "Parallel Computing Forty Years Ago." *Mathematics and Computers in Simulation* 51 (1999):47–62.

Hamblen, Diane. "Editorial." *CHIPS* (April 1992): 3.

"Harvard Computation Laboratory." *Journal of Applied Physics* 17 (October 1946): 856.

"Harvard Receives $15 Million to Benefit Computer Science, Electrical Engineering." *Harvard University Gazette,* October 31, 1996): 1, 6.

Hattendorf, John B. "The Uses of Maritime History in and for the Navy." *Naval War College Review* 56 (Spring 2003): 12–38.

"Highbrow Harvard Bows to a Robot Brain." *Sunday Mirror Magazine*, August 5, 1945.

"John Harvard's Journal." *Harvard Magazine* (September–October 1997): 68.

"Keniston Elected Wolfeboro's New Selectman." *The Granite State News*, Wolfeboro, NH, March 11, 1998): 1.

Leatherman. Robin. "Getting Faster." *Systems for Modern Management* 17 (April 1953): 7–8.

Levitas, Louise. "Thinking Machine Tamer." *This Week* magazine, *New York Herald Tribune*, December 4, 1955: 27.

Light, Jennifer S. "When Computers Were Women." *Technology and Culture* 40 (July 1999): 455–83.

Markoff, John. "Rear Adm. Grace M. Hopper Dies; Innovator in Computers Was 85." *New York Times*, January 3, 1992: A18.

Mason, John F. "Grand Lady of Software." *Electronic Design* 22 (October 25, 1976): 86.

Meier, Mary. "Science Rewards Woman's High Aim." *Boston Evening Globe*, May 21, 1963.

"Navy Computer Grandmother Keeps Moving." *The* [Baltimore] *Sun*, September 26, 1975: B8.

Pearson, Richard. "Adm. Hopper Dies; Pioneer in Computers." *The Washington Post*, January 4, 1992.

Petzinger, Thomas, Jr. "History of Software Begins with Work of Some Brainy Women." *Wall Street Journal*, November 15, 1996.

———. "Female Pioneers Fostered Practicality in Computer Industry." *Wall Street Journal*, November 22, 1996.

"Plainfielder's Niece is Operator of Robot Einstein." *Plainfield* [NJ] *Courier-News*, August 8, 1944:1.

Rausa, Rosario. "In Profile: Grace Murray Hopper." *Naval History*(Fall 1992): 58–61.

Rees, Mina. "The Computing Program of the Office of Naval Research, 1949–1953." *Annals of the History of Computing* 4 (April 1982): 102–19.

———. "The Federal Computing Machine Program." *Science*112 (December 22,1950): 731–36.

———. "The Mathematical Sciences and World War II." *American Mathematical Monthly* 87 (October 1980): 607–21.

———. "The Mathematics Program of the Office of Naval Research." *Bulletin of the American Mathematical Society* 54 (January 1948): 1–5.

————. "Support of Higher Education by the Federal Government."
    American Mathematical Monthly 68 (April 1961): 371–77.
Ruth, Capt. Stephen R. "What Can the Navy Learn from the Air
    Force's Logistics System?" U.S. Naval Institute *Proceedings*
    (February 1977): 100–101.
Schimelpfenig, Ann. "Navy's Computer Expert Carries One in Her
    Purse." [Peoria] *Journal Star,* January 12, 1976.
Smith, Mark. "Adm. Hopper, Computer Pioneer, Had Ties to
    Wolfeboro." *Granite State* [Wolfeboro, NH] *News,* January 8,
    1992.
"Some of the Skills of Program Diplomacy." *Computer Weekly*
    (June 12, 1969): 14.
Stevens, Paul. "New, Faster Mechanical Brain Being Built at Harvard
    for Navy." *The Boston Sunday Herald,* August 22, 1948: 11
Sussman, Doris. "Pentagon Computer Pioneer—They Won't Let Her
    Retire." *Jacksonville* [FL] *Journal,* August 28, 1975.
Tropp, Henry S. "Grace Hopper: The Youthful Teacher of Us All."
    Abacus (Fall 1984): 8.
Wald, Matthew L. "30-Ton 'Brain' Evokes Birth of Computer Age."
    The New York Times, February 16, 1986: 58.
Welch, Gregory W. "Howard Hathaway Aiken: The Life of a Computer
    Pioneer." *The Computer Museum Report* 12 (Boston, MA: Spring
    1985): 7.

Dissertations

Beyer, Kurt. *Grace Hopper and the Early History of Computer Pro-
    gramming: 1944–1960.* Berkeley: University of California, 2002.
Mitchell, Carmen Lois. *The Contribution of Grace Murray Hopper to
    Computer Science and Computer Education.* University of
    North Texas: University Microfilms, 1994.
Welch, Gregory Webb. "Computer Scientist Howard Hathaway Aiken:
    Reactionary or Visionary?" A.B. Thesis, Harvard University,
    1986.

Further Reading

G race Hopper was a prolific author. For those interested in reading her own words, the following are among her most influential works: Grace M. Hopper, *A Manual of Operation for the Automatic Sequence Controlled Calculator* (Cambridge, MA: Harvard University Press, 1946); Grace M. Hopper, "Compiling Routines," *Computers and Automation* (May 1953); Grace M. Hopper, "The Education of a Computer," *Symposium of Industrial Applications of Automatic Computing Equipment* (January 1953); Grace M. Hopper and John Mauchly, "Influence of Programming Techniques on the Design of Computers," *Proceedings of the IRE* 41 (October 1953); Grace M. Hopper, "First Glossary of Programming Terminology," *Association for Computing Machinery* (1954).

Among the most interesting accounts of navy women are: Winifred Quick Collins, *More Than a Uniform: A Navy Woman in a Navy Man's World* (Denton, TX: University of North Texas Press, 1997); Susan H. Godson, *Serving Proudly: A History of Women in the Navy* (Annapolis, MD: Naval Institute Press, 2001); Joy Bright Hancock, *Lady in the Navy* (Annapolis, MD: Naval Institute Press, 1972).

After World War II some official and semiofficial accounts of military women were published. They are now considered classics. More recently, and particularly since the 1990s, interest in military women has revived. For some of each of these genres see the following: Judith Bellafaire, *The Women's Army Corps* (CMH Pub. 72-15. Washington, DC: U.S. Army Center for Military History, n.d.); Martin Binkin and Shirley J. Bach, *Women and the Military* (Washington, DC: Brookings Institution, 1977); Deborah G. Douglas, *United States Women in Aviation: 1940–1985*, Washington, DC: Smithsonian Institution Press, 1991); Jean Ebbert and Marie-Beth Hall, *Crossed Currents* (Washington, DC: Brassey's (U.S.), 1993); Jeanne Holm, ed., *In Defense of a Nation: Service Women in World War II* (Washington, DC: Military Women's Press, 1998); Claudia J. Kennedy with Malcolm McConnell, *Generally Speaking: A Memoir by the First Woman Promoted to Three-Star General in the United States Army* (New York: Warner Books, 2001); C. Kay Larson, *'Til I Come Marching Home: A Brief History of American Women in World War II* (Pasadena, MD: The Minerva Center, 1995); Judith Barret

Litoff and David C. Smith, eds., *We're in This War Too: World War II Letters from American Women in Uniform* (New York, Oxford: Oxford University Press, 1994); Mary C. Lyne and Kay Arthur, *Three Years Behind the Mast: The Story of the United States Coast Guard SPARS* (Washington, DC: n.p., 1946); Lt. Col. Pat Meid, USMCR, *The Marine Corps Reserve Women's Reserve in World War II* (Washington, DC: Historical Branch, U.S. Marine Corps, 1968); Reina Pennington, *Wings, Women and War: Soviet Airwomen in World War II Combat* (Lawrence: University Press of Kansas, 2001); Peter A. Soderbergh, *Women Marines: The World War II Era* (Westport, CT: Praeger, 1992); Mary V. Stremlow, *Free a Marine to Fight: Women Marines in World War II* (Washington, DC: Marine Corps Headquarters, History and Museums Division, 1994); Mattie E. Treadwell, *The Women's Army Corps: The U.S. Army in World War II* (Washington, DC: Department of the Army, 1954); June A. Willenz, *Women Veterans: America's Forgotten Heroines* (New York: Continuum, 1983).

Before an interest in military women began to grow, a movement started in the early 1980s to examine the role of women and society at war. Among the best of these works are: Karen Anderson, *Wartime Women: Sex Roles, Family Relations, and the Status of Women during World War II* (Westport, CT: Greenwood Press, 1981); D'Ann Campbell, *Women at War with America: Private Lives in a Patriotic Era* (Cambridge, MA: Harvard University Press, 1984); Sherna Berger Gluck, *Rosie the Riveter Revisited: Women, War and Social Change* (New York: Meridian, 1987); Doris Weatherford, *American Women and World War II* (New York: Facts on File, 1990); Nancy Baker Wise and Christy Wise, *A Mouthful of Rivets: Women at Work in World War II* (San Francisco: Jossey-Bass Publishers, 1994).

There are a large number of works on the history and sociology of American women, many written within a feminist analytical framework. One or two have been mentioned in the bibliography. This book, however, is grounded in naval history and therefore mention will be made of only one or two additional useful works in the category of women's issues: Sara M. Evans, *Born for Liberty: A History of Women in America* (New York: The Free Press, 1989); and Virginia Valian, *Why So Slow? The Advancement of Women* (Cambridge, MA: MIT Press, 1999).

There is a growing interest in the experiences of women in science and mathematics. A good place to start a search is among some of the most accessible works, that follow: Donald J. Albers and G. L. Alexanderson, eds., *Mathematical People: Profiles and Interviews*

(Boston, Basel, Stuttgart: Birkhäuser, 1985); Susan A. Ambrose, Kristin L. Dunkle, Barbara B. Lazarus, Indira Nait, and Deborah A. Harkus, eds., *Journeys of Women in Science and Engineering: No Universal Constants* (Philadelphia: Temple University Press, 1997); Martha J. Bailey, *American Women in Science: A Biographical Dictionary* (Denver: ABC-CLIO, 1994); Louise S. Grinstein and Paul J. Campbell, eds., *Women of Mathematics: A Bibliographic Sourcebook* (New York: Greenwood Press, 1987); Louise S. Grinstein, Rose K. Rose, and Miriam H. Rafailovich, eds., *Women in Chemistry and Physics: A Bibliographic Sourcebook* (Westport, CT: Greenwood Press, 1993); Caroline L. Herzenberg, *Women Scientists from Antiquity to the Present: An Index* (West Cornwall, CT: Locust Hill Press, 1986); Margaret W. Rossiter, *Women Scientists in America: Struggles and Strategies to 1940* Baltimore, MD: Johns Hopkins University Press, 1982).

Computer science, too, has its own extensive bibliography. The following from various eras give perspective on the development of the field: William Aspray, *John von Neumann and the Origins of Modern Computing* (Cambridge, MA: MIT Press, 1990); Akera Atsushi and Frederik Nebeker, eds., *From 0 to 1: An Authoritative History of Modern Computing* (New York: Oxford University Press, 2002); William Belden and Marva R. Belden, *The Lengthening Shadow: The Life of Thomas J. Watson* (Boston: Little, Brown, 1962); Edmund Berkeley, *Constructing Electronic Brains* (New York: Edmund Berkeley and Associates, 1951); James W. Cortada, *The Computer in the United States: From Laboratory to Market, 1930 to 1960* (New York: M. E. Sharpe, 1993); Richard T. DeLamarter, *Big Blue: IBM's Use and Abuse of Power* (New York: Dodd, Mead, 1986); Nicholas Metropolis, Jack Howlett, et al., eds., *A History of the Computer in the Twentieth Century* (New York: Academic Press, 1980); K. C. Redmond and T. M. Smith, *Project Whirlwind: The History of a Pioneer Computer* (Bedford, MA: Digital Press, 1980); Nancy Stern and Robert A. Stern, *Computers in Society* (Englewood Cliffs, NJ: Prentice-Hall, 1983); W. W. Stifler, ed., *High-Speed Computing Devices* (New York: McGraw-Hill, 1950). For computing and the NSA see: James Bamford, *The Puzzle Palace: A Report On America's most Secret Agency* (Boston: Houghton Mifflin, 1982).

For issues of science and the government/military see: Vannevar Bush, *Modern Arms and Free Men: A Discussion of the Role of Science in Preserving Democracy* (New York: Simon and Schuster, 1949); Vannevar Bush, *Pieces of the Action* (New York: William Morrow, 1970); Vannevar Bush, *Science, the Endless Frontier: A Report to the President* (Washington, DC: U.S. Government Printing Office, 1945); Montgomery

Meigs, *Slide Rules and Submarines* (Washington, DC: National Defense University Press, 1990); Michael D. Reagan, *Science and the Federal Patron* (New York: Oxford University Press, 1969); Harvey M. Sapolsky, *Science and the Navy: The History of the Office of Naval Research* (Princeton, NJ: Princeton University Press, 1990); Kathleen Broome Williams, *Secret Weapon: U.S. High-Frequency Direction Finding in the Battle of the Atlantic* (Annapolis, MD: Naval Institute Press, 1996).

Index

Aberdeen Proving Ground: ENIAC at, 39, 58; and Harvard Computation Lab, 46, 51; Herman Goldstine at, 38; women at, 76

ADA, 170. *See also,* Lovelace, Lady Ada

ADPESO (Automatic Data Processing Equipment Selection Office), 122, 126, 139, 143, 165

Aiken, Howard H.: character of, 25–26, 41, 43, 52, 56; and computing, 31, 50–51; creates Mark I, 29, 30, 47–48; death of, 61; heads Harvard Computation Lab, 45, 56; Hopper on, 31, 32, 35, 40, 41, 43, 49, 56, 62, 66–67, 104–5, 162, 183, 194–95; legacy of, 61–62, 64; on Mark I, 29, 30, 47–48; and Mark II, 99; and Mark III and Mark IV, 101; and navy, 37; and Norbert Weiner, 40; postwar career of, 59–62, 64; on programming, 91; receives Harry Goode Memorial award, 127; and Thomas Watson, 34–35, 64–65

Air Force, U.S.: and computing, 84, 92, 101, 108, 117, 140, 155, 157; and failure of ALS, 159; gets Mark III, 60, 189; and JOVIAL, 94, 118–19; and navy COBOL, 139; and SAGE, 101; tests FLOW-MATIC, 88, 89

Algorithmic Language (ALGOL), 123

American National Standard Institute (ANSI), 118, 122, 132, 136, 139

Andover Academy (Philips Academy Andover), 3, 4, 16–17, 168–69

Applied Mathematics Panel (AMP), 56; computer survey by, 45; and Harvard Computation Lab, 46, 59, 61; and Mina Rees, 40, 48; Stibitz at, 70

Army, U.S.: and computing, 73, 84, 92, 138, 155, 157; and FORTRAN, 118; sponsors ENIAC, 39, 101

ASCC. *See* Mark I

Association for Computing Machinery (ACM), 62, 68, 90, 101, 179; Hopper and, 79, 109, 135, 137, 143

Atanasoff, John V., 27, 39

Automatic Data Processing Equipment Selection Office. *See* ADPESO

Babbage, Charles, 29, 49, 53, 61, 189

Baird, George N., 131, 135, 138, 142, 182

Bankers Trust Company, 16, 17, 20, 98, 169

Barnard College, 5, 6, 21, 22, 23

Bartik, Jean, 179

Bell Telephone Laboratories (BTL), 27, 37, 38, 101, 102

Berkeley, Edmund, 42–43, 45, 62, 101

Bloch, Richard M., 29; at Harvard Computation Lab, 31, 43, 58; and Hopper, 31, 49, 166, 170; on Howard Aiken, 40–41, 43; and Mark I, 39, 45–47, 52, 53; at Raytheon, 62, 99; on Robert Campbell, 44

Brendel, Ruth (Noller), 32, at Harvard Computation Lab, 45, 50, 58, 194; on Hopper, 33, 42, 55–56, 153, 169, 185, 187; on Howard Aiken, 32–33, 40, 41, 52, 56, 62; postwar career of, 62–63

Brewster Academy (Wolfeboro, NH), 166, 174

Brooks Bill (1965), 117, 128, 145, 153, 154, 155

Brown University, 10, 47

Bureau of Medicine & Surgery (BuMed), 138–39

Bureau of Naval Personnel (BuPers), 141, 161; and Hopper, 24, 25, 63, 103, 110–12

Bureau of Ordnance (BuOrd): and Harvard Computation Lab, 44, 45, 48, 58–59, 61; and Hopper, 63, 103, 104–5, 110

Bureau of Ships (BuShips), 35, 81, 110; and Harvard Computation Lab, 25, 28, 31, 36, 46–48, 58–59; Hopper and, 24, 105, 110; and Howard Aiken, 36

Bureau of Ships Computation Project. *See* Harvard Computation Laboratory

Burroughs, 91, 93, 107, 128

Bush, George H. W., 190

Bush, Vannevar, 26, 36, 37,

Campbell, Robert V. D., 76; at Harvard Computation Lab, 31, 58; and Hopper, 31, 166, 170; on Howard Aiken, 33;

Campbell, Robert V. D. *(cont.)*
  and Mark I, 28; and Mark II, 45; at
  Raytheon, 62, 99; on Richard Bloch,
  44
Carter, Jimmy, 154, 165
CDC (Control Data Corporation), 128,
  139
Census Bureau, 70, 73, 84,101
CHIPS Ahoy, 187
Civil Service Commission, 156
Claytor, W. Graham, 154
COBOL, 76, 173; and air force, 139–40;
  for Australia, 143; and CODASYL and
  ANSI, 118; DoD accepts, 94; Hopper's
  role in, 87, 93, 95, 110, 114, 119, 124,
  128, 130, 132, 161–62, 165, 184, 191;
  and IBM, 90, 93, 115, 139; Jean
  Sammet and, 90; for microprocessors,
  161–63, 194; for MIS, 119; for navy,
  114–15, 119, 120, 123, 128, 130, 134,
  142, 148; problems with, 123–24; and
  RCA, 115; for Social Security
  Administration and IRS, 165;
  standards for, established, 94; and
  UNIVAC, 115
Cochrane, Edward L., 35
CODASYL, 92, 114, 115, 132, 135
coding. *See* computer programming
Cohen, I. Bernard, 32, 61, 67
Collegiate School (New York), 5, 16, 169
Columbia University, 12, 39, 48
Communications Supplementary
  Activity-Washington (CSAW), 24, 26,
  36, 99, 100
compilers, 93, 94; ANSI standards for,
  118; at DoD, 157; for federal government, 139; Hopper develops, 77–80,
  83, 84, 85–87, 90, 127, 137; Hopper
  develops for navy, 121–24, 129, 138–
  39, 149; for tactical data systems, 119
compilers, types of: A-O, 79; A-2, 83, 105;
  B-O (FLOW-MATIC), 87, 91; MATH-
  MATIC, 84, 91
computer programming (coding), 31, 33,
  39, 49, 50, 52, 69, 78, 81, 88; Aiken on,
  91; and debugging, 83; Hopper on, 30,
  80, 130; and IRS, 165; and job
  security, 84; and programming
  languages, 123, 127; shortage of
  personnel for, 132, 156; and Social
  Security Administration, 165
computers: air force and, 60, 73, 101, 108,
  117, 155, 189; army and, 39, 73, 101,
  155; Atlas, 99; BINAC, 70, 78; at BTL,
  27, 37, 101; at BuPers, 110–12; CDC

6600, 137; CDC 6700, 147; Colossus,
  27; for commerce, 66, 68, 76–77, 82–
  83; in commercial labs, 37; for
  cryptanalysis, 26; and data processing, 65, 82; DECmate II, 166; for
  defense, 85, 117; in direction-
  finding,106–8, 145; at DoD, 155;
  EDSAC (UK), 78; EDVAC,
  (Raytheon), 71; in government, 113;
  hardware advances in, 108, 157;
  increasing numbers of, 81, 106, 116–
  17; and mathematics, 65, 85; MIT's
  differential analyzer, 26, 37, 47, 52,
  54; in navy, 26–27, 81, 100–101, 108,
  115, 144; software for, 77–78, 123,
  160; for weather forecasting, 85;
  Whirlwind, 68, 78, 99, 101; write
  programs, 80; women and, 75–76,
  178, 180–81, 193; Zuse I and Z3, 27.
  *See also*ENIAC, IBM, Mark I, Mark
  II, Mark III and Mark IV, and
  UNIVAC
Conant, James B., 34–35, 40, 60
Control Data Corporation. *See* CDC
Constitution, USS, 170
Courant, Richard, 24, 61; Hopper on, 17,
  35; at NYU, 10; war service of, 20, 36
Cullins, Peter K., 151

Dahlgren Proving Ground (VA), 42, 45,
  147–48; Hopper at, 63, 102; Mark II
  at, 54, 58, 102
Dalton, John H., 192, 193
Data Processing Management Association (DPMA), 125, 135, 142, 174
Data Processing Service Centers, 157,
  160
David Taylor Model Basin, 20–21, 47, 73,
  81
Department of Defense. *See* DoD
Digital Equipment Corporation, 172–74,
  189–90
DoD (Department of Defense): and air
  force computing, 92, 117, 155, 157;
  and COBOL, 114, 115, 139; and
  computer standardization, 117, 120,
  121, 164, 170; and computing, 92, 135,
  136, 144, 153, 155, 163; consolidates
  ADP, 157; Hopper's influence on, 143;
  Jimmy Carter reorganizes, 154; and
  NAVDAC, 150, 153; and navy, 116,
  118; and size of ADP program, 155–56
DuPont, 82, 83, 85, 89

Eckert, J. Presper, 38; and EMCC, 69, 70; and ENIAC, 56; Hopper on, 73; at Sperry Rand, 95; and UNIVAC, 71, 72, 101

Eckert-Mauchly Computer Corporation (EMCC), 69–76, 100, 104; Hopper at, 69–70, 74, 81, 125

Eckert, Wallace J., 39

Engineering Research Associates. See ERA

Engstrom, Howard, 12, 24, 26, 36, 69, 100

ENIAC, 39, 68, 69, 70; army sponsors, 39, 101; and Betty Holberton, 76; description of, 53, 56–57, 58, 72, 73

ERA (Engineering Research Associates), 69, 71, 100, 104

FLOBOL, 132–35, 138

FLOW-MATIC, 87–89, 90, 91, 93, 133

FORTRAN, 83, 91, 184; and army, 118; for Australia, 143; for navy, 123, 135–36, 138, 140; standards for, 94; and test routines, 122, 125, 129

Fourth Naval District, 101–2, 108, 113

Fredette, Richard, 135, 161; and Adm. Spreen, 138, 147–48; on COBOL, 115; on databases, 160; and Hopper, 131, 176, 187, 190; on Hopper, 120–21, 153, 164, 169, 183, 184; at NAVDAC, 152, 156–57; at NPLS, 140, 142

General Accounting Office (GAO), 153, 160; reports on navy computing (1975), 142, 144–49, 150, 151, 154

General Services Administration (GSA), 175; adopts Hopper's COBOL, 139; and ADP standards, 117; and FLOBOL, 133–35; and navy computing, 144, 148, 153, 158, 163

Gildersleeve, Virginia C., 6, 18–19, 21

Goldstine, Herman, 38, 61

Haak, Frank S., 146

Hancock, Joy Bright, 163

Hancock, Kenton B., 152–53, 170

Harvard Computation Laboratory, 17, 24, 76, 81, 153; alumni of, 99, 100, 166; and BuOrd, 58–59; Hopper at, 25, 26, 68–69, 156; and IBM, 53–54; life at, 37, 42, 130; and Mark I, 31, 36, 44, 64, 129; and Mark II, 54; and Mark III and Mark IV, 101; and NDRC, 36; von Neumann at, 40; work of, 44–51, 55. See also Mark I

Harvard University, 9, 49; computer courses at, 89; and Mark I, 27, 28, 34–35, 36, 72; Maxwell Dworkin Computer Sciences Building at, 61–62; and tenure, 66; war work at, 58

Holberton, Frances E. (Betty): and CODASYL, 93; and computing, 81; contribution to computing of, 179; at David Taylor Model Basin, 81, 84; and ENIAC, 76; and Hopper, 76, 78, 122; on Hopper, 94; at NBS, 122; and Sort-Merge generator, 91

Hopper, Grace Murray: accomplishments of, 90, 93, 95, 127, 179, 187, 193–95; and ACM, 79, 109, 135, 137, 143; awarded Defense Distinguished Service Medal, 170; and awards/decorations, 113, 184–85, 186–87, 190, 192; and Betty Holberton, 76, 78, 94, 122; Betty Holberton on, 94; as boss, 74–75, 130–31, 182, 187; business sense of, 97, 122, 179; character of, 112, 169, 184, 191, 194; childhood of, 1–9, 58, 189; and COBOL, 87, 93, 95, 110, 114, 119, 124, 128, 130, 132, 161–62, 165, 173, 184, 191; and CODASYL, 92, 114, 132, 135; and commercial computing, 66, 68, 76–77, 80, 82–83, 139; and compilers, 77–80, 83, 84, 85–87, 90, 121–24, 127, 137; contributions of recognized by navy, 140, 192, 193; on databases, 160–61; death of, 191; and debugging, 44, 50, 54, 77, 91, 132; at Digital, 172–75; and divorce, 17; at EMCC, 69–70, 74, 81, 125; on ENIAC, 57; and feminism, 125–26, 176–82; and FLOW-MATIC, 87–88, 90, 91, 93, 133, 194; and FORTRAN, 83, 84, 128; generosity of, 183; at Harvard Computation Lab, 25, 26, 68–69, 156; heads Navy Programming Languages Group, 114, 122–24; heads NPLS, 126, 130, 132–35, 138–39, 140, 142; on herself, 17, 91, 121, 125, 149, 170–71, 184, 185, 194–95; on Howard Aiken, 31, 32, 35, 40, 41, 43, 49, 56, 62, 66–67, 104–5, 183, 195; on IBM, 65, 69, 90, 96, 168; John Lehman on, 152, 166–67; on John Mauchly, 35, 73, 75, 78, 183; joins navy, 19, 22–24; and love for navy, 3, 103, 113, 136–37, 184, 193–95; loyalty of, 35, 67, 182–83; makes programming/coding easier, 52–53, 69–70, 79, 84–86; and Mark I,

Hopper, Grace Murray (cont.)
48–50; on Mark I, 26, 27, 29, 39, 51–
53, 57, 67, 78, 156, 162, 195; and
Mark II, 54, 66, 102; on Mark III, 60,
66; on marketing, 88–89, 90, 121–22,
129–30, 181–82; and marriage, 12, 14,
15–16; on microcomputers, 161–62;
named Computer Science Man of the
Year, 125; and nanoseconds, 137; at
NAVDAC, 151, 171; on navy, 119–21,
143; navy fitness reports on, 105–6,
109–10, 111–12, 113; as navy
recruiter, 159; on Norbert Weiner, 40;
obituary of, 54, 191; at Pentagon, 114,
116, 130, 132, 138, 149, 183; persistence of, 9, 33, 86, 90; on programming, 30, 69–70, 77, 80; and promotions, 63, 110, 142, 143, 158, 166–67,
168; publications of, 64, 79, 85, 105–6,
187, 190; as public speaker, 104, 127,
135, 141, 143, 163–64, 185–86;
recalled to active duty, 114; receives
Harry Goode Memorial Award, 127–
28; and Remington Rand/Sperry
Rand, 92, 95, 96–97, 104; retires from
navy, 113, 170–71; and sense of
humor, 44, 56, 130, 143, 163, 177; and
software, 51–52, 69, 89, 123, 138, 155;
strong will of, 1, 6–7, 97; as teacher,
11–14, 18, 33, 63, 74, 109, 128, 135–
36, 137; and UNIVAC, 71, 114, 118,
120, 133, 137, 172; at UNIVAC, 95,
96–97; as Vassar student, 9–11, 77,
97; on von Neumann, 40; on women
and computing, 75–76, 93; work
habits of, 13, 55, 74, 130, 134–35; at
Yale, 11, 12–13, 15, 33, 69, 177
Hopper, Vincent Foster: and Grace, 11–
12; and divorce, 17; and marriage to
Grace, 16, 17, 19; World War II service
of, 20
Hopper, USS (DDG-70), 192–93

IBM: and COBOL, 90, 93, 115, 139; and
computing, 37, 82; creates FORTRAN,
83, 84; and Harvard Computation Lab,
53–54; Hopper on, 65, 69, 90, 96, 168;
and Mark I, 28, 34–35, 64, 187; and
microprocessors, 161; punched-card
equipment of, 48, 54, 82; and SSEC,
65, 96; Thomas Watson heads, 28

Jacobs, Randall, 19
Jones, John L. (Jack), 84, 89, 92, 93, 135
JOVIAL, 94, 118, 119, 123

Kelso, Frank B. II, 192
Knowlton, Ruth, 31, 41, 50, 55–56
Korean War, 103, 115

Lehman, John F., 152, 166–67, 191
Lovelace, Lady Ada, 49, 170

Mark I, 36, 43, 59, 61, 68; description of,
29–31, 51, 57–58; and ENIAC, 53, 57–
58; Hopper on, 26, 27, 29, 39, 50, 51–
53, 57, 67, 78, 156, 162, 195; Howard
Aiken on, 29, 30; and IBM, 28, 34–35,
64, 187; navy and, 35, 36, 99; speed of,
30, 137; and UNIVAC, 72; war work
of, 25–26, 44–50, 60. See also Harvard
Computation Lab
Mark II, 60, 61, 68, 99; creation of, 45, 53;
at Dahlgren, 54, 58, 102; description
of, 54–55; importance of, 66
Mark III and Mark IV, 60, 61, 66, 68, 99,
101, 189
mathematicians: and Bessel functions,
65; in computing, 69, 117; as programmers, 80, war work of, 38, 68
Mauchly, John W., 38, 61, 86; and EMCC,
69, 70; and ENIAC, 56, 101; and
Hopper, 105, 186; Hopper on, 35, 73,
75, 78, 183; at Moore School, 39; and
Short Code, 78, 91; and UNIVAC, 71,
72
McAfee, Mildred Horton, 19
MIT: computing at, 37, 54; and differen-
tial analyzer, 26, 37, 47, 52, 54;
FORTRAN developed at, 83; Ken
Olsen at, 166; Norbert Weiner at, 40;
Radiation Lab at, 25, 38, 47, 58, 59,
101; and Vannevar Bush, 26; Whirl-
wind at, 68, 78, 99, 101
Moore School of Electrical Engineering
(University of Pennsylvania), 37–39,
69–70, 92; and ENIAC, 58, 101;
Hopper teaches at, 74–75, 97, 109,
186, 194
Murray, Grace Brewster. See Hopper,
Grace Murray
Murray, John W. (grandfather), 2, 7
Murray, Mary Campbell (sister). See
Westcote, Mary Murray
Murray, Mary Campbell Van Horne
(mother), 1–8; 16, 20, 95, 98
Murray, Roger Franklin II (brother), 2–8,
12, 19; and Andover, 6, 168; at Bank-
ers Trust, 16, 98, 169; character of, 98,
168–69; on Grace, 192, 194; at NYU,

17–18; teaches at Columbia, 98; and USS *Hopper,* 192; World War II service of, 20; at Yale, 11, 16, 169

Murray, Roger Franklin III (nephew): at Andover, 16–17; on Grace, 7, 167, 176, 177, 191; inherits aunt's farmhouse, 14–15; and USS *Hopper,* 192, 193

Murray, Walter Fletcher (father), 2–8, 16, 20, 63, 65

NARDAC (Naval Regional Data Automation Center), 150, 167

National Bureau of Standards (NBS), 131; and ADP standards, 117; Betty Holberton at, 81; Eugene Smith at, 101; and GAO, 144; oversees navy computing, 153, 154; and Standard COBOL, 124–25, 138, 139; and UNIVAC, 70–71

National Cash Register. *See* NCR

National Defense Research Committee (NDRC), 36, 70

National Science Foundation, 135, 193

National Security Act (1947), 116

National Security Agency, 100

Naval Command Systems Support Activity. *See* NAVCOSSACT

Naval Computing Machinery Laboratory, 26, 37, 100

Naval Data Automation Command. *See* NAVDAC

Naval Ordnance Laboratory (NOL), 39, 47

Naval Regional Data Automation Center. *See* NARDAC

Naval Research Laboratory (NRL), 28–29, 35, 185; direction finding at, 106–8; and Harvard Computation Lab, 46–47, 59; Hopper at, 63; Richard Bloch at, 39

Naval Tactical Data System. *See* NTDS

Naval War College (Newport, RI), 64, 105

NAVCOSSACT (Naval Command Systems Support Activity), 126

NAVDAC (Naval Data Automation Command), 150, 157; Adm. Sutherland heads, 163, 166; Hopper at, 151, 171; and microcomputers, 161–62; and navy ADP reorganization, 159–60; task of, 151; women at, 181

Navy Programming Languages Group, 122–23, 125, 126

Navy Programming Languages Section (NPLS): Hopper heads, 126, 130, 142,

143; work of, 129, 133–36, 138–40, 147–48

Navy, U.S.: accepts COBOL, 93; and ADP management, 118; compilers for, 121–24, 129, 147, 149; and computing, 26–27, 60, 73, 99, 100–101, 139; and computing problems, 108, 115, 145–46; GAO report attacks, 144–49; Hopper standardizes COBOL for, 114; and Mark I, 35, 36, 99; and Mark III, 60, 189; and numbers of computers, 117; precedes Internet, 160; and share of DoD ADP budget, 155–56; shortage of programmers for, 156; and UNIVAC, 105, 107, 119; women in, 18–19, 24, 109, 116, 167, 168, 178, 193. *See also* WAVES

NCR, 26, 37, 128

New York University. *See* NYU

NTDS (Naval Tactical Data System), 100, 110

NYU: and computing, 84; Hopper at, 17; Richard Courant at, 3, 10; Roger Murray at, 17; Vincent Hopper at, 12, 17; war programs at, 21–22

Office of Management and Budget (OMB), 116, 117, 139, 153, 163

Office of Naval Research (ONR), 40, 59, 81, 99

Office of Scientific Research and Development (OSRD), 20, 36, 38

Olsen, Ken, 166, 172, 174, 187

Pentagon, 94, 169; air force at, 139; computing at, 84, 92, 114, 130, 139, 157; Hopper at, 114, 116, 130, 132, 138, 149, 183; NAVDAC leaves, 151

Prager, William, 10

Princeton University, 12, 40

Prokop, Jan, 165

Radio Research Laboratory (Harvard), 31, 38, 58

Raytheon, 62, 71, 99, 119

RCA: and COBOL, 93–94, 115, 122, 139; and computing, 37, 85, 91; and navy, 119

Reagan, Ronald, 167, 171, 183

Ream, Norman, 89, 92, 114, 118, 121

Rees, Mina, 40, 48, 81, 99, 179

Remington Rand, 69, 71, 72, 84; buys EMCC and ERA, 100, 104; builds computers, 85; Hopper and, 92, 104;

Remington Rand *(cont.)*
    James H. Rand heads, 73; navy uses
    computers of, 99–100, 107
Rickover, Hyman G., 170, 191
Russell, Alexander Wilson (great-
    grandfather), 2–3, 20, 168

Sammet, Jean E., 90, 93
Shapely, Harlow, 35, 40
Smith College, 168; Northampton
    Midshipmen's School at, 22–24, 25
Smith, Eugene, 36, 40, 81, 84, 92, 101
Sperry Rand, 69, 95
Spreen, Roger E., 146; and Hopper, 128,
    133–35, 139; on Hopper, 140; as OP-91,
    126; and Richard Fredette, 138, 147
Stibitz, George R., 27, 61, 70–71, 101
Sutherland, Paul E., 163, 166, 167, 170,
    192

Turing, Alan M., 27, 85–86

Underwater Sound Laboratory
    (Harvard), 38, 59
UNIVAC, 69–70, 101, 108; and COBOL,
    115; commercial uses for, 82; and
    compilers, 83, 87, 90, 128; description
    of, 71–73, 80; and FLOW-MATIC, 89,
    93; and FORTRAN, 122; and Hopper,
    71, 114, 118, 120, 133, 137, 172; and
    IRS contract, 165; and navy, 105, 107,
    119; overtaken by IBM, 95–96; at
    Smithsonian, 95; speed of, 137; and U-
    1100, 160; and UNIVAC 418, 138–39
University of Pennsylvania. *See* Moore
    School of Electrical Engineering

Vassar College, 5, 8, 24, 38; and Hopper,
    77, 97, 175; Hopper teaches at, 12–22;
    Hopper student at, 9–11;
Verdonck, Frank, 34, 43, 50, 58–59

Vietnam War, 103, 115, 116, 136, 146–47
Voight, Wilma, 164
von Neumann, John, 10, 39, 40, 46, 61

Washington Navy Yard, 149–51, 173–74,
    189
Watson, Thomas J. Sr., 28, 34–35, 64–65
WAVES, 54; disestablishment of, 178;
    establishment of, 18–19; history of,
    109; and Hopper, 102, 163, 171; and
    officer training, 22–24; and service
    overseas, 32; and two-tier system,
    103–4; and Vietnam War, 116. *See
    also* Navy, U.S., women in
Weaver, Warren, 46, 61
Weiner, Norbert, 40, 61, 62
Wellesley College, 19, 21, 31
Westcote, John (nephew), 56
Westcote, Mary Murray (sister), 2, 9, 19;
    on Grace, 4–5, 18, 19, 177, 183, 190;
    on Roger Murray II, 16; and USS
    Hopper, 192; and Vincent Hopper, 12;
    and World War II work, 20
Westcote, Walter (nephew), 17
Wilkes, M. V., 52, 78
Women: and careers, 11, 15, 185; and
    computing, 68–69, 75–76, 93;
    education of, 5, 8–9, 15; perception of,
    125; and war work, 20–22. *See also*
    Navy, U.S., and WAVES
Women's Armed Services Integration Act
    (1948), 63, 109

Yale University, 2, 3, 9, 11, Hopper at, 11,
    12–13–15, 33, 69, 177; Howard
    Engstrom at, 24, 69; Roger Murray II
    at, 11, 16, 169; Walter Westcote at, 17
Yavinsky, Rita, 172–76, 186, 190, 192

Zumwalt, Elmo, 142, 178

About the Author

K athleen Broome Williams was born in Charlottesville, Virginia, in 1944, grew up in Italy and England, and returned to the United States to attend Wellesley College. Since then she has lived in Germany, Puerto Rico, Japan, and Panama. She holds an MA from Columbia University and a PhD in military history from the City University of New York (CUNY). A professor of history at Bronx Community College, CUNY, she is also a member of the history doctoral faculty at the CUNY Graduate School and University Center. The author of *Secret Weapon: U.S. High-frequency Direction Finding in the Battle of the Atlantic* (Naval Institute Press, 1996), her most recent book, *Improbable Warriors: Women Scientists and the U.S. Navy in World War II* (Naval Institute Press, 2001), was awarded the John Lyman book prize for U.S. naval history. She is currently doing research on her father, a World War II Marine, who died as a result of wounds sustained during the American landings on Saipan.